To Roger Kahn
from his friend
Robert Frost
After a good afternoon of real
talk together at the cabin in Ripton
September 1960

# Into My Own

# Into My Own

The Remarkable People and Events That Shaped a Life

# ROGER KAHN

THOMAS DUNNE BOOKS

*St. Martin's Press* ❧ *New York*

THOMAS DUNNE BOOKS.
An imprint of St. Martin's Press.

INTO MY OWN. Copyright © 2006 by Hook Slide, Inc. All rights reserved.
Printed in the United States of America. No part of this book may be used or
reproduced in any manner whatsoever without written permission except
in the case of brief quotations embodied in critical articles or reviews.
For information, address St. Martin's Press, 175 Fifth Avenue,
New York, N.Y. 10010.

www.stmartins.com

Design by Ruth Lee-Mui

Library of Congress Cataloging-in-Publication Data

Kahn, Roger.
    Into my own : the remarkable people and events that shaped a life / Rober Kahn.—1st
ed.
        p.  cm.
    ISBN-13: 978-0-312-33813-8
    ISBN-10: 0-312-33813-9
    1. Kahn, Roger.  2. Sportswriters—United States—Biography.  I. Title.

GV742.42.K35  A3  2006
070.4'49796092—dc22

                                                                    2006040394

First Edition: June 2006

2  4  6  8  10  9  7  5  3  1

*To my wife, Katy, with gratitude, appreciation, and love;*

*To my children, Gordon J. and Alissa A.;*

*To my loving stepson, Edgar Galloway;*

*And in memory of Roger Laurence Kahn*

# CONTENTS

# WORDS OF THANKS

One is often asked, "How long did it take you to write the book?" In the case of *Into My Own,* a fair answer is, "All my life." If you believe in the unconscious, that includes even sleeping time. Obviously an author, or anyone else for that matter, must experience people and places, events and emotions, before he or she can set them down.

Al Silverman, a prominent New York editor, remarked several years ago, "With the people you've known and the life you've led, you simply *have* to write a memoir. But in publishing today, a memoir could be a hard sell. Center on the great stars you've known, Jackie Robinson, Robert Frost, and the rest who became friends, and you'll have something that will spark interest in any market. I'm recommending a *cloaked* memoir." I here uncloak Al Silverman.

Walter Rich, the president and CEO of the New York, Susquehanna, and Western Railroad, was encouraging across many summer evenings at Edgewater, his estate in Cooperstown, New York. We gather annually there to celebrate ballplayers and politicians. Three of my favorite fellow celebrants are Congressman Sherwood Bohlert; the retired right hander, James Timothy (Mudcat) Grant; and the gentlemanly former Dodger pitching star Clem Labine. As a source of inspiration, Walter presented me with a copy of William L. Shirer's memoir, *Nightmare Years.* Let this be a public thank-you to my tycoon friend.

Samuel S. Vaughan, formerly editor in chief at Doubleday, suggested that I write about my late son. Indeed the chapter title "Rescuing Roger," with its deliberate ambiguity, came out of a conversation with Sam. He said such personal matters would be difficult to write; it turned out also to be joyous. For when I wrote about Roger throwing passes, scoring hockey goals, or just being a kid, he was alive again and at my side.

My agent, Robert Wilson, found me a happy home at St. Martin's Press and an amazingly energetic editor in Pete Wolverton. Rob Wilson was encouraging, cheerful, and supportive throughout all my efforts on this book. Pete Wolverton scanned every word and was alive with comments, suggestions, and even demands. The committed editor, who works on a manuscript as though it were his own, is an endangered species. I can't remember encountering a more committed editor than Pete Wolverton, and I'd suggest that the Wolverton species is in no way endangered.

I benefited from research assistance supplied by two journalism graduates of The State University of New York, New Paltz, a college not far from my Hudson Valley home, where recently I served as Distinguished Ottaway Fellow in Journalism. Adam Bosch ran down any number of elusive details, including many on the demise of the DeSisto School. Stephanie Rogers pursued facts and photographs and kept files, and the author, generally organized. She even located copies of every issue of *Our Sports,* the now obscure magazine that Jackie Robinson and I put out fifty-three years ago.

Bill Francis of the National Baseball Library at Cooperstown always knew what ballplayer threw to which base and how accurately. Carole Thompson, curator of the Robert Frost Stone House Museum in South Shaftsbury, Vermont, showed me a good deal of fresh Frost information when I spoke there in the summer of 2005. Mark Reese, Pee Wee's son, a poet and filmmaker (and retired outfielder) maintained a steady drumbeat of support. They have my gratitude.

"But *really,* how long did it take to write the book?"

Really, it took all my life.

ROGER KAHN
Stone Ridge, New York
November 4, 2005

They would not find me changed from him they knew—
Only more sure of all I thought was true.

—*"Into My Own,"*
ROBERT FROST

# Into My Own

# Brooklyn Overture

PEARL BUCK once warned aspiring writers—"little embryo novelists," she called them—not to be born under a great creed. It was better, she said, for a writer to be born among thieves and gypsies. A writer's life flourishes amid wildness, sometimes visible, as in a prizefight, sometimes within, as in a breakdown. But without that wildness, Pearl Buck maintained, the fires that make a writer do not burn.

As things happened some seventy-seven Octobers into the past, I myself was born under a great creed. In a word, that creed was intellectuality. As playthings and nursery rhymes, so to speak, my mother offered Greek myths, the searing tales of the house of Atreus; classical music, the keyboard works of Bach, the violin sonatas of Beethoven; and poetry, poetry; indeed, all was poetry in my mother's house long ago, where the twilights rang with Homer, Shakespeare, and Housman and Edna St. Vincent Millay, whose haunting elegy, "The Ballad of the Harp-Weaver," made my mother's eyes grow moist.

My mother, Olga Rockow Kahn, had graduated from Cornell University in 1923 with a major in ancient history. She was an early female Ivy Leaguer, Jewish to boot, and on top of *that,* a Socialist, small, dark, and fiery, a woman whose dream was that I publish new and acclaimed translations of the plays from Athens's heroic age. In later years one of my responses was to post a D minus in a college course in classical Greek, which I accomplished by declining to learn the letters of the

Greek alphabet. It is difficult to translate Aeschylus if you cannot make out the spelling of his name.

Straining against the creed, I longed for the ways of thieves and gypsies, and I was not denied. My father, Gordon Jacques Kahn, an unpretentious, onetime college infielder, from a mixed Jewish–Catholic Alsatian background, came into the world, walked to and fro with a lurching stride, and by and large liked what he saw. Among his interests were botany, crossword puzzles, Thomas Jefferson, Venice, detective stories by Ellery Queen, and the Reconstruction period in the South. Among his loves were Gibbons's *Decline and Fall of the Roman Empire* and the four symphonies of Johannes Brahms. But his great passion, aside from my mother and Pall Mall king-size cigarettes, was the game of baseball. I never entirely escaped my mother's great creed. Indeed, our final conversation, after time and a brutal mugging had diminished her, was a courtly debate about Prince Hamlet and King Lear. But my lust for thieves and gypsies never waned. I would find them, as perhaps my father had, in baseball . . .

# CHAPTER I

# The Coach

Reality brightens my dream, to become a writer.

## I

It may seem curious, at least it does to me, that an old *Herald Tribune* hand tapping a keyboard would so soon cite a primal dictum of *The New York Times,* as quoted by Arthur Gelb in the 662-page memoir he called *City Room.* Early in the book, along about page 136, Gelb quotes Adolph Ochs, paterfamilias of the family that runs the *Times,* as saying, "The most useful man on a newspaper is one who can edit. . . . Writers are galore."

Quoting Ochs around the *Times* may not be precisely like spouting Luke in a Southern Baptist church, but it comes close. The old man burst out of Chattanooga and took control of *The New York Times* in 1896, a publisher of ferocious ambition, an astounding work ethic, and a brilliant head for business. Even in the twenty-first century, six decades after his death, he remains the principal architect of what is probably the most successful newspaper on earth. There is a nice ring to his surprising phrase "writers are galore," but in this instance, as in a few others, Baron Ochs was wrong.

The greatest newspaperman I have known was R. (for Rufus) Stanley Woodward, a huge, myopic former Amherst lineman whose glory days came when he was sports editor of the New York *Herald Tribune*. During that stretch, from the 1930s into the 1960s, "Coach" Woodward pitched batting practice for the Yankees in a uniform borrowed from Lou Gehrig, discovered Red Smith, saved the baseball career of Jackie Robinson, and invented the modern sports page. He also took time out to cover World War II and, in 1944, armed with a Boy Scout knife and a sheaf of pencils, landed behind Nazi lines in a glider, the better to observe the horrific Battle of Arnhem. He did all these high deeds, and, on another level, he managed to convince me in my youth that if I worked hard, double-spaced my copy, read *Paradise Lost,* and learned to remain vertical after drinking four martinis, there was no reason, no reason at all, why I could not become a writer. Woodward was the man Ernest Hemingway wanted to be.

Woodward's credo, which he learned as a cub reporter at the Worcester *Evening Gazette* from an editor named Nicholas J. Skerrett, went like this: "The American newspaper is the greatest institution in the world." I think all of us who have worked for American newspapers feel that way, at least some of the time, which is why we get so upset when we see the art and craft of newspapering abused. Within Woodward's mighty frame—six feet two, 230 pounds—beat the sensitive and vulnerable heart of an idealist. He was a classicist, a humanist, and a liberal, who loved farming and played the violin. But above all he was an idealist.

Ogden Mills Reid, who had inherited great wealth, ran the *Trib* for four decades, until his death in 1947. In a staunch Republican way, old Ogden was an idealist, even as Woodward, and he championed the sometimes combative Coach. But Reid's will left the paper in the hands of his widow, Helen Rogers Reid, who had started her career as an impecunious social secretary. Helen was slight, strong-willed, jut-jawed, and tightfisted. She appointed herself publisher and designated her son "Whitie" editor in chief. Both these people were kind to me. Each took a personal interest in my work. But neither had old Ogden's overall tolerance for nonconformists, rebels, or, for that matter, martinis. After some clashes, which I'll get to presently, Helen and Whitie fired the best sports editor in the country and replaced him with a onetime col-

lege hockey star named Bob Cooke, formerly Whitie's Old Blue classmate at Yale.

Jolted, his adrenaline pumping wildly, Woodward immediately dictated, not wrote but *dictated,* a remarkable, forgotten book called *Sports
Page,* which could be used as a primer today by every publication covering sports, although, Woodward being Woodward, it is livelier and better
written than standard texts. In *Sports Page,* Woodward warned of "the
unholy jargon, the tendency to call things by names other than their
own." Typically that would be describing a shortstop's error as a "mis-
cue." The shortstop, of course, does not carry a cue stick. Woodward
ruled that "horrendous clashes of fearsome Tigers and snarling Wolverines, usually concluded in purple sunsets, are taboo." Copyreaders,
whom he called "the comma police," sometimes may cut a good writer
to dullness, "but they are essential if the vehicle [sports section] is not to
be smeared with wild and indiscriminate pigments." Good copy editors
were rare and valuable, but the lifeblood of a great sports section and a
great newspaper flowed from its writers, or at least it should. "The giants
of our craft," Woodward asserted, "Grantland Rice, W. O. McGeehan,
and Westbrook Pegler, each gave something to today's school of writing.
Rice contributed rhythm and euphony; Pegler a grumpy and grudging
curiosity for fact; and McGeehan a certain twist, in the likeness of Anatole France, which could make an ordinary sentence interesting."

Rice is best remembered for creating the most remarkable lead ever
written on a football game. Covering Army–Notre Dame in November
1924—Notre Dame, 13; Army, 7—Rice began:

> Outlined against a blue-gray sky, The Four Horsemen rode again. In
> dramatic lore they are known as Famine, Pestilence, Destruction and
> Death. These are only aliases. Their real names are Stuhldreyer, Miller,
> Crowley and Layden. They formed the crest of the South Bend cy-
> clone before which another fighting Army football team was swept
> over the precipice at the Polo Grounds yesterday afternoon as 55,000
> spectators peered down on a bewildering panorama spread on the
> green plain below.
>
> A cyclone can't be snared. It may be surrounded but somewhere
> it breaks through to keep on going. When the cyclone starts from

South Bend, where the candle lights still gleam through the Indiana sycamores, those in the way must take to their storm cellars at top speed . . .

Over drinks Red Smith liked to ask archly, "From what angle was Granny watching the game if he saw the Notre Dame backfield outlined against a blue-gray sky?" Further, there was no precipice below the Polo Grounds; the old ball park actually sat *under* the precipice called Coogan's Bluff. But such specifics are piffle. Rice's lead itself was a cyclone that swept away all before it. Or so I believe. (So did Woodward, and so did Red Smith when he wasn't being arch.)

William O'Connell "Bill" McGeehan, called Sheriff, had his golden years in the 1920s, which used to be called the Golden Age of Sport. When Luis Angel Firpo, nicknamed the Wild Bull of the Pampas, fought Jack Dempsey, the Manassa Mauler, for the heavyweight championship in 1923, Firpo knocked Dempsey through the ropes in round one. Sportswriters shoved Dempsey back into the ring and, although dazed, he continued to fight fiercely. Dempsey won by a knockout in round two, the ninth knockdown in about four minutes of championship boxing. Ring Lardner commented that Dempsey had turned big Luis Firpo into "the Tame Cow of the Pampas." More seriously Sheriff McGeehan wrote in the *New York Tribune*: "A pair of wolves battling in the pines of the Northern Woods, a pair of cougars in the wastes of the Southwest, might have staged a faster and more savage bout, but no two human beings."

Pegler is remembered, if at all today, for his venomous old age, when he moved into the western desert and wrote column after column attacking Franklin and Eleanor Roosevelt. But the earlier Pegler had been a superb and salty journalist who wrote that only two varieties of sportswriter existed on earth, "the ones who go 'gee whiz' and the one who say, 'aw nuts.'"

Why is it that none of these worthies worked for Ochs's *New York Times,* or wanted to. First, to be sure, such writers as Rice and McGeehan were not "galore" and would not care to be so labeled. Besides, like most fine craftsmen, they did not want editors touching their stuff and, to repeat one of Adolph Ochs's graceless phrases, making their values "brought within the understanding of the reader." They were not, after all, writing for simpletons or, in Pegler's term, "the great unwashed."

Woodward was proud of his chief copyreader, a bespectacled character named Arthur Glass, who could and often did read works in Latin or classical Greek. But he would never have called Glass the most important man in his sports section. One result of Adolph Ochs's dictum about copyreaders was a concentration of power within the walls of the Times Building, where Ochs was most comfortable. The copyreader comes into the office, and there he stays, in the old days wearing a green eyeshade. Reporters, moving about the rough and tumble of their beats, become rough and tumble themselves, and independent. When I first was anointed a baseball writer, Red Smith told me that there could now be only two excuses for my appearing at the *Herald Tribune* offices on West Forty-first Street. One was to pick up a paycheck. The other was to drop off an expense account.

When the inside people, the copy editors and the rest, become empowered, as they were at the *Times,* they tend to develop a generic arrogance. They can change, cut, and edit a writer's stuff as suits their needs and pleasure. These folk may be pleasant and cordial in many ways, but they see as their duty correcting and improving prose written by others, whether or not they have the ability or understanding to do so. A notable example of editing by arrogance befell Red Smith after the *Times* hired a woman named Le Anne Schreiber as sports editor, in a partial (and unofficial) settlement of a sexual discrimination lawsuit brought against the paper in the 1970s by several female staffers. (That story was covered by the late Nan Robertson of the *Times* in her book *The Girls in the Balcony.*)

Smith had been visiting one of his favorite haunts, the racetrack at Saratoga, and was sitting beside a friend who owned a horse that was running comfortably ahead. Then the horse slowed—"flattened out" is the racetrack term—and most of the field galloped by. The horse finished far out of the money. Smith said, "Sorry," then considered the owner's face and presently wrote, "He looked as though he had just bitten into an apple and found half a worm." Without consulting Smith, Schreiber changed the sentence to read that the man looked as though he had bitten into an apple "and found a worm." The cream of Smith's jest was soured. Recounting this episode, and a few others, to me, Smith summed up Le Anne Schreiber in one sentence. "She is," he said, "the only editor who has ever made me scream."

The Ochs system of coronating editors created generations of misery on the *Times*'s writing staff. Gay Talese, as a young man in the 1950s, complained consistently about what "the desk" was doing to his stuff. In time, pursuing happiness, he married a beautiful woman named Nan Ahearn and quit the paper. Years later Molly Ivins, the spicy, gifted coauthor of *Bushwhacked: The Short but Happy Political Life of George W. Bush,* signed on with the *Times* but quit soon afterward. Her style and the *Times* desk people did not mesh. During my own years covering the Brooklyn Dodgers my *Times* rival, an earnest, elderly, and somewhat deaf sportswriter named Roscoe McGowen, used to wind down his daily stint by downing "three fingers"—sometimes six or nine—of good bourbon whiskey supplied by the ball club, after which he began to grumble, "I'd wish they'd let me write, really write, but they just won't." He wanted not simply to report ball games, he said, but also to contribute a regular column of chatty Brooklyn baseball notes that he would call "Oil for the Lamps of Flatbush." "Similar to the sort of conversational stuff they let you get into the *Trib*." Like Talese and Ivins after him and scores of reporters before him, Roscoe got nowhere suggesting something new to the ruling class of copy editors. He died at 80, not bitter, but surely disappointed. (In fairness, my own most recent original article in the *Times,* a 2005 op-ed piece, edited by one David Shipley, ran as written, and Shipley sent a note of thanks.)

But it was a wonder then and it remains a wonder today that I found a job at the *Herald Tribune,* not the *Times.* My classroom record had been erratic; the portfolio of my campus writing was slim. I was fortunate to come aboard at all. It was yet a greater wonder that my first *Trib* guide turned out to be Rufus Stanley Woodward.

Prep school days had been reasonably happy at a now defunct Episcopal Brooklyn institution called Froebel Academy. I retain a writing prize I won there on May 31, 1937, for commentary on stories read in the assembly by a commanding woman named Ida Bentley Judd. The prize, inscribed to me by Mrs. Judd, took the form of an illustrated edition of

*Huckleberry Finn,* "copyright, 1923, by The Mark Twain Company." I still grin at the "Notice from the Author": "Persons attempting to find a motive in this narrative will be prosecuted; persons attempting to find a moral in it will be banished; persons attempting to find a plot in it will be shot."

From the time that I was seven or eight I felt that I could write. It was nice to have someone else say the same thing, and nicer still to win Mrs. Judd's prize over students three or four years my senior. If I had to name a date when my dream of becoming a writer first took serious hold, I would select May 31, 1937.

The Froebel headmaster, Carlton M. Saunders, M.A., drafted my father, the onetime college third baseman, to serve as athletic director, without pay, this being the 1930s, when Depression ruled the land. My family was comfortably fixed, and my father, who loved athletics, mapped out a three-sport program for about forty boys as we stood in an uneven mass on the gravelly field behind the Froebel mansion. His basketball plans were hooted down by some preppie louts who insisted that basketball was a sissy sport. "Why do you have to *bounce* the ball?" asked one of my louder classmates, "Fats" Scott. We all agreed that soccer was strictly for girls. There being no hockey rink, that left us football in the autumn and baseball in the spring.

Unlike even the youngest Little Leaguers today, we played baseball without wearing uniforms. We must have looked like a rabble going to our big game against Adelphi Academy at Cunningham Park in Queens, some wearing tan work pants, some corduroy knickers, some blue dungarees. Our football was more formal since my father decreed that every boy who played had to wear a helmet, cleated shoes, and shoulder pads. By a vote we selected blue and gold as the Froebel football colors and the parents of all the boys, also comfortably fixed, chipped in and bought leather helmets, pads, cleats, moleskin pants, and jerseys. They bought just one set; we practiced in our game uniforms and some glory shone right there. After tussles with elementary French, I still remember going down to the shop which was our dressing room and changing from classroom clothes into my football uniform. Then clacking down some steps that led to the gravelly field, I experienced a metamorphosis. No longer the bumbling French student—is a female horse *la cheval* or *le cheval?*—I was now a helmeted, padded running back.

My father hired a full-time coach named Red Grogan, who taught me a number of things. You followed blockers closely enough so that no tackler could move among you, but not so closely that if a blocker went down, you went down, too, in a tangle of legs and a rumble of grunts. You ran not like a long-striding sprinter, but like a ballcarrier, legs pumping up and down, which made you harder to tackle. You tapped your blockers on the shoulder pads, left side or right, to let them know which way to block a tackler. It was exciting stuff if you were not afraid to be tackled, which I was not. The Froebel classroom time itself was tolerable, except for the chatter of the class anti-Semite, whom I shall call "Neil Rafferty." He would say such things as, "Louis Pasteur discovered the cure for *rabbis.*" This emboldened a pretty girl named Jean McGovern to chant at me during one recess:

> *Oh, they don't wear pants*
> *In the southern part of France,*
> *And the dance they do*
> *Is enough to shock a Jew.*

I can't recall if I was offended or aroused by Jean's impish, impudent manner. A good guess would be both. But Jean was only the second-prettiest girl in Froebel; the most attractive, ladylike Janet Arpert, was unattainable. She had fallen in love with the music teacher, Dexter Davison, whom she would marry just about as soon as that was legally possible. As for Rafferty, he lacked the guts to play football, so I never did get back at him. He was one of the few Irish Catholics at Froebel—Peter O'Malley, later the bumbling president of the Los Angeles Dodgers, was another—and followed the preachings of Father Charles Coughlin, the infamous radio priest whose message over a hundred American radio stations insisted that poor Jews were Communists and rich Jews were international bankers. Since all Jews were either poor or rich . . . Well, Coughlin's asinine points won a good deal of credence. He was a classic scoundrel, cloaked in the robes of the clergy and the First Amendment.

My Froebel class graduated in June of 1940, which was, to use Thomas Hardy's term, a time of the breaking of nations. In less than a year of fighting, Nazi armies had conquered Poland, Norway, the

Netherlands, Belgium, and France. The Nazi leader had been photographed beside the Eiffel Tower. However disastrous the idea, however horrifying the thought, a world dominated by Adolf Hitler appeared to have become a possibility. Against this background, I recited an Old Athenian Oath during commencement ceremonies at St. Bartholomew's Episcopal Church in Brooklyn: "We will never bring disgrace to this our city by any act of dishonesty or cowardice, nor e'er desert our suffering comrades in the ranks."

That was at best remotely relevant to the disintegrating state of civilization. Next one of the girls sang, "When you come to the end of a perfect day . . ." Nothing could have been less appropriate. This was 1940. This was the year of the blitzkrieg. Then a Brooklyn judge, an old Brooklyn Protestant judge—sadly, I have forgotten his name—delivered a stunning address. The world was in dreadful shape, he said, and it was his duty to apologize to the young graduates for the cauldron into which they were going. He talked about the Great Depression, the Fascists, the Nazis, and the Japanese militarists ravaging China. We adults, the judge said, have done a terrible job in our time, and, as I say, young people, I apologize. My greatest hope is that you Froebel graduates somehow can do a better job than we have done.

In the reception that followed, my parents said that they had considered the judge's talk extraordinary. They found themselves alone in their enthusiasm. Most of the other parents, *all* of the other parents, disagreed. The prevailing mood was, *Facts be damned. You should not say disturbing things to children.*

Gordon and Olga seemed surprised. They were naive about the depth and power of American isolationism. They did not seem to have recognized the extent of American indifference to Hitler's anti-Semitism. A few days later I heard my mother, the old Cornell Marxist, say, "We simply must pull the boy out of prep. If we don't, we may have a Fascist in our home."

"Not that," my father said, "but possibly a Republican."

"Almost as bad," Olga said.

That fall I was dispatched to Erasmus Hall, a vast public school in Flatbush, where sports were big-time and commercial, with no spots open to 120-pound running backs. Without varsity sports my experience there was less happy than at Froebel, at least until fourth-year Latin. There I encountered my first great teacher, a Scottish Jew, Dr. Harry Wedeck, who taught two books of the *Aeneid,* Vergil's epic, which glorifies the legendary Trojan origins of the Roman people. Fifteen of us who had survived Caesar (easy) and Cicero (windy) convened daily in a studio in one of Erasmus Hall's Gothic towers, where Dr. Wedeck held forth. I enjoyed the wanderings of Aeneas, and one day Wedeck sent me to the blackboard, there to write and parse fifteen lines of Vergil that I had been assigned to memorize. Somewhere about line six, I could not recall whether a particular letter was an "i" or an "e." I had developed a limited academic shrewdness, and I made a letter with a narrow loop, which I then dotted. Next I accented appropriate syllables as Wedeck wanted. (In teaching Latin Dr. Wedeck was also teaching three fundamentals of writing, in Latin or in English. These were and are grammar, syntax, and rhythm.)

Back at my desk, the text revealed that the uncertain letter was an "i."

"Mr. Kahn," Dr. Wedeck began. (He was the first teacher to grace me with an honorific.) "Is that an 'e' or an 'i?'"

"An 'i,' sir."

"But, Mr. Kahn, I do not detect a dot."

"I made a dot, Dr. Wedeck, but it was obliterated by the accent mark."

"I don't believe you, Mr. Kahn, but at least you used the word 'obliterated.' Full credit." Soon afterward I was wandering with the Cumaean Sybil into an underworld illuminated by the genius of Publius Vergilius Maro and the wit and learning of Dr. Harry Wedeck.

On the good earth, I became enamored of two pretty girls, one named Naomi Fox and the other Nancy Wolf. This led my father to ask if I were interested in zoology. I was not. Elementary biology was more like it. Then college came and proved mostly a time of grief.

New York University Uptown, officially the College of Arts and Pure Science, located on University Heights, site of the present Bronx Community College, was separated from what the school song called "the grim, gray Palisades," by the Hudson River, a cliff, and a colonnade housing the Hall of Fame for Great Americans, Eli Whitney first entry. My daily trip to the Bronx Alps meant an hour-and-twenty-minute subway ride each way from Brooklyn, a noisome, jolting trip that sucked the joy out of my college experience somewhere between 96th and 161st Streets at about 8:20 A.M. Worse yet, the college was designed for premedical students who hoped attending an NYU undergraduate college would help them gain admittance to the NYU Medical School. Most of the premeds were Jewish, and various quota systems at the time sharply limited the number of Jews medical schools would accept, which created a carnivorous, or perhaps I should say cannibalistic, intercollegiate climate. Grades, as opposed to learning, ruled the joint. My maternal grandmother, Emily Rosenfeld, had graduated from medical school in Berne, Switzerland, and following a stay in Paris become one of the first female physicians to practice in Brooklyn. This was so long ago, around 1900, that there is no telephone number on her professional card. Although my mother was clearly independent and spirited, enough cliché Jewish mother resided in her to insist that I become a doctor. My counterinsistence that I had no interest whatsoever in medicine, provoked a blare of nasty scenes, climaxed by Olga's war cry that I had better prepare to be a shoe salesman because that was all my intelligence would allow.

My father, one of the creators of the enormously popular radio quiz program *Information, Please,* wanted me to go to law school and practice "radio law." He was reasoning correctly that show business law was a growing field, but it was also one in which, like medicine, I had zero interest. I was still trying to become a writer, although I wasn't close enough to either parent to say that out loud very often at home. My father's family, which came to America in 1848, was a mix of Jews called Weill, Joseph, and Lazar, and Roman Catholics, with the formidable name of Villipigue. Maurice Kahn, my grandfather, was imported from the Alsatian village of Dahlingen to marry my grandmother, Sophia. Her dowry was a butcher's shop. I sometimes wondered if I preferred putting up with a bit of anti-Semitism that came with the name Kahn to going through life with the porcine, albeit Christian, handle Villipigue. (I'm still not sure.) The Weills owned a wholesale meat business on Washington Street near downtown Brooklyn with the Brooklyn Navy Yard and the U.S. Navy itself as major clients. During the 1890s the Villipigues opened a restaurant at the fashionable Sheepshead Bay Racetrack. In my father's favorite cautionary tale, he told me that one of the Villipigues had a weakness for gambling: After losing a great chunk of the family fortune on ambling ponies, this character committed suicide by hanging.

My father had little tolerance for foibles. Dropping the weary zoology joke about Wolf and Fox, he told me often, loudly, grimly, that if I ever got a girl pregnant, he would physically throw me out of the house "for good." Gambling was yet a worse sin, but he could be a bit lighter there. If I performed some chores, weeding the gardens at his country place and asked for a tip, he responded more than once, "Don't bet on horses." And as for my actually impregnating a Wolf or a Fox, if I'd tried that in the back row of the Brooklyn Paramount, I would have been arrested. For good or ill, virginity ruled my corner of old Brooklyn. Groping girls, many who were eager to be groped, and watching shabby black-and-white pornographic movies, was as far as anybody got in the skin game that was played in my old neighborhood.

I did find one splendid teacher at NYU. Dr. Theodore Francis Jones, a World War I aide to Franklin D. Roosevelt, presided over a course that covered the period of ancient Hellenism (about 800 B.C.E.) through the reign of the Byzantine emperor Justinian, which ran to 565 A.D. In short, the origins of western civilization with side trips that interested Dr. Jones. He did three lectures of the history of the persecution of Jews, though 1492, and another three on the history of heraldry. He threw out stimulating questions. "If Christ were alive today, would he be considered a Communist?" I sat fascinated, and the result was the one A I posted in college. But the rest of the curriculum and much of the faculty were dreary, and many of the courses were rigged so that it was all but impossible to get a grade higher than a C. The biology chairman, Dr. Horace Wesley Stunkard, who delivered a killer set of lectures, began one: "Protoplasm is a polyphasic colloidal emulsion in electrostatic and dynamic equilibrium, the phases of which are reversible." My memory was strong and on the Friday quiz I gave Stunkard all his words back verbatim. I got a C.

"What the hell is this?" I asked a graduate assistant, who was an albino.

"It's a C," he said, "That's the third letter, in case you didn't know. If you wanted a better grade, you should have done outside reading on the nature of protoplasm."

"It's a way," said my friend, big, black-haired Hershey Marcus, "of keeping Jewish premeds out of medical school. Stunkard gives everyone a C. Then when you get interviewed for med school, if you do get that far, you'll be asked, How can you expect to be a doctor when you only got a C in freshman bio?" (Hershey took his biology at a less demanding college and in time became a psychiatrist, a field which I don't believe gives much prominence to polyphasic colloidal emulsions.)

I took to skipping classes in the required courses biology, organic chemistry, and calculus, hanging out in the gym. Soon I had developed one of the best outside shots in the Bronx and at about that time found myself placed on probation. I might have played varsity ball at Middlebury or Amherst, but NYU basketball was strictly for pros, recruited to play in Madison Square Garden and assigned to snap courses at the School of Commerce. "They're mostly taking Snow Shoveling 30–40," someone said. "The prerequisite is Snowing 10–20." I wrote some pieces for *Medley*, the campus humor magazine. I hired out to a few medical students, ghosting themes they had to write for courses in English composition. But when not typing or shooting hoops, my main thought at NYU was simple and constant. "I have to get the hell out of here." I was seventeen years old.

I found work successively as a delivery boy for Ludben Stationary on Twenty-third Street; as an assistant electrician at a fluorescent fixture shop on Bedford Avenue, across the street from Ebbets Field; and as a sheet metal solderer for Espy Products, which manufactured two-way radios for the navy in a factory on East Sixty-fifth Street. The money was fair, and I managed to keep attending just enough classes at NYU to avoid outright expulsion.

Crisis came in the summer of 1947, when I was nineteen. The Harmony Country Club of Hurleyville, New York, hired me as a busboy, a job which made me be responsible for setting places, clearing dishes, and bringing specialty items for forty-eight people three times a day. Harmony was called a "hash house," which meant that there was one entrée, and only one entrée, for all. Better hotels, with menus, were called "blue plates." The salary was $10 a week; sleeping quarters were in an airless barn, but with good fortune a busboy could earn serious money in tips.

We worked in tuxedo pants, white shirts, and black bow ties, standing at attention as the hungry guests came marching in. Harmony advertised itself as "150 Acres of Everything for the Young of All Ages," but most of the vacationers were fiftyish people, cutters, sewing machine operators, and pressers, from New York's garment industry, more comfortable with Yiddish than with English. My own Yiddish vocabulary at the time consisted of two words, both derogatory, "schmuck" and "schlemiel," and the language and dialect barrier struck me at my first breakfast. "Bring me," said a bald, openmouthed diner, "ha bissel potsis."

"Peaches, sir? I'll see if the salad man has any."

"No! Not peaches. *Potsis!*"

"Do you want a pitcher, sir. I'll bring one."

"Not pitcher, schlemiel. *Potsis!*"

I sent out an emergency call to a Yiddish-speaking waiter, who listened and quickly translated, "He wants a little [*bissel*] pot cheese." I soon learned that a "stickele herring" meant a piece of pickled herring, a "glassele tay" was a glass of tea and an order for "ganzen brennen" meant that the guest was enduring a bout of constipation. "Ganzen brennen" was Yiddish for All-Bran. Many of my diners greeted me with a joke, the same joke. "Hey. Lemme esk you. Are you da bus boy?"

"Yes, sir."

"Well, if you da boss's boy, you must be rich, so I won't hef to give you a teep."

"Ha, sir. That's a good one."

"Mine husband," one woman said, "You know what he is? A regular Milton Berle."

But the diners did tip, and generously. Over July 4 weekend I earned $150, and that was when the crisis struck. I'd kept my NYU grades away from my parents for some time by intercepting the mail. But now, with my parents at their Westchester summer home and me anchored in Sullivan County, my college transcript fell into the hands of my father. Mostly D's and C's, with perhaps a single B. Enraged, my father wrote me a long hand letter saying that I had better start thinking of some other place to live. I was not likely again to be welcome in his home. Then, in cold fury, he wrote, "You may not drag this family back to the jungle."

I was upset, of course, but I was also thrilled by a wallet bulging with $150 in small bills. I thought of writing Dad, smirking, "Precisely what jungle does one find in the province of Alsace?" But I chose another stratagem. I bought a $150 postal money order and mailed it to my father with a note directing him to open a savings account in my name. I concluded, "I'm assuming I can trust you with this sum." From the day he got my money order, my father never threatened me again. I may have remained a bit of a boob in his estimation, and certainly an undisciplined student, but I was a boob who knew how to make money. An inept businessman himself, he respected that.

By Labor Day my bank account exceeded $1,000, probably equal to $10,000 today. I was also exhausted because the work week at Harmony Country Club was seven days long, and the work schedule ran from six A.M. to nine P.M. After sleeping for a few days, I thought of transferring to a smaller college, where liberal arts dominated, but my spirit weakened and I registered at NYU again, pretty much as a conditioned reflex.

I sometimes wonder what sustained me during these years of drift. Probably it was the dream that I could somehow, someday, become a writer. Certain signposts encouraged me. I had won the Ida Judd writing prize. I had been Dr. Wedeck's favorite student. All of my ghosted essays for the NYU premeds drew grades of A. But I was not Truman Capote or Françoise Sagan, able to write a smashing novel while emerging from adolescence. "Write what you know," generations of English teachers have said. "Write about what you have seen." Fine, I thought, but limiting. Vergil never saw Troy. Shakespeare never knew Macbeth.

I sketched out plots for three novels. None pleased me. My youthful writing efforts, mostly poetry, fell so far short of my ambitions that I knew some hard and very lonely afternoons and nights. It was a lot more difficult writing a sonnet, I discovered, than John Keats made it appear.

Trying to make sense of a great many things all at once, I escaped into imagining the life of a writer. On dust jackets, writers were described as having experienced intriguing and varied careers. Typically, "Renowned author J. Edgar Schimmelpfennig has been a homicide detective, a soda jerk, a furniture mover, an elephant trainer, a diamond miner, a male nurse, and a piano player in the House of the Rising Sun."

I often thought of what might be said on the dust jackets of my books, none yet written. *Running back.* (Could follow blockers.) *Latin star.* (Won gold medal at Erasmus Hall.) *Busboy.* (Never dropped a tray.) Even to me that sounded skimpy. Maybe I could get a job at an advertising agency. Advertising messages seemed vaguely related to creative writing and were said to pay nicely. Work in advertising, salt away some cash, then rent a flat in Paris or London or Rome and start a book. But what book would I start? One of the nicest things about youthful dreams is that they don't have to be practical. No book came to mind, but the dream of authorship sustained me.

One October evening in 1947 my father asked if I still harbored notions of becoming a writer. A friend of his and colleague on the editorial board of the *Information, Please Almanac,* was Joseph G. Herzberg, city editor of the *Herald Tribune.* If I telephoned, Joe Herzberg would grant me an interview for the position of copyboy, which, my father said, could conceivably lead to "something more than that, if you're good enough."

Herzberg was a stern, deep-voiced character whose hands shook as he read newspapers, which he did throughout the interview. I talked about my fondness for writing and journalism, to what appeared to be his profound uninterest, so it surprised me when his secretary, Eve Peterson, telephoned one February day and said that if I reported for work promptly at four P.M. tomorrow a job would be waiting. When I arrived at the fifth-floor newsroom, breathless with excitement, I found, as Keats described George Chapman's translation of *The Iliad,* "a realm of gold." From that day forward I never again entered a college classroom, except to teach.

I joined the *Trib,* red-faced and eager, on a twelve-degree day in 1948 three and a half months after my twentieth birthday and became, to use one of Stanley Woodward's pet words, a troglodyte. Technically my job was night copyboy, four shifts running from four P.M. to midnight and one running from eight P.M. to four A.M. The pay was $24 a week, or as I soon learned to say, "A cool $24 a week," but the job was almost impossible to get. The *Trib* generally was regarded as the best-written newspaper in America, as the New York *World* had been acclaimed during the 1920s. Just wedging a toe inside a door at the *Trib,* any toe, any door, drew graduates of Columbia Journalism, a former Harvard football captain, and a star college editor from NYU, to mention a few of my impecunious, pale, and overqualified troglodyte colleagues. We were all part of a generation that Wanted to Write, and I had read pretty much everything by Sinclair Lewis, Thomas Wolfe, John Steinbeck, John Dos Passos, and Ernest Hemingway. Writers I have come to regard as larger talents—Hardy, Dostoevsky, and Joyce—lay beyond my twenty-year-old ken. After Herzberg interviewed me, I would learn long afterward, he remarked to my father, "I'll see what I can do, but the boy seems awfully *young.*"

In 1948 most outstanding newspaper people wanted to work in New York City. *The Los Angeles Times* and *The Washington Post* were growing up. *The Chicago Tribune* was hopelessly right-wing. The *St. Louis Post-Dispatch* still identified people by color, as in "John Smith, 38, Negro, was struck and killed by a trolley car yesterday." Certainly there had been exceptions, such as H. L. Mencken, the grouchy sage of Baltimore, but New York was the capital of American newspapering, and the *Tribune* had the best writing staff in town.

The chief night copyboy, frail, bent Benny Weinberg, a rarity in that he was a career copyboy, showed me around. Here in a row of teletypes were the Washington wires transmitting sixty words a minute. That struck me as a technological marvel. Here in a room full of Western Union "bugs," men typed national news and sports stories that were being transmitted in Morse code. "Never whistle in this room," Weinberg said. "It can confuse the telegraphers." Here were the overseas cables and here were the wirephoto machines. "That gentleman is Mr. Herzberg, our city editor," Benny said. "Over there is the night desk. The night editor, the person in charge, is Everett Kallgren, who everybody calls 'the Count.' Behind that little fence is the sports department. The big fellow with the eyeglasses is Mr. Woodward, the sports editor."

Much of a copyboy's job consisted of carrying stories, "copy" in the argot, from reporters to editors or more generally from point to point. But we also answered phones, took messages, and performed personal services for the staff. We were addressed not by name but as

"Copy," or in the case of Everett Kallgren, with a sneering cry of "Boy." Ken Bilby, a good foreign correspondent who later became an executive at NBC, won a measure of infamy in our ranks by flipping a cigarette on the linoleum floor, yelling, "Copy," and then ordering, "Kid, step on that butt."

On my first night at work, Kallgren glared at me and called, "Boy, take this over to the man at the end of the left side of the copydesk." It was a comment on a headline that the man had written. "Do better than this," it read in large letters, "or you're fired."

The copyreader read the message and slid quietly from his chair to the floor. He had fainted. The Count pretended not to notice. After the copy editor recovered, he moved to the business news section, which operated beyond the range of Kallgren's glares.

I had been reading the *Herald Tribune* for some years because its sports section surpassed that of the *Times* and also because, not being owned by a self-conscious Jewish family, it seemed to give more honest accounts of such major issues as the Nazi's slaughter the Jews of Europe and Israel's struggle to be born. The *Trib* officially was "liberal Republican," and, as my father put it, more liberal than the *Times* three years out of every four, the exception coming with presidential elections. Hoover, Landon, Dewey—the New York *Herald Tribune* backed them all. I knew the bylines of most of the *Tribune* stars before I got there, and in the first exciting nights I looked about to see, actually to see, the celebrity journalists.

Virgil Thomson, the music critic, was an intimate of Gertrude Stein—he wrote the music to her libretto *Four Saints in Three Acts*—and worked within a glass-walled office. He detested what I regarded as gorgeous symphonies by Jean Sibelius, but breathes there a critic without critical quirks? Walter Lippman, the distinguished political commentator, operated out of Washington and seldom visited the New York office. But John Crosby who wrote a column of commentary on radio, later TV, which is still the standard for that craft, sat out in the open, just like a reporter, except that he was guarded by attractive female assistants who came and went. Probably the most famous foreign correspondent was Marguerite Higgins, a radiant and willowy blonde with a breathy, bedroom voice. Probably the best correspondent was Homer Bigart, a rumpled, bespectacled fellow who stammered. When the *Tribune* folded in 1966, Bigart moved to the *Times*. (Arthur Gelb devotes parts of fourteen pages to him in *City Room*.) Stanley Woodward was more succinct. He summed up this brave newspaperman with a nickname, "Cannon's Mouth" Bigart.

Kallgren was, of course, ferocious, and Joe Herzberg, once he had gotten me my job, became glacial, but the mood in the editorial offices generally was nurturing to young people. I talked a bit with William Zinsser, the youthful drama editor, and he mentioned a story idea. A figure skater named Andrea McLaughlin would be appearing at Madison Square Garden for two weeks, during which time, given the relative seating capacities of the Garden and New York theaters, more people would see her than would see a Broadway play across three or four months. There was a story there, Bill said; did I want to try my hand at writing it? The skater was pretty, the interview went well, and Zinsser paid me $10 for the piece. Plus, and it was a big plus, at the age of twenty my byline appeared in the Sunday drama section of the New York *Herald Tribune*. Old newspaper men sometimes said, "You can't pay the grocer with a byline." The hell with that. At twenty I was feeling Miltonic, as in the wonderful line from *Lycidas*: "Fame is the spur that the clear spirit doth raise."

What did I know about the Irish playwright, Sean O'Casey, Zinsser next asked. Actually much less than I would claim. "Many think he's the greatest playwright in the world," Zinsser said, "but he can't get produced on Broadway. One of his very good ones, *The Plough and the Stars,* is about to open, but off Broadway, at the Hudson Guild Theater. Why don't you catch the show and give me another piece." In the next two days I read four O'Casey plays, something like three months' worth of reading during my downbeat college days. O'Casey captured me with the vital beauty of his language and his uncompromising social conscience. I wrote the longest story of my life, two thousand words, and Zinsser ran most of it, apologizing for his cuts, but that, he said, was the nature of the newspaper beast. This time he paid me $15.

But good writing assignments came hard. Most of my working time was still spent as a copyboy, carrying paper, running chores, and being addressed not by name but as "Copy." I thought then of a Roman term for slave that Dr. Wedeck had taught: *instrumentum vocale,* an instrument with a voice. The nightly pace was frenetic, until about 9:30, when the city edition closed and much of the staff repaired to the Artist and Writers Restaurant, a former speakeasy called Bleeck's, after its onetime owner, Jack Bleeck, where executives and reporters drank side by side. Copyboys were as welcome there as anyone else from the *Tribune,* but we could not afford the drinks.

As spring came, I took to spending the slow period in the sports section, where I answered phones and sometimes tore copy from the two sports teletypes, saying, with careful nonchalance, "Here's the White Sox story. They lost again." The chief copy editor, the so-called slot man, always responded, "Thanks, copy."

One or two nights a week, Stanley Woodward assigned himself to the desk. He was a complete newspaperman and liked to keep his touch at such skills as writing headlines. He also knew that the presence of the boss on the scene kept everybody else focused.

"Copy," Woodward said to me one night. "Go down to Bleeck's and get me a couple of packs of Camels." He handed me two dollars. The cigarettes cost fifty cents, and when I came back and tried to return the $1.50, Woodward said, "Keep the change, son." He was the only staffer at the *Trib* who seemed to know or care that a $1.50 tip meant a lot to a $24-a-week copyboy.

Some nights, after the city edition had gone to bed and he had drunk a few (or a flagon of) martinis at Bleeck's, he returned to the desk and started discussing journalism. I asked if I might sit in, and Woodward said, "Sure, son. What's your name?" Hosanna! No more *instrumentum vocale.* I was a person.

When he was young, about my age and working for the Worcester *Evening Gazette,* Woodward said, he got to handle an unusual late-breaking story. A fireman had married a local girl, and as he left the church, some of the fireman's pals handcuffed him to the bride. Woodward batted out the piece, then wrote this head:

### BLACKSMITH IS REQUIRED
### TO SEPARATE NEWLYWEDS

"It never ran," Woodward said. "The printers who saw it started to giggle, and the chief makeup man caught the thing. He replaced it with something duller."

Woodward was classically educated and proud of it. About once a year he journeyed to Yankee Stadium to cover a game and write a story that always included this line: "Casey Stengel stared out of the Yankee dugout under brows of dauntless courage and considerate pride." Regularly a copyreader changed the word "considerate" to "considerable." Next day Woodward marched into his sports department and yelled at the deskman. "I don't mind you changing my stuff, but you just changed John Milton. 'Considerate pride' comes from *Paradise Lost*." This was not simply braggadocio. Woodward wanted, indeed, demanded, that his staff be literate. "Do you happen to know Rogers Hornsby's lifetime average?" he asked me one night, seemingly out of nowhere. "Something outrageous like .350," I said. "I don't know the exact number."

"That's fine," he said. "I don't like figure filberts. You can always look up the numbers. But take a pennant race between mediocre clubs and call that 'a dubious battle.' That's the ticket. Where does it come from, the phrase 'dubious battle'?"

"A novel by John Steinbeck. He took the title from Milton: 'In dubious battle on the plains of heaven.'"

"You know Milton and you like baseball," Woodward said.

"My mother thinks baseball is my religion."

"Keep running errands and answering the phones," Woodward said. "Something may turn up for you in sports."

Woodward's overview was towering—he surely is the spiritual father of the well-tempered sports page—but he had the good sense to keep things, or at least the appearance of things, light. That is, when he was not intimidating those who fell into the unholy jargon. Uniquely among editors I have known, he tended to leave copy alone, even copy that he didn't like. But the clichés that sprout on sports pages moved him to fury. A baseball writer named Ed Sinclair once described a close Yankee victory as "a spine-tingling game." When Sinclair next appeared in the office, Woodward greeted him with a sustained fortissimo. "Next time you use that phrase, Mr. Sinclair, I am going to assign you to the

Yankee Stadium bleachers and you are going to have to ask every fan, every single one, whether or not his spine actually is tingling." Sinclair never became an outstanding baseball writer; neither did he use "spine-tingling" again.

Al Laney was a gifted writer who had been a secretary to James Joyce during the 1920s in Paris. He had written a fine memoir, *Paris Herald,* but even the best of us knows weak moments, and one day I was jolted to hear Woodward shouting at Laney, "If you refer to Chicago as 'the windy city' in my sports section one more time, out, out! OUT!" To this day I cannot type the words "windy city," without suffering a spasm of anxiety.

"You have to excise what is libelous or incoherent," Woodward said, "as when they drink themselves silly in a press box, but with these damn clichés, I'll simply leave them in. No one really suffers except the English language. Then, when I point out to a good writer that a cliché has appeared under his byline in my sports section, he will feel, to say the least, embarrassed. If I raise my voice, he'll be more embarrassed still. But if I had cut the cliché in the first place, the writer might have gone right on using it for years, pummeling the hell out of good English."

The only woman in sports was Woodward's secretary and editorial assistant, the very able Verna Reamer, and one of her tasks was keeping the big fellow organized. As baseball teams maintain scouting reports on prospects, "Coach" Woodward maintained scouting reports on sportswriters. He frequently handed stacks of stories to Verna for filing, stories from good papers and from bad ones. Reviewing an undistinguished and now defunct publication, the *Philadelphia Record,* he found a man he called "the original glutton for punishment," writing seven sports columns a week and in addition composing news reports on the top stories that broke in baseball, football, boxing, and horse racing. "He obviously was doing too much," Woodward later wrote, "probably 500,000 words a year, but he made it all good and much of it excellent. Some of his columns were afterthoughts, conjured up out of thin air, written perhaps between innings at a ball game. However they were never dull. When he came into our department and discovered that he only needed to write one story a day, he reacted amazingly. He was turned into a columnist and his product became brilliant." The formerly overworked

Philadelphia newspaperman whom Woodward scouted and hired was Walter Wellesley "Red" Smith. (Woodward at length discovered a small woman's college called "Walter," after which he sometimes told Red, "You're the only sportswriter in the annals who is named after three girls' schools.")

Verna alphabetically filed stories Woodward liked—fortunately my O'Casey piece was among them—in large beige envelopes marked "Good Stuff," and she also was required to keep a sort of counter-file of pieces Woodward called "Miasma from the Past." (Miasma is not a bronchial condition; it describes a noxious or poisonous atmosphere.) He used this file to show developing newspapermen such as myself the sort of jargon he would not tolerate. Here is one from 1933:

Navy's ship of success foundered on the banks of the Severn today, wrecked by the rugged rocks of Pittsburgh. After a safe passage past Columbia, Penn and Notre Dame abroad, the gallant craft came to grief at its home port, sunk by the waves of Pittsburgh's power . . .

"You are aware," he said, "that this was a football game not a boat race because you are reasonably bright. Others might find themselves confused."

Another went like this:

Sixty thousand hats were hurled into the air at Belmont Park yesterday afternoon as Zev, the American colt, came splashing down the muddy stretch an ever increasing five lengths ahead of Papyrus, Great Britain's best horse of the year. Twenty dollar beaver felts from Fifth Avenue shops sailed high into the air, along with three-dollar caps, cheap black derbies and carload lots of wilted fedoras. This was patriotism.

"This sounds like some sort of silly fashion show," Woodward said. "Writing a lead that bad would be a firing offense, firing without severance pay, except that the fellow who wrote it, Granny Rice, seldom went that purple."

"Even Homer nods," I said.

"I learned that, too," Woodward said, "back in Amherst and from

Robert Frost, no less. He talked about a lot of things in a course I took with him called Non-Shakespearean Elizabethan drama."

"That must have been thrilling."

"It was not. I didn't like their stuff much and I don't think Frost did, either."

"I was wondering who wrote that Navy-Pitt lead, Coach?" I said.

"Fellow who used to work here named Richards Vidmer. He had a column called 'Down Front.' One day he announced he was quitting the paper to marry a maharani and as far as I know he hasn't worked since, unless you call riding elephants work, which I do not. Come on. I need some more cigarettes and I'll buy you a drink."

We took the rear, Fortieth Street, elevator down five floors and walked a few dozen yards to Bleeck's, entering under a large sign that read ARTIST AND WRITERS RESTAURANT (FORMERLY CLUB)." The last was a reference to speakeasy days and prompted the gifted journalist, John Lardner, to name a Saturday luncheon group to which he belonged "The Formerly Club." A long, dark wooden bar dominated the front room at Bleeck's, where a framed stuffed marlin caught by J. P. Morgan hung on one wall. A suit of armor (unoccupied) guarded the entrance to the main dining room. The presiding bartender, Leo Corcoran, had mastered the art of filling martini glasses so that a silvery crown of gin rose above the rim. Surface tension kept the drink from spilling but it was impossible to lift a fresh Corcoran martini without wetting at least one of your cuffs. For your first sip you had to bend and slurp, making an unseemly noise. Bleeck's was egalitarian. The talented assistant managing editor, Everett Walker of Short Hills, New Jersey, bent and slurped; so did the chief editorial writer, Geoffrey Parsons; so did sexy Maggie Higgins when she was in town; so did Woodward, so did I, and so, I was told, did the late and well-liked publisher, Ogden Reid, who had died recently. That was part of the Republican *Herald Tribune*'s de facto egalitarianism—publishers, reporters, and even a copyboy, bending and slurping very dry martinis side by side without regard to race, income, or previous condition of servitude.

"I've got some concerns about our new management," Woodward told me. "Mrs. Reid suffers from frugal tendencies, common to self-made women, and Whitie seems too anxious to please too many people.

So I'm probably going to have a full plate to deal with. But I want you to know that I've asked [assistant sports editor] Irving Marsh to keep an eye on you. You'll be getting some assignments from him. Work hard, but don't expect wealth. If you want wealth, do what Dick Vidmer did. Find yourself a maharani to marry."

Leo's martini was relaxing me. "I don't speak Hindi, Coach," I said.

I was undergoing a rigorous, if informal, apprenticeship. Woodward talked to someone at the Associated Press, where I was hired as a stringer. I took Saturdays off from the copyboy chores and covered eight college football games for the AP. I wrote to space and met the deadlines. (The AP, never noted for profligacy, paid me $24 for the season.) After I had passed the wire-service test, the *Trib* came through with modest sports assignments: a speedboat race from Albany to New York, a walking race from City Hall to Coney Island, cross-country meets in Van Cortlandt Park. I had to show that I could write coherently at the rate of about eight hundred words an hour. That was part one of the apprenticeship. The other aspect, as you probably realize, came from Woodward's conversational lectures. No spines tingled at any event I covered back then, nor, I hope, have any in what I've written since.

Woodward's greatest sports story had been published May 9, 1947, on page 24, under an eight-column line, the shouting type that laymen call "a banner headline."

### NATIONAL LEAGUE AVERTS STRIKE OF CARDINALS AGAINST ROBINSON'S PRESENCE IN BASEBALL.

A subhead suggested even more:

### GENERAL LEAGUE WALKOUT PLANNED BY INSTIGATORS.

The importance of the story was underscored by a line that ran before the text began: Copyright 1947 New York Tribune, Inc. A distinct copyright line ran only with pieces of the brightest magnitude. The byline read Stanley Woodward. The magnificent piece of reporting was and remains the sports scoop of the twentieth century.

That is not to say, for no one really can, that this was the single biggest sports story across a hundred years. During the twentieth century sports icons emerged, with names such as Dempsey and Ruth, Rockne and Tilden, Mantle and Mays. Blacks came to dominate heavyweight boxing. Women came into press boxes and locker rooms. For one single shocking sports news story, it would be hard to beat the fixing of the 1919 World Series. In this company, Woodward's 1947 piece remains important in baring the overall racism of post–World War II America. More specifically, it unmasked a movement, whites only, that in time could have destroyed major-league baseball. But most important to my purpose here is the monosyllable "scoop." This story was developed through the enterprise and courage of *Herald Tribune* staffers. It belonged to the *Trib*. Everything that followed the *Tribune*'s scoop was not news so much as commentary.

Even today, almost sixty years later, questions persist. In the first place, how on earth did Woodward get his hands on a story in which all the principals swore virtual blood oaths to secrecy? Then why did the *Herald Tribune* bury its exclusive on page 24 on a day when the front page included such tepid stuff as an account of a spring cold wave? Finally, why did the doyens of the Pulitzer Prize committee choose to ignore Woodward's work and splash their 1947 awards on lesser and now mostly forgotten stories?

The last question is easiest. The Pulitzer Prize people at the time were not great fans of the idea that black men should be allowed to play major-league baseball. Journalism at large was unenlightened. Robinson broke in with the Brooklyn Dodgers in 1947. As late as 1953, reporters from the so-called Negro newspapers were not allowed to sit in the front row of the press box in St. Louis. No New York newspaper employed a black sportswriter until 1959, when the *Times* hired a reporter named Bob Teague. In short, the baseball fields were integrated many years before integration came to sports departments and newspapers generally.

As for sticking the strike story back on page 24, Woodward had a theory. "It's Old Double-Rubber," Woodward said. "He comes from a town called Demopolis that's in the heart of the Hookworm Belt." The man Woodward called Old Double-Rubber was the managing editor,

George Anthony Cornish, a tall, courtly figure who had grown up in west central Alabama. Cornish worked out of an office generally called the inner sanctum and distinguished by a bust of Adolf Hitler that Allied forces had shot full of holes during World War II. Department editors gathered in that office late every afternoon, under the mutilated Hitler, and described their daily budget of stories, Cornish then decided what would and would not appear on the front page. Woodward was a risk taker; Cornish was not, whence the condom nickname. Woodward further believed that Cornish retained some of the bigotry endemic to his native state and that bigotry, not impartial news judgment, kept the Robinson story "back of the corset ads," as Woodward put it.

In my formal meetings with Cornish, a few years down the line, I found him courteous and concerned. His voice was soft, and his manner, behind dark-rimmed spectacles, was gentle. He would be managing editor for a period of nineteen years (1940–1959), and if he ever shouted at anyone during all that time, under all that pressure, I never heard about it. This first time I asked Cornish for a raise he told me that "with your writing flair you should be selling stuff regularly to all the big magazines." It was half a day later before I realized that for all the pleasant talk, my salary had not increased. In a genteel way I had been hustled. When I asked a second time, I said I might have to look for another job. Cornish took no affront. "There will be a $50-a-week increase on your next check," he said. But later when I ran into trouble with subeditors over some hard-edged reporting on the integration of baseball, Cornish did not become involved. Long afterward, when relating that to Woodward, I said, "Actually, this censoring of my stuff happened at a lower level. Maybe George never knew about it." Woodward would have none of the apologia. He said simply, "Managing editors are supposed to know what's going on."

Woodward protected his sources, so some details of how he came by his greatest sports story remain unknown. But working at the *Trib* and drinking with the Coach and other *Trib* staffers, I managed to get a fairly complete picture. The baseball writer assigned to the New York Giants, a trim, handsome Canadian named Cecil Rutherford Rennie, who wrote as Rud Rennie, was something of a gay blade. He had lady friends in several National League towns, and he sang in a boozy barbershop quartet with a doctor named Robert Hyland, the St. Louis Cardinals' team physician, and a man who liked to hear himself called "the surgeon general of baseball." During one convivial night of song, Hyland remarked to his friend Rennie that it was a shame Rud was traveling with the Giants this year because when the Brooklyn Dodgers came to St. Louis—the date would be May 21—"one hell of a story is going to break."

Hyland said that on May 21 the Cardinals would strike, that is, refuse to suit up and take the field, in protest against Jackie Robinson's appearance at Sportsman's Park in a big-league uniform. "And not just the Cardinals. If this thing goes through the way they're planning, no team in the National League will take the field on May 21. Not one. And no team will take the field again until Robinson is released."

Containing his excitement, Rennie remarked that the ballplayers were under contract and legally obligated to play. "What I understand," Hyland said, "is that they want the contracts changed, giving them the right to approve or disapprove of the people they play with and play against."

"When I heard this from Doc Hyland," Rennie later told me, "one word came into my mind. In large letters. INSANITY. Next, What a story! But I couldn't write it. If I did, people who knew of my friendship with Hyland would trace it back to Bob. So I telephoned Woodward, told him what I had, and asked the Coach to take it from there."

Now comes the mysterious part. Woodward worked on developing the story for some time. How? "Myself and some of the boys put our microscopes on the Cardinals and the rest of the league." That is vague, and Woodward was hardly a vague fellow. He talked to Sam Breadon, a one-time garage mechanic who was president of the Cardinals, a strong-minded sort who had made a fortune in baseball and formerly employed such worthies as Rogers Hornsby (manager) and Branch Rickey (general manager). Breadon denied that a strike plan existed. So did various white ballplayers who were party to the plot. These included Terry Moore, a superb center fielder who was captain of the Cardinals; Ewell "the Whip" Blackwell of the Cincinnati Reds, a tall, sidearming right-hander out of Fresno, who later settled in North Carolina; and, most distressing in these circumstances, Fred "Dixie" Walker, Robinson's teammate, a vastly popular right fielder out of Villa Rica, Georgia, who was batting .411 on the day Woodward broke the story. Dixie, a warm and sophisticated man, apologized years later, saying that helping to organize the strike attempt was "the stupidest thing I've ever done." But that was in the 1970s. In 1947, there he stood. A pseudo-Klansman.

A number of club owners supported the idea of the strike. One was Larry MacPhail, president of the Yankees. "When Rickey brought in the colored boy," MacPhail said, "he depressed the value of every franchise in the majors. Our fans don't want to watch colored baseball. We oughta sue Rickey's self-righteous ass."

One man did not deny the story. His name was Ford Christopher Frick, and he was a gaunt, former newspaperman who had once ghost-written stories for the barely literate Babe Ruth. In 1947 Frick was the president of the National League. "I talked to Ford," Woodward said. "I'll tell you that much, and I'll tell you something else. I know Ford Frick to be an honest man."

"Did you talk to Branch Rickey? Did you talk to Dixie Walker?"

"I've told you everything," Woodward said, "that I'm going to. Drink your drink."

The problem with running the story, Woodward felt, was that it would arouse a tidal wave of denials and beyond that whoops of derision from racists, semiracists, and lummoxes on other newspapers and throughout baseball. The night riders still were mighty in '47. After three days of thought and on the basis of his faith in one honest man, Ford Frick, Woodward decided to run the piece. It began like this:

A National League players' strike instigated by some of the St. Louis Cardinals against the presence in the league of Jackie Robinson, Brooklyn's Negro first baseman, has been averted temporarily and perhaps permanently squashed. In recent days Ford Frick, president of the National League and Sam Breadon, president of the St. Louis club have been conferring with St. Louis players at the Hotel New Yorker. . . .

The strike plan, formulated by certain St. Louis players, was instigated by a member of the Brooklyn Dodgers. The original plan was for a St. Louis club strike on the occasion of the first game in Brooklyn, May 6. Subsequently the St. Louis players conceived the idea of a general strike.

The article went on to report that Frick spoke to the players as follows:

> *If you do this you will be suspended from the league. You will find that the friends that you think you have in the press box will not support you, that you will be outcasts. I do not care if half the league strikes. Those who do it will encounter quick retribution. All will be suspended and I don't care if it wrecks the National League for five years. This is the United States of America and one citizen has as much right to play as another.*
>
> *The National League will go down the line with Robinson, whatever the consequences. You will find if you go through with your intention that you will have been guilty of complete madness.*

Woodward continued: "The New York *Herald Tribune* prints this story in part as a public service. It is factual and thoroughly substantiated. . . . Since Robinson has played in Brooklyn many difficulties have loomed; sometimes forbiddingly, but all have been circumvented. It is understood that the St. Louis players have been talking about staging the strike on the day that Brooklyn plays its first game in St. Louis. Publicity probably will render the move abortive."

It did. Verbal abuse, beanballs, and redneck threats continued to assault Robinson until the end of his ten-season major-league career, but Woodward shattered for all time the players' strike.

Significantly, Woodward did not mention a single ballplayer's name in his story. Frick, Breadon, and Robinson were the only names that appeared. Was that to offset opportunities for denial, or from a fear of libel suits or, as I suspect, a bit of both? Woodward would not comment. The *Herald Tribune* published the story in its city edition, which hit the streets at about ten P.M., and gave the *Times* two hours of opportunity to counter with a story of its own for the more widely circulated late city edition. But all the *Times* did was pick up an unimpressive five-paragraph Associated Press brief in which Frick spoke four sentences of confirmation.

A day later Woodward wrote an impassioned column, "The Strike That Failed," opening with a flourish. "The blast of publicity which followed the revelation that the St. Louis Cardinals were promoting a players' strike against Jackie Robinson probably will serve to squash further strolls down Tobacco Road. In other words it can now be honestly doubted that the boys from the Hookworm Belt will have the nerve to foist their quaint sectional folklore on the rest of the country." Next he called Frick's statement "obviously the most noble ever made by a baseball man." He made one correction. The Frick declaration was delivered to Sam Breadon, and it was Breadon who actually read Frick's harsh, stirring words to the St. Louis ballplayers. A strike meant suspension. Suspension meant no paychecks. Suspension would cause hardship at the dinner table for many strikers whose salaries then were a small fraction of what ballplayers earn today. Some could lose their homes or farms. Even in a fever of racism, economics outpointed bigotry, and Robinson's career, armored by his great athletic ability, went forward.

Newspapers around the country picked up the Woodward story. Breadon quickly denied that anything had happened. "Laughable," Woodward said, "because even as Sam Breadon is denying what I wrote, Ford Frick is confirming it." Most of the press conceded, however grudgingly, that Woodward had scooped them all. One newspaperman who did not was the late Bob Broeg, who covered the Cardinals for the *St. Louis Post-Dispatch*. An otherwise reasonably sound newspaperman, Broeg maintained that no strike threat had existed and what Woodward wrote was "barnyard journalism." St. Louis was a segregated city in 1947; because of his color Robinson was barred from registering with teammates at the Chase Hotel. For decades Broeg remained loud and persistent in his denial, trapped by misguided loyalties into mendaciously defending an indefensible cause. A spokesman for the NAACP summed up matters more rationally with a comment on May 16. "The Frick statement reported by Stanley Woodward has been applauded by all lovers of fair play and especially by Negro citizens and sports fans. The consensus of opinion is that it is the most pointed and unequivocal statement on fair play in sports, so far as racial minority participation is concerned, that has ever been made."

My own researches led me in 1992 to the town of Collinsville, Illinois, and the retired Terry Moore. By then Moore was afflicted with prostate cancer that would kill him three years later. He met me on his small front porch—a painted cardinal brightened his mailbox—poured me a soda, complained a bit about his health, and, an old man making peace with his conscience, confirmed the Woodward story. "I ain't gonna give you no names," Moore said. "That wouldn't be right. But most of us had got pretty worked up. Stan Musial was against the strike. I can't recall any others that were. Was other teams in the strike deal? Every team in the whole damn National League, except the Brooklyns.

"What happened was that Sam Breadon got us all together and read us this statement from Ford Frick. After that there was some phone calls and the whole strike deal died.

"I come from a little place called Vernon, Alabama. If you write this sometime, please put that in. I was only acting on what I'd been taught to think as a boy.

"The Dodgers beat us out of the '47 pennant by five games and I don't believe they would have without Robinson. He was a great player.

"Put on the radio in your car when you move on. The sky looks nasty to me and you want to listen sharp for tornado warnings. . . ."

As Woodward foretold, the management of the widowed Helen Rogers Reid was significantly different from that of Ogden Reid, who had died on January 3, 1947. Reid was a hard drinker who inherited a fortune, which his father, Whitelaw, had built on exorbitant profits harvested from Cuban sugar canebrakes before and after the Spanish-American War. By all accounts, Ogden Reid truly loved the newspaper business, right down to the public bar at Bleeck's where the publisher sometimes, it was said, fell into one of Leo Corcoran's martinis nose first.

Helen Rogers Reid came from a Wisconsin family of modest means, which managed to send her to Barnard College. As a student Helen ran a tutoring service, typed in the bursar's office, and in her senior year edited the yearbook. Following her graduation in 1904, she found her job as social secretary to Elisabeth Reid, the wife of Whitelaw Senior. The romance with Ogden followed.

Now, some four decades later, Helen Reid was sole proprietor of the *Herald Tribune,* and with it the Reid fortune. She immediately set about saving money. It is axiomatic that no one can publish a great newspaper primarily by saving money, something Adolph Ochs probably understood better than anyone, which is why the *Times* for years maintained a bureau in, say, Karachi. But the heiress-through-marriage Helen Reid believed the *Trib* could keep going its successful way even if she enforced certain economies.

New York City at the time was divided into six police districts: Manhattan north and south, Brooklyn, the Bronx, Queens, and Richmond. The *Trib* like the *Times* employed six so-called district men, reporters who worked out of the district headquarters and telephoned crime stories through the city desk to rewrite men. One *Trib* district man once was connected to Bob Peck on the rewrite bank who wrote a story about an argument following a snowstorm. A landlord and his tenant in South Brooklyn disagreed about which man should shovel the driveway. Tempers boiled, and the landlord finally hit the tenant over the head with a shovel, killing him. Police then arrested the landlord, which, as Peck wrote in his droll way, "left no one to shovel the snow."

Mrs. Reid decided the paper could save money by firing the six district men and replacing them with two reporters, who would drive about in cars equipped with two-way police radios. The economy here was false. The district men had developed great police sources, born of long contact with the desk sergeants and captains at the headquarters. You can't nurture sources like that while tooling around in a Chevrolet. But no one strenuously objected, and the *Trib*'s police reporting simply got a little worse.

Next Mrs. Reid issued a memo through George Cornish asking department heads to name two staffers who could be dismissed with the least damage to the paper. Dutifully, Joe Herzberg, Norman Stabler, the business editor, and the rest submitted the names of marginal people. Only Stanley Woodward's list was surprising. The two men, he wrote, that the sports department could best afford to lose were Stanley Woodward and Red Smith. Helen Reid took Woodward's defiance as disrespect. Several firings followed, none in sports.

Finally, in the spring of 1949, Mrs. Reid directed Woodward, again through Cornish, to cover a women's amateur golf tournament scheduled for a tony club in Westchester. Woodward refused. He said the women were by and large poor golfers, not worthy of professional sports coverage. "That isn't the point, Stanley," Cornish said. "Some of these women are married to our wealthiest and most prominent advertisers."

"George," Woodward said, "the sports section of the *Herald Tribune* is not for sale."

Within the week, Cornish summoned Woodward and told him that the Reids, Helen and Whitie, the editor in chief, had decided to fire him. "We're all arranging a fair severance settlement for you now." His replacement would be Robert Barbour Cooke, thirty-six, who had been covering the Brooklyn Dodgers (and had completely missed the Robinson strike story). As I mentioned, Cooke was Whitie Reid's classmate at Yale, a former hockey star, tall, handsome, and nonrebellious.

Near the Hitler bust in Cornish's sanctum, Woodward rose without comment and took a taxi to the apartment he was renting at 77 Park Avenue. There he said to his wife, Esther Rice Woodward, "Ricie, mix me a batch of martinis. A large batch, please, and very dry."

As word of the firing spread, Irving Marsh, the deputy sports editor, and Red Smith agreed that the Reids were making a disastrous mistake. They huddled with Bob Cooke and told him politely that, while he had a nice baseball writing style, he was too young to be sports editor. The three then walked down a long hall and presented themselves in Whitie Reid's office. Marsh and Smith spoke; Cookie nodded. Whitie finally telephoned his mother in her sixth-floor office and after a bit she agreed: The firing of Stanley Woodward was rescinded. "We appreciate that, Whitie," Marsh said. "It takes a big man to admit that he's made a mistake."

"I'll call Stanley myself right now," Whitie said.

Quite a few hours had elapsed since the firing, and, as requested, Ricie Woodward had made her husband's martinis numerous and dry. When Reid telephoned and offered Woodward his sports editorship back, the answer was short. "Take that job," Woodward said, "and shove it up your ass."

A bookend to Arthur Gelb's guarded, politic *City Room* exists in *The Paper: The Life and Death of the New York Herald Tribune,* by Richard Kluger, the final editor of the *Tribune*'s Sunday book review. In its 799 pages

Kluger, who calls himself "the last literary editor of the New York *Herald Tribune*," came late to the *Trib*, and devotes too much space to the paper's last days, when he was employed there. The dying *Trib* was sometimes brilliant, often shrill, and frequently just plain silly.

Kluger, who attended the Horace Mann School, a New York prep not noted for sports excellence, and moved on to Princeton, misses the artistic and commercial significance of the Stanley Woodward sports section and is blind to the catastrophic results of Woodward's firing. After meeting Princeton undergraduates across a number of years, Woodward had described them collectively as "implausible brats." With Woodward safely dead, Kluger wrote, implausibly, "A still more troubling loss [than Woodward] was the departure of foreign editor Joe Barnes. . . ." Woodward liked to say, "If we didn't print something, then when it turns out to be wrong, we don't have to deny it. Never use the *Trib* to rectify a *New York Times* mistake." But correcting Kluger's misinterpretation is important here because his 1986 book is widely accepted as an accurate account of the way things were at the *Trib*. Actually, Woodward's firing uniquely shocked newspapermen throughout the country. It was both iron-headed and petty, and people knew it. Never again would the *Trib* shimmer quite so brightly as a beacon to nonconformists with talent. To equate this with Barnes's dismissal is what Woodward might have called a rookie mistake. (During a mild moment.)

In reality the paper's foreign news coverage under Joe Barnes was episodically distinguished, as in Woodward reporting from behind Nazi lines, John Steinbeck writing from Russia, and Homer Bigart filing from anywhere. But overseas the *Tribune* was outmanned by the *Times,* which had more correspondents, more bureaus, and consequently delivered fuller coverage. Despite the *Times*'s self-consciousness on Jewish issues, it sold a lot of copies on the basis of its far-ranging foreign stuff, many to readers who were themselves Jewish. (I still remember my socialist dentist grandfather reading a fudged *Times* story on Hitler's anti-Semitic terrorism sixty-five years ago and asking rhetorically, "Why am I looking at the Fascist *New York Times*?" I would not like to have been Dr. Rockow's first patient that day.)

Barnes did a good job with the correspondents he had, but so did his successor, Frank Kelley. Under Kelley the Korean War correspondence of Bigart and Marguerite Higgins won two Pulitzer Prizes in a single year, 1951. Higgins behaved heroically during the perilous Inchon landing far behind North Korean lines, but generally the *Times* overseas staff, in the words of a recently deposed *Times* executive from Alabama, "flooded the zone." As an earlier Southerner put it, overseas the *Times* usually "got there fustest with the mostest."

By contrast the *Tribune* sports section during the Woodward years outclassed the rival pages of the *Times* both in news judgment, hard reporting, and the quality of its prose. Red Smith became the most widely syndicated sport columnist in the country. Joe H. Palmer created the best horse-racing column ever. ("However," Palmer wrote, "I am not a horse lover. A horse lover is a horse that loves another horse.") Bob Cooke developed into a witty and deft baseball writer. Jesse Abramson's track and field stuff was so authoritative that he was nicknamed "the Book." Al Laney's feature stories were matchless. When Laney wrote about a great old Negro boxer, Sam Langford, "the Boston Tar Baby," who was blind and penniless but somehow cheerful in a Harlem slum tenement, readers spontaneously mailed in thousands of dollars to help, making Langford's final Christmases joyful. And so it went. Woodward, of course, had assembled this staff from his scouting reports, and he went to pains to keep it disciplined. Before each football season he hired coaches to run clinics. Sports reporters were required to attend such lectures as "The Techniques of Stunting and Looping in Intercollegiate Line Play."

Writers on different sports needed different skills and outlooks. "The boxing business," Woodward wrote in *Sports Page,* "is full of liars as well as hoodlums, and the isolation of truth from ballyhoo requires a man who is discriminating and hard-boiled." Then, famously, on the Dodgers: "For some strange reason baseball writers develop a great attachment for the Brooklyn ball club if long exposed. . . . The transpontine madness seems to affect all baseball writers, no matter how sensible they outwardly seem. You must watch a Brooklyn writer for symptoms and, before they become virulent, shift him to the Yankees or tennis or golf."

Woodward appointed himself overall guardian of what Smith called "the mother tongue," the English language. The word "win" was a verb not a noun. Anyone reporting that a pitcher had accumulated twenty "wins" faced a blast. "The word you should have used and the word you will use in the future is victories." In Woodward's sports section no batters flew out. They flied out. Infinitives were not to be split. None, the contraction of not one, was singular as in "none was." You never wrote "none were" under Woodward, or anyway you never did it twice. As with another large character, Jack Dempsey, Woodward's high tenor voice at full volume could stop a locomotive. When too many baseball writers used the word "paced," as in "Paced by the six-hit pitching of Ed Lopat . . ." Woodward issued a growling memo headed "Requiescat in Pace." He frequently held forth on the keys to forceful writing: precise nouns and active verbs. "Consider the lowly single. A batter can line a single, ground a single, bunt a single or loop a single and when you use the proper verb the reader has some picture of what happened. When you write that a batter 'made a single,' he does not."

"I'd like you to notice something in John Lardner," Woodward said to me one day. "He never uses italics. When he wants to emphasize a word, something ordinary writers accomplish by employing italics, he changes the rhythm of the sentence. The word he wants you to notice is rhythmically stressed. No slanted type for John. He works with rhythms. That's a nice trick to learn, if you can learn it."

One of his demands seemed odious. To cover football you carried a large chart book into the press box, its pages marked with grids covering the 100 yards of the field where most of the action takes place. (Counting the end zones, a football field is 120 yards long.) You also carried four or five sharpened pencils, each blue on one end and red on the other. You then charted the progress of the game, following one team in red and the other in blue. A solid line meant a run, a dotted line indicated a pass, and a wavy line represented a kick. You wrote notes and comments in the margins. On Tuesdays Woodward called staffers in and examined their weekend football charts. "I'm so busy switching from the blue side of the fucking pencil to the red that it's tough to follow the game," one reporter complained.

"Not if you concentrate," Woodward said, "which is what this is about. Also," he added, addressing the reporter by name, "it is a terrible idea to bring a date to a football game you're covering, as you did last Saturday. You'll find yourself worrying about whether the hot dog man got mustard on the young lady's dress, instead of considering why that last double reverse gained twenty-two yards. Dates and assignments from me do not mix, and the prettier the girl the more your concentration will be divided. Meet her after you've met my deadline, at which point your behavior, or lack of it, becomes your own affair." For all of his bluster, confidence, and authoritarianism, Woodward was modest about his own prose. "I'd put it like this," he told me once. "Over the years I've tried to write English and I've tried to see that others did, too."

According to the best surveys available in the late 1940s almost 30 percent of the *Herald Tribune*'s readers bought the paper for its sports section. They liked the way the *Trib* covered big stories, like the Robinson strike and the Kentucky Derby and the World Series, but also the way it handled smaller ones: Williams-Amherst football; Columbia-Navy basketball, and a track meet called the IC4A, the Intercollegiate American Amateur Athletic Association. The *Tribune*'s daily circulation oscillated about the number 350,000, so we had something like 105,000 people stirring each morning to find change in their suit pants with which to buy Woodward's sports pages. How many people bounded from bed at dawn to study the foreign news Joe Barnes edited? No hard figures exist, but circulation men at the time put Woodward way ahead. (In those days the New York *Daily News* was outpeddling everyone, with sales of 2 million copies a morning, but it catered to a different breed of reader. "Mass not class," the saying went. "People who buy the *News* move their lips as they read.")

Still, for all Woodward's newspapering genius, the big feller found himself canned. As I've suggested, I don't think the *Herald Tribune* ever really recovered. In firing Woodward, the Reid widow and her eldest son indicated that willful and independent-minded people, however talented, were no longer secure at the *Trib,* which under the earlier Ogden Reid, had employed, albeit uncomfortably, the willful and doggedly Democratic columnist Dorothy Thompson. Further, the Reids irreparably depleted one of their greatest assets, the Stanley Woodward sports section. Thus did the Reid family, a generally attractive lot, emulate the actions of losing Roman soldiers. They fell on their swords.

Why, some wondered, didn't *The New York Times* immediately hire Woodward to vitalize its torpid sports section? Harrison Salisbury, once a prominent *Times* editor, put it this way: "His free-spirited, quick-thinking, hard-drinking liberal ways would not have worked at our shop, given the bureaucracy that ran things." When the *World Journal Tribune,* successor to the *Herald Tribune,* folded in 1967, it took fully four years for the *Times,* evolving into a less rigid paper, to get around to hiring Red Smith. Overlooked by the Pulitzer Committee during his prime years at the *Trib,* Smith won a Pulitzer for the *Times* just four seasons later. That, he said, shows, "if you live long enough and work for the right employer . . ."

## II

Following the firing, our roads, Woodward's and mine, diverged, although not in a yellow wood. After leaving the *Tribune,* Woodward started a magazine called *Sports Illustrated.* It ran some interesting features, but Woodward was not a general journalist. He was a newspaperman. His magazine died and the publisher eventually sold the title to Henry Luce. After dropping $10 million or so, Luce and his minions began to make money with their version (or versions) of *Sports Illustrated,* ultimately hitting a jackpot with an annual "swimsuit issue" offering color photographs of attractive, bikini-waxed young women. Not exactly a Stanley Woodward sort of feature.

Woodward then worked as sports editor of a small, liberal New York tabloid called *The Compass,* with a sports department consisting of three people (including Woodward) when he began. *The Compass* employed good staffers, including a few who had been fired by bigger papers because they were leftists during a nightmare of right-wing frenzy. But the paper in no way approached the *Herald Tribune.* Stanley Isaacs, whom Woodward recalled as a "bright young fellow," signed on as a sportswriter at *The Compass* after graduating from Brooklyn College. "Woodward," he says, "was a burly man with a gruff exterior that quickly disappeared once you got to know him. He occasionally burst into the Amherst song, with Lord Jeff something or other in the lyrics." (Lord Jeffrey Amherst, a revered nobleman in his day, has recently been accused of wiping out Native Americans in New England by giving them blankets laced with smallpox bacilli.)

"Woodward often went down to the bar around the corner on Hudson Street for a midafternoon drink," Isaacs recalls. "When he first sent me out to cover a live event, a Knicks basketball game, he said, 'Make sure you get the attendance in the story.'" Were the embryonic Knicks succeeding or were they not? Quite obviously attendance was a key.

Woodward composed numerous *Compass* pieces about "the Reliable Jersey House," a very elegant and entirely theoretical bookmaker who wore a homburg. This fellow's paternal grandfather, Woodward maintained, had taken horse bets from Queen Victoria's regent, Prince Albert, while his maternal grandparent handled wagers for "the czarevitch, Prince Ivan Petrovsky Pickoff." That was in fun, but Woodward also wrote seriously about a system whereby bookies made monthly payoffs to the New York City police. "And the cops demanded that they be paid for thirteen months, the twelve regular ones and Christmas." All this graft growing out of sports betting eventually erupted into a public scandal that drove the mayor, William O'Dwyer, to Mexico City and sent the police bagman, Harry Gross, to prison. But few crooked cops were indicted. "There were a lot of hoodlums on and off the police force, and some judges were in on things, too," Woodward said. "This was damn dangerous stuff to print. But I got away with it."

Ted Thackrey, who published *The Compass,* had previously run the *New York Post* along with his wealthy wife, Dorothy Schiff. In those pre–Rupert Murdoch days, the *Post* was the most liberal of the major New York dailies, but Thackrey and Schiff had a political falling-out. Thackrey supported Henry Wallace of the Progressive Party for president. Schiff preferred the centrist Republican Thomas E. Dewey. Neither Thackrey's position at the *Post* nor his marriage survived the 1948 election—a victory for Harry Truman—and with somewhat shaky financial backing Thackrey started *The Compass.* He signed Woodward to a one-year contract, during which Thackrey constantly sought new investors and varied his political slant to suit the most recent investor. "Some weeks," Woodward wrote, "the paper was light pink. Others it was red as Marx." He was through at *The Compass* after his year. Thackrey told him in sorrow, "This paper simply can't afford you, Coach."

Woodward took farming seriously. While raising chickens near Princeton, he brought cartons into the *Herald Tribune* marked "Modern

Eggs." He priced them at sixty cents a dozen and, peddling them from a desk in the sports department, consistently sold out. Now he invested much of his savings in a 125-acre farm near Circleville, in the pretty, rolling country of Orange County, west of the Hudson in southeastern New York State. He bought bulldozers, power shovels, and trucks and built a new road and created a lake in front of the house. He acquired a large net, which he baited with dog food, and plunged it repeatedly into a nearby pond. That was how he stocked his new lake with bass and bluegills. The farmhouse kitchen with its large country fireplace was his favorite room. In the cold of winter he drove a Gravely tractor into the kitchen to join the family at dusk. "That way I knew I could get the damn thing started in the morning." But after a while his savings ran out—the same thing happened to Thomas Jefferson at Monticello—and Woodward had to sell the farm and take the best job he could find. That turned out to be sports editor of the *Miami News,* a now defunct evening paper in Florida.

By this time we were corresponding and Woodward wrote me that he had moved into "a rentable house in the South Miami boondocks. One problem is that when the wind blows off the swamps, it brings with it biting insects, just a bit smaller than the openings in the screens. Malaria has not appeared among us yet, but we are watchful. Another problem is that we (Ricie, our two daughters and Thelma Burgess, the housekeeper) are sharing our home with a large number of scorpions. The paper isn't much, but I'm doing what I can. It doesn't snow down here. Ever think of working in Miami?" Woodward datelined this letter, as he would several others: "Green Hell, U.S.A."

The publisher required him to promote a Golden Gloves Boxing Tournament, which was fine with Stanley until he found out that the fighters were to be divided into two major divisions: white and black. At the risk of losing another job, Woodward said, "Dempsey fought black men. He had a black sparring partner. Joe Louis fought whites. I only promote integrated boxing." The publisher backed down.

After the U.S. Supreme Court made its epochal ruling against-school segregation in 1954, Woodward wrote me that "a bunch of our executives, all from Georgia, gathered round my desk and asked what I thought of the decision in *Brown vs. Topeka.* I told them I didn't like it one bit." The Southerners looked incredulous. "The reason I don't like it," Woodward said, "is because it will force self-respecting colored children to go to school with you goddamned wool-hats."

In the summer of 1955, the managing editor of the *News,* a Mr. Welsh, wrote Woodward, who was preparing a series of columns from New York, that "though you are a marvelous operator, your salary is too high for our paper." In short, Woodward was fired yet again. His friend Walt Kelly, who wrote and drew the witty comic strip *Pogo,* spoke to executives in the Newhouse newspaper chain and Woodward promptly became sports editor and columnist for the *Newark Star-Ledger.* He called Newark "a huge slum across the river from New York," but added, "I find the people friendly and the standard of newspaper work high."

After Woodward's forced exit from Manhattan, my own *Tribune* experience spun out into halcyon days. As Woodward asked, his deputy, Irving Marsh, began looking after me, in Marsh's term, "like a Dutch uncle." I have never known a kinder, gentler man, but as with Woodward, Marsh had a disciplinary side. "Get the athletes' first names," he said. "We don't care for initials. And something else. I'm not paying you to write essays. Worry less about literature and more about getting the important facts up high."

"I'd like to write literature," I said.

"I'm sure you will eventually," Marsh said. "For now, get the salient facts up high."

Marsh found a full-time spot for me on the *Tribune* sports copy desk, at $48 a week. It would not be the most exciting of jobs, but I was jubilant. Never again would I have to leap at the bray of "Copy!" Nor would I be required to put away other peoples' mail, mix pots of noxious white paste, or serve as errand boy to a reporter who grew meaner with each drink he swigged from the $4 bottle of Four Roses Blended Whiskey he kept in a desk drawer. To me the modest promotion was nothing less than manumission.

As often happens when one is developing a career, I had drifted away from my parents. But my father now said, "Twenty-two years old and a full-fledged copyreader on a great American newspaper. Not bad, son. Not bad at all."

My mother remained determined to be unimpressed. "You," she said, "responsible for punctuation and grammar? Where on earth do you imagine *you* ever learned grammar?"

"In Dr. Wedeck's Latin class. Once you master Latin grammar, English is relatively easy, Mom. Anyway, I certainly didn't learn English grammar from you."

My mother threw me a hard glance and presently we were exchanging looks of loathing love. Olga, the fierce Cornell socialist, was a reasonably exact opposite of the cliché Jewish mother. She took little visible joy in my accomplishments, seeming to feel that the more prominent I became, the more she herself was diminished. In frustration I sometimes thought, "This woman has given me *nothing*." Then another voice reminded, or copyedited, me, as it does to this day, "Nothing, except your affinity for Shelley and Keats, Brahms and Beethoven, the Greek myths, A. E. Housman, T. S. Eliot, and even Robert Frost." I know little of my mother's own childhood, so the source of her conflicted emotions continues to be elusive. Certainly the persistent baseball chatter that went on between my father and me left her excluded at her own dinner table. But perhaps it was more basic than that. Perhaps she could not bring herself to forgive me for the indignities and agony I imposed on her during the process of childbirth. As I write these lines, fifteen years after her death, my mother remains a mystery. To some extent, all interesting women are mysteries. Mystery is one of the things that makes them interesting. My own mother may be the most mysterious woman I have known.

At the *Herald Tribune* Irving Marsh was telling me he would not let me get lost on the desk. "The Coach thinks you're better than that, and so do I. You'll stay there just until a writing job opens up. A hitch on the desk is a good way to learn the insides of the newspaper business." I was handed soft early-edition stuff and managed to write some headlines, such as:

**HARVARD NEXT
ON DARTMOUTH
FOOTBALL SLATE**

"No verb," Marsh said.

"But it fits," I said.

"Try writing heads that fit and also include a verb."

With the outbreak of the Korean War in 1950, Everett B. Morris, a naval reserve commander who covered yachting and basketball, was called to active duty, and in the ensuing staff shuffle I became "school-boy sports editor." No raise, but also no more writing heads, no football slates. I was empowered to hire stringers at various high schools and preps and pay them each $3 a month. I wrote and rewrote their earnest reports and both Marsh and Bob Cooke liked the results. The next year, at twenty-three, I was promoted to general assignment sports reporter. The tutoring continued. When I covered a City College-Columbia baseball game, I dutifully reported the score and how the runs came home, which made for an acceptable, flat piece. "That isn't the way to write baseball," Bob Cooke said. "You want to comment more, try as the innings go by to tell an interesting story." With that he handed me a yellowed clipping from the New York *World* of October 12, 1923, in which Heywood Broun proclaimed the ascendency of Babe Ruth and the decline of John McGraw's so-called scientific game, bunts, steals, and hit and run.

Broun began with a play on words from the Bible: "The Ruth is mighty and shall prevail. He then quoted McGraw: "Why shouldn't we pitch to Ruth [as opposed to deliberately walking him in a tight spot]? I've said it before and I'll say it again, we pitch to better hitters than Ruth in the National League." Ruth then hit two home runs and a 450-foot sacrifice fly and his Yankees defeated McGraw's Giants, 4 to 2. Broun summed up McGraw's bravado: "His fame deserves to be recorded along with the man who said, 'Lay on, Macduff.'" Those were just about the last words uttered by Macbeth before the sword fight in which Macduff lops off his head. Less violent, the Yankees that year won their first World Series, four games to two.

Although matching the style of Heywood Broun was, to put this softly, difficult, my own baseball writing began to improve. I came to recognize that it was a good idea to have the lead sentences and the conclusion relate to one another. The intervening paragraphs then became building blocks. You would not and should not merely report the story, itself no tiny task given the standards of the *Herald Tribune*. You would simultaneously report and write a narrative interweaving the two into a single seamless fabric, and, as I've observed, do it at a rate of 800 words an hour. That is rather more difficult than it may appear.

The following year Harold Rosenthal, the *Tribune*'s Dodger beat man, decided that the constant travel required to cover the major leagues was ruining his family life, and about halfway through spring training in 1952 he asked for another assignment. Bob Cooke called me at my modest apartment in a forlorn corner of Brooklyn. "Do you know what you're doing Tuesday?" he asked.

"I haven't checked the assignment sheet."

"You don't have to. On Tuesday you're flying to Vero Beach to begin covering the Dodgers."

I splurged and took a taxi to the office. Cooke was beaming and said that the secret was simply to write what I saw, report and narrate, and apply a light touch. "You remember that Heywood Broun piece."

Marsh, sitting next to Cooke, looked dour. "I want to tell you just what I told Bob," he said. "At twenty-four you're too young for this assignment. That's my opinion. Too soon. Now go out there and make me look bad."

This was a wonderful Brooklyn team, with Jackie Robinson, Pee Wee Reese, Duke Snider, and Roy Campanella, just to mention the Hall of Famers. But Marsh's remarks stayed with me, and when I checked the birth dates in the Dodger roster I discovered that I was younger than anybody in the starting lineup. Still, things went well. Cooke asked me to write "a guest column" in May, and I chose the late Joe Black as the subject. Black, a gifted, intelligent African American from Plainfield, New Jersey, had pitched from Maine to Venezuela in a variety of ramshackle leagues before the color barrier dropped and he was allowed to become a major-league rookie at the age of twenty-eight. He told his story passionately and well. I typed the column in a Pittsburgh hotel room, and a few hours after I filed it, a telegram arrived. "You are making me look worse every day. Keep it up." The wire was signed Irving T. Marsh.

Cooke took pride in my work, and when my father died suddenly on a Brooklyn sidewalk in October 1953, he was the first *Tribune* staffer to pay a condolence call. Dad's death shocked his survivors. He was only fifty-two, and the previous August, during a softball game, he had hit two long doubles. He couldn't run much, but he still had imposing power. In my youthful sorrow I wondered how a man could hit hard on a summer day and early that autumn, not two months later, fall dead. I still wonder about that.

Bob Cooke told my mother that he felt he had known my Dad through me and now it was as if he had lost a friend. Olga spoke afterward of Cooke's elegance and breeding. We had gotten close, and Bob asked one weekend if he could borrow my car, a Chevrolet convertible, with a color General Motors called Honey-Dew, for a trip to the Hamptons. "Sure, Bob," I said, "but I must be in the wrong business if the boss can't afford a car of his own."

"My wife," Cooke said, "likes to live very well and, by the way, you are in the wrong business. If I were you, I'd find a way to get into television. That's where the real money is."

One afternoon, an off day, I was chatting with John Winders, the best copyreader in the sports department, when Cooke joined us and remarked that he had recently appeared on a new radio show featuring Jackie Robinson. "He talks as though somehow he got a tongue depressor stuck inside his tongue," Cooke said. His eyes went flinty. "Branch Rickey did more to damage big-league baseball than anybody in history when he brought in the colored guys. When I was playing hockey at Yale, I had a harder shot than any of the Rangers, but I couldn't make the NHL. The Canadians were faster skaters. They had the legs. That's what's going to happen in baseball. The colored guys have the legs. They're going to run the whites out of the game. You fellers agree with me, don't you?"

I was shocked into silence. John Winders said calmly, "No, Bob. I don't agree with you at all." Cooke's look softened and he changed the subject. I never again heard him bring up race and baseball. I found the friendship between Jackie Robinson and Pee Wee Reese to be nothing less than an advertisement for America, and here I was covering the athletes and their team for a man who didn't believe Robinson belonged in the National League. Or Roy Campanella for that matter. Or Joe Black. Or Willie Mays. I was still covering the Dodgers, but that single dreadful moment, to cite Wordsworth, "killed the bloom before its time."

I continued to write stories about Robinson's ongoing struggle for fair play. Sol Roogow, the night sports editor, shared Cooke's prejudice and killed most of the pieces. But some made the paper, and during spring training in 1953, I broke a scoop that put a spotlight on some nasty racism.

A black rookie infielder from Tennessee named Jim "Junior" Gilliam excited Charlie Dressen, the Dodger manager. "I been watching close," Dressen said, "and he hasn't missed the ball completely on any swing he's taken all month. He's got one hell of an eye." After consulting with Buzzie Bavasi, the general manager, Dressen decided to switch Jackie Robinson, now thirty-four, to third base and install Gilliam as the new second baseman. That meant benching the incumbent third baseman, Billy Cox, who had just about the best glove in the league. Bavasi directed Dressen to tell Cox he'd be paid a bonus ($1,500) for switching to "utility man," but the manager never got around to doing that. One evening, over a late snack, Cox said to me, "How would you like a nigger to take your job?" His roommate, the pitcher, Preacher Roe, said, "It's all right to have them in the game, but now they're taking over."

John Lardner had been writing about a new baseball doctrine he called "the fifty per cent color line." That meant it was fine to play four blacks and five whites in your nine at any one time, but if you dared to play five blacks and four whites you would upset the twaddle known as White Supremacy. So nobody had dared. But now, with Gilliam playing alongside Robinson, Campanella, Sandy Amoros, and Black, the Dodgers would occasionally have five blacks on the field. A few other Brooklyn players chimed in with racist comments. I then wrote a careful story, that ran on March 21, and began, "While Charlie Dressen fiddles with his Brooklyn infield, Billy Cox burns." To get the piece past Cooke and Roogow, I confined the racial nastiness to the last three paragraphs and as a matter of personal ethics, I mentioned no specific names. The ballplayers had been "just talking," not holding a press conference. The *Tribune* printed the piece I wrote untouched, but when the Associated Press picked up the story and moved it nationally, the AP editors focused entirely on racial problems infesting the team that just six years earlier had integrated the major leagues.

Within two days a legion of sportswriters reached the Dodger camp at Vero Beach. The *New York Post* immediately began publishing a five-part series "The Roots of Prejudice." The *Journal-American* fabricated a front-page piece denying that dissension existed and bearing the byline of Jackie Robinson. "I never talked to them and they stole my name," Robinson said. "I'm gonna sue the fuckers."

"If he does," said Michael Gaven of the *Journal,* who had written the spurious story, "every Hearst newspaper in the country will tear that coon apart." Editing the epithet—I made the offensive word "guy"—I reported Gaven's threat to Robinson. Probably wisely, Jack elected not to litigate.

Presently I noticed a large, familiar form among the swarming newspapermen. "Come have a drink," Stanley Woodward said. "How did you get that story past Ol' Double-Rubber?"

"I wrote it ass backwards, Coach. I made what should have been the lead the end. I guess that threw off everybody. At least that was the plan."

"Would you want to give your old boss the names of the Brooklyn players who talked to you?"

"Just as soon as you tell me the names of the players who talked to you about the Robinson strike."

A nod. "You've done well, young man. The best way to deal with these primitives is to smoke 'em out. There won't be any more trouble." There was none. "If you'd like to work in Miami, just give me a call. Our winters are unbelievably mild."

Although I never did work for a Miami newspaper, I left the *Trib* a year later. Cooke had shifted me away from Jackie Robinson to the Giants, and I set down much of a Leo Durocher tantrum against players he felt were not hustling. The next day he denied most of what he had told me, and Cooke said I would have to apologize to Durocher. Cooke himself was trying to get into television—"where the real money is"—and he wanted Durocher to appear on a pilot show. If I declined to apologize, said Roogow, Cooke's hit man, I would be permanently assigned to the copy desk, there to work the eight P.M. to four A.M. shift, writing headlines about football slates and growing more pallid each night until the end of time.

I resigned. Red Smith later wrote, "The *Herald Tribune* fired Roger Kahn for quoting Leo Durocher accurately." After some shuttling about,

I became sports editor of *Newsweek* in 1956, on the recommendation of John Lardner, soon after Woodward became sports editor and columnist for the *Star-Ledger*. The Coach began appearing in Bleeck's again, but having been dismissed by two newspapers in less than a decade, he had become grumpier and generally more angry.

My *Newsweek* salary was modest, $14,000, but Frank Gibney, in charge of the so-called back of the book, said that the job required only three days' work a week and I could spend the rest of my hours free-lancing for any other magazine except *Time*. I hired a hardworking young assistant out of Columbia Journalism School, Dick Schaap, who was never the strongest of writers but from the start was an indefatigable and nervy reporter. When I dispatched him to pre-Castro Havana to cover a Grand Prix competition, I said it would be worthwhile just before the start of this perilous event to ask the world auto-racing champion if he were thinking about the possibility of death. Schaap did just that. "Death?" said Juan Manuel Fangio of Argentina. "I only give it a quick, glancing thought."

During my Dodger days I sometimes had postgame drinks with Duke Snider, a marvelous center fielder. One night, in a shabby Milwaukee bar called Holiday House, Snider said, "You may not believe this, but if it wasn't for the money I'd be just as happy if I never played another game of baseball again."

"If you want to say that on the record, Duke, I think I can make us both some money." In time, I sold a piece to *Collier's* magazine, which carried both our names and was published in the issue of May 25, 1956, under the title "I Play Baseball for Money—Not Fun." The "I" of course was Duke. To this day I myself still play baseball as best I can—for fun.

I taped Snider at his home in Compton, California. He said, "The truth is that life in the major leagues is far from a picnic. . . . There are youngsters who throw skate keys and marbles at my head when I'm backed up close to the stands. . . . There are older fans who try to bounce beer cans off my legs. . . . There are the sportswriters who know just as much baseball as my four-year-old daughter but who write expert articles about what's wrong with me every time I go a few games without a hit. . . . There is the travel that makes me spend half my life in strange towns, a thousand miles away from Beverly and the kids. You know, it isn't just one of these things, but when they all come at you at about the same time, when you get off the train after a couple of hours' sleep, and a manager snipes at you before the game, and the fans during the game and the writers after the game, you begin to wonder about baseball as a trade." He then told a semicomic, semiangry story about how Charlie Dressen had berated him at a team meeting for having ordered creamed cauliflower, a seventy-five-cent à la carte item, before signing a check which the Dodgers would have to pay.

"Can we just go out on the field and warm up?" Snider said. "I'll give you the the seventy-five cents after the game."

"Are you trying to run this #$%&# ball club?" Dressen said.

Read today, the original article rings with candor—Snider usually said just what he felt—but there is no booze in the piece, no drugs, no sex. By present standards then, it's a malted milk, with just the lightest lacing of tequila. But in 1956 it kicked up a tsunami. (Snider has since denied reading the story before it was published. That may be so, but to block that sort of questionable claim, Gordon Manning, the managing editor of *Collier's,* had him initial every one of the eighteen pages "EDS," for Edwin Donald Snider, before releasing a check to the Duke.)

The press generally commented that Snider was an ingrate and a complainer, although all the points he made were factual. Red Smith got a column out of the concept that Duke had clutched the lapel closest to my heart and wept. The roughest comment appeared in the *Newark Star-Ledger.* Without asking either of us about it, Woodward wrote that such pieces as my Snider collaboration come about like this: A writer gets an idea that can make money. He writes a story. Then he approaches athlete after athlete until he finds one willing to affix his name to the synthetic stuff.

I confronted Woodward in Bleeck's, told him how the article had in fact developed, and said, "Your column was wrong. Absolutely wrong." He heard me out with an expression of distaste, then said, "The piece I wrote was entertaining and short of libel and that's my definition of a good column." I turned away to drink with John Lardner. From behind me Woodward said quietly, "Drink as much as you want. I'm getting the tab."

I said loudly enough for Lardner to overhear, "I accept your apology, Coach."

Although comment on my work has been mostly pleasant, occasionally someone lobs a grenade. My response over the years has been consistent: anger. But not this time. My esteem for Woodward, as opposed to my contempt for slashing hacks, produced a different emotion: hurt. Lardner went home and composed the most profound of all the commentaries on the article. Snider had once dreamed of becoming a major leaguer, Lardner wrote, and Duke thought, as young people will, that if only his dream came true he would know heaven on earth. Now the dream had come true and Snider was discovering day by difficult day that earth still was not heaven. That was the essence of the Snider story, something I certainly did not realize myself until the matchless John Lardner pointed it out.

Although Woodward enjoyed working in Newark, he didn't want to live there. He was a farm or city person—he cared for neither Greenwich nor Scarsdale—and now, after a spell in Princeton, he took an apartment in an art deco building at 315 West End Avenue, on the southwest corner of West End and Seventy-fifth Street. I had moved into a rambling two-bedroom place at 320 West End diagonally across the street. (The rent in the 1950s was $220 a month, with the landlord throwing in a paint job and free new toilet seats as an inducement for me to sign a two-year lease. Most similar places on the Upper West Side of Manhattan now are co-ops. They sell for about $1.4 million and if you want new toilet seats you have to buy them.) Both Woodward's apartment and mine had bars, and we began to spend more hours together than we ever had. In time I heard enough to recognize his life as an American saga.

Woodward built up the the *Star-Ledger* sports section with such skill that he soon was awarded the title of supervising sports editor for all newspapers in the Newhouse chain. "I appreciated the recognition," Woodward said, "and even more the raise that went with it. Financial acumen is not among my virtues." He brought a few of his best Miami people into Newark and encouraged a promising feature writer, and later columnist, Jerry Izenberg. Meanwhile, as the *Star-Ledger* prospered, the *Herald Tribune* experienced disorder and early sorrow. The *Times,* of all places, began introducing fresh talent into its sport section, notably the late Howard Tuckner and the acute and gifted Gay Talese. Later the *Times,* not the *Trib,* integrated New York press boxes with Bob Teague.

John Denson, the *Tribune*'s editor during a tumultuous stretch near its end, once complained to Woodward: "Everybody on this damn sheet thinks he has a proprietary interest in it." Denson's complaint did not go far enough. Pretty much everyone who had ever worked for the "damn sheet" continued to believe that he or she retained a proprietary interest in it, even after moving on to magazines or books or public relations or Hollywood. We held no stock in The New York Tribune Inc. Our interest was that the paper remain as splendid as the paper we had known.

At a lunch one day in Costello's, a popular Irish pub, I sat with John Lardner and Joe Mitchell of *The New Yorker.* At coffee Mitchell remarked that we had spent the entire lunch talking about the *Herald Tribune.*

"That's probably because all three of us worked there," I said.

"That's true of any three people sitting at any table in this place," Lardner said.

With the *Times* drawing farther ahead of the *Trib,* notably in Sunday circulation, Helen Reid replaced Whitie as editor with her second son, Ogden, nicknamed Brown. (He had answered to "Brownie," but felt the diminutive was no longer suitable.) Unsettling staff changes followed as Brown demoted those he regarded as Whitie loyalists. If I had to pick an ebb in the Brown Reid regime, and there were many, it was his association with a self-proclaimed "mole" in the Communist party named Herbert Philbrick, who carried about a membership card marked Communist Party of the U.S., 1946, and numbered 56988. Philbrick reported on Communist activities for the FBI and in 1952 published a popular book called *I Led Three Lives.* These were, Philbrick said, "citizen, 'communist' and counterspy." During those high and nasty red-herring times, the book sold well. Philbrick asserted that "a hard core of 30,000 Communists agents" existed in America, striving tirelessly to seize the government. Further, "since World War II, Communists have been taking over territory at the rate of 8,000 square miles a day, every day, and the free people of the world have not taken back an inch." (He apparently slept through Douglas MacArthur's Inchon landing, which briefly seized a significant portion of Communist North Korea.)

Working with Philbrick, Brown Reid began a *Herald Tribune* column called "The Red Underground," and started toting a holstered pistol because "you never can tell when one of those Reds is going to try to kill me." The Reid-Philbrick column embarrassed many of us who were apolitical or Democrat or Republican. One sample of embarrassing stuff was a listing of "secret Commie meetings," which were simultaneously advertised publicly in the Communist newspaper, *The Daily Worker.* The tone varied from shrill to hysterical. If "The Red Underground" belonged anywhere, we thought, it should appear in Hearst's right-wing *Journal-American,* not in the enlightened *Trib,* or as we felt, *our* enlightened *Trib.* At length, Mrs. Reid recognized that her son, Brown, could not restore the *Tribune.* Preserving her inherited fortune, she peddled the paper in 1958 to John Hay "Jock" Whitney, who was often described as "art patron, financier, and sportsman." Whitney was also President Dwight D. Eisenhower's ambassador to the Court of St. James's. He possessed a prodigious private fortune.

"A lot of people are worried about Jock taking over," Bob Cooke told friends. "Not me. Whenever Jock is in town, we play bridge together Thursday nights." Within days a Whitney deputy dismissed Cooke, who never did cash in on "the big money" of television. As far as I know, he spent his remaining years selling real estate.

Over a scotch in Bleeck's, Irving Marsh told me happily, "Woodward is coming back. Whitney wants him to be our sports editor again."

"Is this official?"

"Absolutely. It will be announced next week."

Whitney's primary sports interest was horse racing, but he knew some football and baseball. He saw Red Smith in racetrack clubhouses from time to time, and when Whitney's acquisition of the *Tribune* neared, Smith made a case for bringing back Woodward. "Jock didn't need much convincing," Smith said.

At Bleeck's I reminded Marsh that I was the sports editor of *Newsweek* and that I now felt I had to write a Woodward piece for the press section.

"That wasn't my intention," Marsh said, "but I can't tell you not to go ahead. Just don't name me as your source."

I asked Woodward to my apartment, mixed drinks, and told him what I had. "It surprises even me," he said. "Old Double-Rubber took me to lunch at Whyte's, on Fifty-seventh Street, where he figured no one would spot us. The offer was fine. I've had a nice situation at the *Star-Ledger,* but what I can't resist about coming back to the *Trib* is this: I'm giving the Reids a stiff poke in the eye. I'm going to restructure the old place, but first I have to write an opening column. Any ideas?"

"Why not begin, 'As I was saying . . . '" Woodward gave that some thought. His first column on returning to the *Trib* actually began, "As I was saying when I was so rudely interrupted eleven years ago . . ."

In his prime, it had taken Woodward more than a decade to create a great sports section. Now he was sixty-four years old; time was winding down for him and for the *Herald Tribune* as well. He felt he had to fire "the semi-competents" who drifted into the department during his absence. But a union, the American Newspaper Guild, had won certain guarantees that kicked in after a new staffer had worked at the paper for a mere four months. Unless the boss could prove "gross negligence, gross incompetence, or gross insubordination," a dismissed employee drew significant severance pay. "It's almost impossible to prove gross anything," Woodward said. Woodward promptly collided with an attribute not usually associated with Jock Whitney. For all his wealth, Whitney turned out to be as parsimonious as Helen Reid.

Whitney had inherited his fortune from a grandfather who consolidated streetcar and railway lines in New York City and from an uncle named Oliver Payne, an early partner of the first John D. Rockefeller. When Whitney was a young man, Hollywood lured him—Paulette Goddard and Joan Crawford were principal attractions—and he became chairman of the board of Selznick International Pictures and chief financial backer of *Gone with the Wind*. That was risky, but at length increased his fortune. By the time he bought the *Tribune,* an older Whitney had grown more cautious. He deputized a frugal lawyer-financier named Walter Thayer to run things on a daily basis and to hold down expenses. Whitney was an affable, unpretentious man who refused to allow his name to be listed in the *Social Register*, which he called "a travesty of democracy." He was a political centrist who said of himself, "Some nights I go to sleep a Democrat and wake up a Republican." But for all his egalitarian merits, Jock Whitney was no newspaperman. He began brilliantly by rehiring Woodward, but when he installed a Wall Street lawyer as publisher, Whitney courted doom. He had been investing in television stations and establishing a company called Whitney Communications, imagining a media conglomerate of the sort—but not the political slant—that Rupert Murdoch has since built. The *Herald Tribune* was to be Whitney's centerpiece. Soon I began to hear grumbling from *Tribune* people at the bar in Bleeck's. "Why the hell does Jock have a lawyer running things? Doesn't he know that a newspaper ought to be run by a newspaperman?" When Woodward dismissed his hunting and fishing writer, Ed Gilligan, Thayer said he could not hire another until Gilligan's severance had run out, a matter of at least three months. Woodward held his tongue and simmered.

Thayer clashed with George Cornish, who shocked everyone, even Woodward, by resigning and moving on to the quieter world of the *Encyclopaedia Britannica*. His replacement, one Robert M. White II, came from a small Missouri town called Mexico, where he had been running the family newspaper. In a relatively short time White left—"not budget minded," Thayer said. "He also," Woodward said, "didn't know a damn thing about New York." White was replaced by a tall *Tribune* veteran named Fendall Yerxa, who was, in turn, superseded by John Denson, that brilliant, demonic, mass of energy, talent, prejudice, and chaos.

Denson ran *Newsweek* during my years there alongside John Lardner, generally with great success. He was a reformed alcoholic who had stopped drinking and kept a case of Jack Daniel's bourbon under his desk to show us all that he could spend hours near the stuff without touching it. When challenged, Denson was given to tantrums for which the warning sign was a clacking of his dentures. During one departmental conference a prim, flirtatious research assistant named Elizabeth Knox remarked in seeming innocence, "When Mr. Denson gets angry, it sounds as if he is chewing on nuts."

Hard-boiled Gordon Manning, now Denson's deputy, said, "He is. Mine!" Elizabeth managed to blush.

Denson tried to read every word that was to appear in each edition of *Newsweek* and he rewrote most of the heads. Despite ranging prejudices—he disliked African Americans, Jesuits, and Frank Sinatra—the magazine became livelier, and when Denson moved to the *Herald*

*Tribune* in 1961, he tried the same omnivorous editing approach. That did not work; it could not work. No single individual can edit all the copy and all the headlines of a large metropolitan newspaper under the constraints of daily deadlines and remain sensible or, for that matter, actually meet those deadlines. Denson did neither.

During Woodward's absence the New York sports scene changed radically. In 1954 the New York Giants won a World Series. The 1955 Brooklyn Dodgers did the same. But after the 1957 season, both teams abandoned New York for California. Woodward was coming back to a one-team town, even as, say, Cincinnati. The baseball beat became roughly two-thirds smaller than it had been, which made producing interesting summer sports sections that much tougher. (The Mets were not created until 1962 with the principal financial backing coming from Jock Whitney's sister, Joan Payson. That season they managed to lose 120 games. They finished 60½ games behind the San Francisco Giants, who won an exciting play-off from the Los Angeles Dodgers. When Woodward came back to New York, Willie Mays was gone and Sandy Koufax was performing before home crowds that included Cary Grant and Doris Day. This exciting stuff was taking place a long way from Brooklyn. Woodward's transpontine madness was no more.)

The coach plunged into his second term at the *Trib* with full energy but he had a bumpy ride. Years of smoking left him with a chronic shortness of breath. Some of the people he fired tried to dismiss him as, in one man's impertinent phrase, "a wheezy old drunk." He was able to hire Jerry Izenberg from Newark, but most of the time the parsimony of the Whitney regime tied his hands. He appreciated Talese's work at the *Times,* but lacked the budget to make an offer. He had no use for an ambitious young freelancer named Jimmy Breslin. "He makes things up and he invents quotes," Woodward said.

"He tries for special effects," I said. "Some people are calling that the new journalism."

"Then," Woodward said, "the new journalism is the old bullshit."

I can't argue that Woodward II matched Woodward I, but on the occasion when I worked for him again, he was formidable and at the top of his game. One of the interesting heavyweight boxing pairings of the mid–twentieth century matched Floyd Patterson, a smallish champion from a Brooklyn ghetto, against Ingemar Johansson, a former street laborer in Gothenburg, Sweden. Neither was a Dempsey, or even close, but their distinct styles created significant excitement. Patterson was fast and held his gloves high in a manner the writers described as "peekaboo." Johansson relied on a right-hand punch that he called "Toonder." He declined to show the right when sportswriters were watching, but after workouts he liked to lift his right fist, clench it, and announce, "No man can stand up to Toonder." With amused skepticism, John Lardner named Johansson's unseen right "the Hammer of Thor," after the Norse god of thunder who hurled a hammer at his foes. After slaying them, the hammer magically returned to Thor's massive hand.

The boxers met first at Yankee Stadium on June 26, 1959, and for two rounds Johansson looked lackluster. Then, in the third, he hurled the mighty right through Patterson's gloves, catching the reigning champion squarely between the eyebrows. When Patterson rose, at the count of seven, he walked vacantly across the ring, a glove to his nose, like a little boy who was hurt and didn't want to fight anymore. Six knockdowns later, referee Ruby Goldstein stopped the battering. Ingo Johansson was heavyweight champion of the world.

They met again at the Polo Grounds on June 20, 1960, and this time Patterson eluded the right and knocked out Johansson in the fifth round with a leaping left hook straight to the point of the jaw. Johansson lay unconscious for almost five minutes, with his left leg twitching. Later, media people were barred from his dressing room. Elizabeth Taylor, who displayed a startling décolletage, was not. "Hey, what paper is she working for?" reporters called to a sullen phalanx of policemen.

The press conference the next day started with awkward silence. Johansson had prepared no statement, and everybody seemed reluctant to question a man so soon after he had lain on his back, unconscious and quivering. Finally I said, "Ingo, was that the hardest you've ever been hit?" He met my eyes and said, loudly and clearly, "I tell you." He grinned slightly amid general laughter.

A third match, promoted by Roy Cohn, of all people, took place on March 13, 1961, in Miami Beach. Johansson had moved his official residence to a Swiss village where taxes were only a whisper. But still he found himself engaged in a money spat with the New York State Tax Commission regarding the state's cut of his purses from the previous fights. By fighting in Florida he sought to elude the hounds of Albany.

Woodward invited me to lunch at Bleeck's, said he'd heard I was going to be in Florida for spring training, and asked whether I wanted to take a break from baseball and cover the fight at the Miami Beach Convention Center. "Smith's doing the column. Abramson's doing the lead. What would you like to do?"

"Notes," I said, shorthand for a free-form color piece about the fight, the fighters, and the people and events around them.

"Fine," Woodward said. "You can get that done before the fight. Afterward, work the Swede's dressing room. The late city closes at midnight."

I was thrilled to be a newspaperman again and thrilled to be working for Woodward again. I was not upset when he said, "I'll pay you ten dollars."

"I'm not going to bargain off ten dollars, Coach, but I'll need about three days in Miami Beach to gather string."

"Mr. Whitney," Woodward said, "will pick up those expenses."

The day of the fight Woodward spent time on the phone with Smith, Abramson, and myself checking the themes we had in mind so that his sports pages would be free of repetition. The bout itself was another rouser. Johansson's right knocked down Patterson twice in the first round and then Patterson's left hook floored Ingo. The free swinging continued until round six when Patterson landed two rights to the head and Johansson went down. He pulled himself up by the ropes at the count of eleven. The fight was over. Patterson had retained his heavyweight championship. Then an unusual and touching thing occurred. The men had met three times in furious battle. Now Patterson, the winner, walked across the ring and lightly kissed Johansson on the cheek. Ingo nodded and a tear ran from one eye.

The Johansson dressing room was not pleasant. Xenophobic cracker security police used nightsticks to pound the skulls of European journalists whose credentials were even slightly out of order. As Johansson stepped naked out of a shower, New York State tax men ringed him and thrust papers into his hand. He would not be able to leave the county until he settled his Albany bill. "You could have waited till he put on a bathrobe," I said to a tax man. He glared. Fortunately, this character was not carrying a nightstick. I wrote the dressing-room story quickly, pleased that a newspaper deadline held no insurmountable terrors. I had taken a long time composing my notes, and noticed with some distress that Max Schmeling of Hamburg, a former heavyweight champion but also a former Wehrmacht paratrooper, was applauded as he strolled down Collins Avenue and that many cheering him seemed to me to be Jewish. I then wrote: "Max, like sixty-seven million other Germans, was never a Nazi. As I get the picture, there were never more than five or six Nazis in Germany, but, of course, they worked very hard."

On some level I recalled all the *Tribune* censoring under Bob Cooke. I knew the paper drew copious advertising from Volkswagen. I put the Nazi note in the middle of my color story, hoping that placed there, it might survive.

When I got home to West End Avenue, a letter from Woodward awaited. "I liked your stuff so much I have decided to pay you five times the agreed-upon price and it would have been more if the expense bite hadn't been so high. Meet me in Bleeck's."

I walked into the bar expecting a flourish of trumpets. Instead Woodward said, "Why did you bury your lead note?"

"I thought if you saw it you might kill it."

"Sometimes" the Coach said, "you can be a stupid son of a bitch." I had offended one of the press's great champions of free expression, and Woodward made me pay for my own drinks.

The lesson here could well be engraved on the portico of every school of journalism in the country. You can't do much, or sometimes anything, about censorship from above. But if you're going to be a reporter, never, *ever*, censor yourself.

Woodward's own passion for free expression shortened his second term. A prime condition for the National League to return to the New York market was the construction of a new ball park, and here inside politics came into play. Robert Moses, "the Power Broker" in Robert Caro's phrase, chose a site on old world's fair land in Queens, the same site he had offered to Walter O'Malley, the Dodger president, in the mid-1950s.

O'Malley declined, saying he was damned if he was going to build on filled-in land. "That filled-in stuff sinks," O'Malley told me. "In five years my upper deck would be my lower deck."

With O'Malley gone, Moses extracted $24 million from the municipal budget and commissioned plans for what would eventually become Shea Stadium. From its earliest drawings Shea looked small and undistinguished. "What New York needs," Woodward said, "is a place that seats 100,000, not half that. This is the premier city. It deserves the premier ball park, something that would also attract the Army-Navy football game and heavyweight championship fights. Why on earth would Moses draw up something so small?"

"Perhaps," I said, "he has an edifice complex."

"As you well know," Woodward said, "anything you say to me enters the public domain." In a column that pilloried the projected ball park, he helped himself to my phrase. Meanwhile, Jock Whitney's sister was working at founding the Mets. A Whitney-Moses tie existed, creating a conflict of interest that Whitney chose to ignore. Moses called Whitney, lambasted Woodward, and insisted that Shea Stadium would be the most remarkable arena built since the Flavian Amphitheater, the Colosseum in Rome. The Colosseum, inaugurated in 80 A.D. by the Emperor Titus, remains a monument to Roman architectural and engineering genius. Shea, formally opened in 1964, was and is a mediocre park. But instead of challenging Moses or simply defending his editor's right to express opinion in a column, Whitney sent a sharp memo to Woodward saying that the job of the sports editor was not to make enemies. Woodward muttered but made no formal response. Then came Denson.

Traditionally the *Tribune* sports department was an independent state. After the sports editor was allotted his daily space, say twenty-six columns, roughly 2,600 lines, he used it as he chose. The sports staff prepared its own layouts, wrote its own heads, and only on those rare occasions when a sports story made the front page was there a final review by such outside editors as Everett Kallgren. Denson elected to work not from Cornish's old sanctum but from the so-called night desk, out in the open, close to the geographic center of the main editorial floor. He revamped the paper's look, introduced headlines that ended with question marks and came to be regarded variously as a journalistic wonder and an unconfined lunatic. His special concentration was the front page, but he wanted to oversee the sports section as well. Denson tampered with a few Woodward columns—no one had done that before—and finally killed a column outright.

Woodward had written that he was one editor with admittedly Democratic leanings on a Republican paper, but the *Trib*'s latest slogan— "Who says a good newspaper has to be dull?"—summed up an affection that was stronger than party politics. As for the *Times,* notably the Sunday *Times,* growing ever larger with what Woodward called "interminable advertising," that paper really *was* dull. However, Woodward wrote, he had made certain arithmetic calculations. Buying the Sunday *Times* was the cheapest way New Yorkers could acquire wrapping for fish.

Denson sent the column back to Woodward marked, "Killed!" When Woodward challenged him, Denson said that "playing around" with the *Tribune*'s advertising slogan was "insulting to Mr. Whitney."

Woodward said, "I have no wish to insult Mr. Whitney, but I'm not trying to please him. I'm trying to amuse and entertain the readers of Mr. Whitney's paper."

"The column is facetious," Denson said. "It's dead."

The next conversation between the two concerned the financing of Woodward's retirement. He could not work for as choleric a boss as Denson, "who recognized nobody's editorial judgment but his own." Another source of anger was the juxtaposition of their jobs. Why hadn't Jock Whitney thought to make Woodward managing editor? "I was," he said, "an extremely well-established newspaper editor who had worked cityside as well as sports and put in two good turns as a war correspondent, during both of which I carried on under fire. I knew the newspaper business as well as I knew the Boulevard in Worcester, where I raced horse-drawn sleighs when I was a boy. Specifically, I knew the *Herald Tribune* as well as I knew my mother's kitchen. And I liked to eat."

In a final column, published on March 31, 1962, Woodward put up a stoic front, writing, "The sports department seems to run as well as ever without my help and that's the real tip-off that it's time to quit." Upon his resignation, effective April 1, he accepted the title of sports editor emeritus, realizing as he did that there was no such job.

★ ★ ★

By the accounts of most people who knew him, "Jock" Whitney was "a nice rich guy." During World War II, he served heroically as an intelligence officer. He collected Impressionist paintings, raced horses, supported good causes, and gave generously to his alma mater, Yale. In many ways Whitney was a model citizen, but as I've remarked, he was no newspaperman. Before he became a publisher, he showed no signs of understanding the way things were in the newspaper fraternity.

Joe H. Palmer, the *Herald Tribune*'s gifted horse-racing columnist, died in his midforties. This was six years prior to Whitney's purchase of the paper, but Jock was already a well-known and well-liked figure in racetrack clubhouses. Palmer left a widow and two children, but little money, and Red Smith gathered his columns into a book called *This Was Racing*. The publisher printed a special leather-bound edition of one hundred copies, to sell at $100 each. The proceeds, $10,000, would go to Palmer's widow and orphans. Smith explained the circumstances and showed the premium version of the Palmer book to Whitney.

"I liked Joe's columns very much," Whitney said. "I'll buy one."

Smith, who did not rattle easily, told me he found himself speechless. "I meant for Jock to buy up the whole edition," Smith said. "The nice rich guy" just didn't get it. Whitney's greatest failing, of course, was his unwillingness to put a healthy portion of his inheritance behind the *Herald Tribune*. He kept looking for quick fixes. When none worked, he bailed out and folded the paper after he had been at the helm for only eight years. It was said at the time that Jock Whitney felt himself under pressure. He was down to his last $950 million. He may have been a prisoner of the Old WASP business commandment: *Never touch capital*. Whatever, the Whitney publishing legacy turned out to be dismal. In the end he became a newspaper mortician.

"I never set out to be a sports editor," the Coach was telling me. "That was something that just happened. What I set out to be was a newspaperman." We were sitting in the living room of a small red house off Route 133, near the village of Brookfield Center in what was then rural Connecticut, not far from from Danbury, where Woodward was trying to settle into retirement. He was pleased to see someone with *Herald Tribune* memories, and after only the slightest prodding he began to tell tales of his seventy years. I don't believe I'd ever asked about his background when we were in New York, and he certainly didn't volunteer much. It was a matter of etiquette at Bleeck's that one discussed issues, not personal history. Perhaps it was the country setting—"enforced bosky relaxation" he called it—but now he spun out fabrics from an extraordinary life.

Growing up comfortably in Worcester, where he was born in 1895, he played most sports until early adolescence, when his eyesight began to fail. The diagnosis was cataracts, a condition handled with relative ease by contemporary surgeons, but "back in 1912, they could treat cataracts all right, but the method they used affected your vision for life. I remember being angry that a big strong kid like me had to wear thick spectacles."

The bad vision interfered with baseball, although he developed into a pretty fair country pitcher, but not football, where his size and strength lent weight to the Amherst line. "My academics were never much more than adequate," he said. "I could never balance scholarship and football. I always sank in class work during the fall and I'd barely make the alkaline side of the ledger with some all-night study between the Williams game, which ended the football season, and the midyear examinations."

After graduating in 1917, he took an army physical, failed because of his eyesight, then joined the merchant marine. "I wasn't going to miss the whole damn war." He put in time on freighters named *Amphion* and *Pawnee* in a dangerous North Atlantic that merchant ships shared with German U-boats. He remembered visiting "every French port between Le Havre and Bordeaux, steering ships into New York Harbor and shivering in my boots as our gun crew opened up on a periscope half a mile astern." But he relished the sailing life and said he would have become a sea captain, "except that was impossible. In peacetime you couldn't get licensed if you were an optical cripple." He sent long letters home, which his mother, Stella, carried to the Worcester *Evening Gazette*. None survives, but they impressed Nick Skerrett, the city editor, who printed them and after the armistice gave Woodward a job as a general assignment reporter. "From that day in 1919 until my recent forcible retirement," Woodward said, "I was never out of the newspaper business except for some foolish dabbling with a magazine. I think that works out to forty-three years."

In Worcester he absorbed a heavy journalism course from Skerrett, who said such things as "The creation of heaven and earth is told in ten words in the Bible. It is a good story, well reported. Be concise! Be accurate!" Woodward covered murders, strikes, skulduggery, speakeasies, the Irish of Vernon Hill, the blacks of John Street, the Jews of Providence Hill, the Italians of Shrewsbury Street, the Swedes of Belmont Hill, and a Protestant upper stratum "that was just as hard-core as Beacon Hill." After becoming city editor in Worcester, he moved on to the *Boston Herald* in 1922, where his background as a pitcher and lineman landed him in the sports department. His father said, "Now that you're leaving Worcester, Stan, and becoming a sportswriter, it appears the only practical thing I've ever done for you is teach you how to score a ball game."

He had written a few books, he told me, but he hoped he wasn't done yet. He thought there still was "a big one in a big guy like me." Someone had placed a stack of papers on an end table. "I've been working at it," Woodward said, gesturing toward the stack, "but my wind isn't what it used to be. I need some help."

He was asking, I realized, if I would work with him. I was quite startled. "After that Duke Snider column you wrote, I thought you didn't like my collaborations."

"You were wasting your skills working with a ballplayer of limited depth. This is different."

"Actually, *I* don't much like my collaborations."

He pressed no further. But as we talked from time to time he consulted the stack of papers. He wanted to make sure, he said, that he was being accurate. Accuracy and color, he said, were the keys to the kingdom of journalism.

He remembered his first big-city sports scene in vivid bloom, bursting from youth. "Ruth was three years gone from the town after pitching the Red Sox to victory over Chicago in the World Series of 1918 and winning the home run championship with 29 in 1919. Man o' War was in his second year of retirement. Bob Jones was a year away from his first golf championship. The United States had held the Davis Cup for three years. Jack Dempsey was the world boxing champion. We had two big-league ball clubs, big-time football at Harvard and Boston College, three or four boxing clubs, the Patriots' Day Marathon, dog shows, horse shows, and the Charles River alive with eight-oared crews from Harvard, MIT and sundry schools. Boston was a perfect place to get a start in sports."

The editor of the *Herald,* Robert Lincoln O'Brien, was a grammarian. Infinitives were not to be split on O'Brien's *Herald,* nor were verb forms to be divided. Writing "Yale had utterly routed Harvard" drew a reprimand. One was instructed to write "Yale had routed Harvard utterly." At the *Herald* Woodward performed intelligently and grammatically—he himself never ceased to be a grammarian—and moved out of sports and became a crack general assignment reporter, which was what he was doing in 1930 when the *Herald Tribune* offered him a job writing sports for $135 a week, $45 more than he was earning in Boston. In those Depression days, that salary shone like silver, gleamed like gold. "A five-course steak dinner at a fine restaurant, the Basques," he told me, "went for $1.50. A bootleg martini sold for sixty cents. I was out of Boston like a shot." Woodward moved merrily into a large railroad flat on the West Side. Somewhere along the way—Woodward never discussed the details—he had been married and divorced. Then he remarried, a strong-willed, attractive Connecticut girl named Esther Rice, who as Ricie Woodward became his lifetime companion. Stanley and Ricie relished 1930s Manhattan, where the Empire State Building was being completed on the site of the old Waldorf-Astoria at Thirty-fourth Street and Fifth Avenue and plans for a great riverfront urban throughway, the West Side Highway, were just about complete, and theater, opera, speakeasies, later saloons, filled the nights. They remained Manhattanites until Woodward, missing the sea, moved to Port Washington, where he sailed a skiff in calm waters and rough, in summer and in raw Long Island winters, plowing through nasty, frigid swells to the alarm of Ricie, who sometimes watched from shore. Adventuring laced with danger gave him joy.

In 1935, the *Trib* sent Woodward to Orlando to cover the spring training of a pretty fair Brooklyn Dodger team. Stars included the hard-drinking hard-throwing righthander Van Lingle Mungo; a pleasantly eccentric outfielder named Stan "Frenchy" Bordagaray; and the catcher, Al Lopez, who before his death in 2005 was the oldest member of the Baseball Hall of Fame. (Mungo had a lot of stuff, John Lardner wrote, possibly because he drank a lot of stuff.) Woodward's favorite was the manager, Casey Stengel, who frequently left a note in Woodward's mailbox, "Mr. Stengel is pouring in suite 601." During one game, Woodward said, Bordagaray doubled and presently stood on second base tapping his foot. An opposing infielder tagged him and the umpire called Bordagaray out.

"How in hell," Stengel roared in the dugout, "can you get called out when you're tapping your foot on second base?"

"I guess," Bordagaray said, "he caught me between taps."

This jolly band, which included a shortstop named Lonny Frey, who made 41 errors in 131 games, finished fifth in an eight-team league. A year later the manager, whom Woodward dubbed Field Marshall Casey von Stengel, was dismissed. Stengel would not know major-league success for another thirteen years, when he won what was the first of five consecutive World Series for the Yankees. "I always knew he was an outstanding baseball man," Woodward said, "but it is difficult to win in the major leagues while managing a team stacked with comedians."

Woodward switched to the Yankees in 1936, Joe DiMaggio's rookie year. "You could just look at this hatchet-faced kid on the field and say, without any chance of making a mistake, 'There's a great ball player.'" That was the Connecticut Woodward talking in 1962. In 1936 he wrote from St. Petersburg: "The question still exists whether DiMaggio can power the offerings of the American League brothers after they start cutting loose, whether he can go and get them in the outfield, and whether he can throw as well as his enraptured ex manager, Lefty O'Doul, says he can." When I confronted Woodward, cordially but firmly, with his old on-scene view of DiMaggio, he was in no way embarrassed. "I was exercising caution," he said. "I was still young enough to believe that caution was a virtue."

"Some still believe it is," I said.

"Perhaps, but caution tends to be boring. There are few worse attributes to a good sportswriter than being a bore in print."

The Yankee manager, a dour Buffalo Irishman named Joe McCarthy, did not care for the press. Having heard that Woodward could throw hard, as most well-coordinated big men can, McCarthy asking in a teasing way if he wanted to throw half an hour of batting practice.

Pitching batting practice to big leaguers has certain similarities to standing up against a firing squad. After releasing the ball you are perhaps fifty-seven feet from home plate and line drives up the middle will, as the players like to say, "get your attention." Many travel at more than a hundred miles an hour. Undaunted, Woodward agreed. He borrowed a shirt, number 4, from another big, muscular man, Lou Gehrig, but Gehrig's pants were too tight a fit. Woodward cadged a baggy pair from a portly relief pitcher named Pat Malone. "It was the first time I ever pitched to big-league hitters," Woodward said, "and I was forty-one years old." Today batting practice pitchers are protected by a screen, but in 1936 batting practice pitchers worked figuratively naked, and more than one was seriously injured. "I survived without damage [and without showing fear]," Woodward said, "although a couple of drives whistled close to my ears." As he walked off the field, arm weary and proud, a female fan, noticing the number on his back, called, "Mr. Gehrig."

Woodward looked up. "It was a thrill to see you pitch batting practice, Mr. Gehrig, "but I had always heard you were left-handed. How come today you did your pitching right-handed?"

"Madam," Woodward said, "I am indeed left-handed, but I make it a point to save my good left arm for the regular season. To keep it rested until opening day I throw right-handed."

The lady thanked Woodward and he proceeded to the clubhouse where he returned the uniform shirt to Gehrig. "I actually had a case of the giggles," Woodward said. "Lou stayed deadpan. He didn't want me to know that he was impressed."

Ogden Reid promoted Woodward to sports editor in 1938. "He did it through his managing editor, Grafton Wilcox. My pals in the sports section were as pleased as I, and we all went down to Bleeck's to celebrate. As a result I didn't get home until three thirty A.M. Mama was pleased with my new job, and salary, but a little put out about my lateness and unsteady gait."

The *Times* sports section in the 1930s was indisputably complete, covering such events as Harvard-Princeton junior varsity rugby and offering the daily standing of the clubs in the Three-Eye League (Illinois, Indiana, and Iowa). But the writing was pedestrian, and feature stories were all but unknown. Even into the 1930s, the *Times* declined to give bylines to most of its sportswriters. One of Adolph Ochs's favorite editors, Carr Van Anda, asserted, "We are not running a register of reporters."

At Woodward's first staff meeting he announced, "It is impossible to outcrap the *Times*. Let's not try. Let's outthink the bastards and by all means let's outwrite them. That shouldn't be hard. But I expect I'll have to spend rather a bit of the publisher's money."

That memory made Woodward laugh in the small red house off Route 133 in Connecticut. "You know that James Gordon Bennett at the *Herald* sent Stanley to Africa in search of Livingston. The *World* sent Nelly Bly around the earth. Somebody else sent Richard Harding Davis to cover the Spanish-American War in Cuba. All these assignments cost a lot, but they won renown. So I realized I'd have to start moving my people around to where the good stories were developing. Otherwise I'd be remembered as the old feller with the spectacles who was tight with expense money."

Woodward stopped covering events he thought had minor interest. Good-bye Union College-Hamilton lacrosse; farewell Navy-VMI electrical épée. But, rethinking and reworking his budget, he began sending baseball writers out of town to cover important series, in addition to staffing the three local clubs. In the fall he dispatched reporters to the South and West for major football games, the first time any New York newspaper had done that. "Whenever anything important was going on, we had a man there. It made a great hit and drove the *Times* into revolving fits."

After the Japanese attack on Pearl Harbor, Woodward's interest in sports withered. He kept working hard but all the while campaigned to quit the press box and become a war correspondent: "Al Laney can sit in as sports editor." Finally, in the summer of 1944, the *Herald Tribune* sent Woodward to England aboard the former luxury liner *Ile de France,* so famous for the romantic lyric from "These Foolish Things."

> *The park at evening when the bell has sounded;*
> *The Ile de France with all the gulls around it . . .*

That was in tuneful peacetime. Now amid the blast of war the vessel had been converted into a troop transport. "The quarters were not bad. Twenty-eight of us shared a room that formerly housed one rich first-class passenger and his wife." After a few weeks in England, Woodward encountered a Royal Air Force officer he remembered as "Wing Commander Budcroft." The British officer dispatched him on what he called "the great adventure of my life."

The Battle of Arnhem, code-named Operation Market Garden, began on Sunday, September 17, 1944. The plan, largely devised by Field Marshall Bernard Montgomery, Britain's hero of El Alamein, called for three divisions of glider and parachute troops—about 35,000 soldiers— to drop from the sky as much as sixty miles behind Nazi lines in Holland. They were to seize four German-held bridges, after which tank and heavy artillery units would join them. The combined forces would then outflank the Nazi Siegfried Line, the *Westwall,* sweep into Germany, and win the European phase of World War II by the end of the year.

Some official histories attribute the ensuing Allied difficulties to the fact that "by a complete fluke two elite German SS Panzer Divisions were billeted around Arnhem." British and American soldiers soon found themselves fighting heavy tanks with rifles. "That 'complete fluke' theory is complete nonsense," Woodward told me in the tranquillity of the Connecticut woods. "There was a leak from within the British high command. Some goddamned spy had penetrated. The Nazis knew we were coming, if not each exact drop point, then pretty close. After the initial surprise of our attack they damn near wiped out the entire British First Airborne. That is, out of the 10,500 British troops that landed around Arnhem, only 2,400 returned."

Back in London, Commander Budcroft was telling Woodward that he was offering him a chance to go on a great airborne invasion of continental Europe on a scale never previously approached. "It is above average in danger," Budcroft said. "You can either go in aboard a glider with troops of the [American] 101st Airborne [commanded by future chief of staff Maxwell D. Taylor] or else you can fly over the invasion area in a photographic plane, which will return to London before dark. Personally if you are really looking for a story, I suggest you go in a glider."

Woodward said fear gripped his gut. He said, "All right. I'll go in a glider."

"Because of the danger of the mission," Budcroft said, "we'll have an M-1 rifle ready for you at takeoff. You can learn how to use it on the trip. Someone named Walter Cronkite from your United Press will ride in another 101st glider. We're letting Bill Boni of your Associated Press go in with the 82nd Airborne.

"One more thing, Mr. Woodward. If you talk, you will be jeopardizing thousands of lives. Don't have a drink with anyone you don't know very well."

Now in Connecticut Woodward grinned at the irony. "Budcroft didn't realize some bastard had already jeopardized the mission. I called another *Trib* correspondent, Dick Tobin, and we met at the best pub in London, the Kings and Keys on Fleet Street. After I downed three American-style [5-to-1] martinis, the glider ride did not seem quite so perilous, and, for what it's worth, I never mentioned Operation Market Garden, even to my colleague."

Two days later Woodward reported to the 101st Division Headquarters near Windsor, fifty miles west of London. He was outfitted with an army uniform with a small insignia of an American flag wrapped around one arm. A staff sergeant confiscated his portable typewriter saying, "You can't run carrying that thing and you'll probably have to run." He was allowed to retain a small bag containing paper, pencils, a sweater, and a carton of cigarettes. He would have to do his writing in longhand. "We'll be setting up radiophones," the sergeant said, "so you'll be able to call your stories into London [from where they would be relayed, also by phone, to the *Tribune* offices in New York]."

"What about my rifle?" Woodward asked. There was none and there would be none. A slipup somewhere. He was to land behind Nazi lines armed with a pocketknife and a sheaf of pencils. "All you needed to be really secure, Coach," I said, "was a yellow Star of David sewn onto your uniform."

"I would have been proud to wear it," he said.

He excused himself and returned in a few minutes carrying a martini for himself and a scotch for me, with a bulky scrapbook wedged under an elbow. "Someone in my family saved my stuff. You were not going to get copies of the New York *Herald Tribune* delivered behind German lines. My glider group was headed for a small town in Holland called Zon. The British 1st Airborne was headed for Arnhem across what the Dutch called the Nether Rhine. The 82nd would land at Nijmegen. Then the soldiers were suppose to seize bridges, and our tanks and big guns would roll across." He opened the scrapbook. "Look at this." The headline read:

### OVER ACK-ACK INTO HOLLAND: THE GLIDER TRIP
**TOUGH AMERICANS DIDN'T SCARE AS THE BULLETS AND SHELLS FLEW AROUND THEM**

Under Woodward's byline (and a *Tribune* copyright notice) the story began:

WITH THE AMERICAN AIRBORNE FORCE IN HOLLAND—The German ack-ack told us that the greatest airborne invasion in history had crossed into enemy territory. Machine gun bullets ripped through the fuselage and wings and the flimsy glider lurched with the explosion of German shells. I was riding in the fourth glider which entered Holland. Hordes of tough parachutists had gone in ahead.

Then we landed. . . . Dutch patriots were swarming to our support, the Dutch flag was flying from every house and the colors of the House of Orange were displayed in every buttonhole. After one look at the airborne force, the Dutch decided the Germans were gone for good.

"Would it had been so," Woodward said. "I remember that glider ride as vividly as anything in my life. There were thirteen men in our glider and the back of it was filled with cases of ammunition. If flack slammed into that stuff, we'd blow up. If flack took off a wing, we'd drop like a stone, 1,200 feet. I remember thinking 1,200 feet was about the height of the Empire State Building and it surprised me then, as it does now, that I was not frightened. The Empire State got me thinking briefly of New York where my will was up to date and in my desk drawer. It also struck me that death would be instantaneous if the ammo went and reasonably quick if we fell to earth. You know Tennyson?"

I anticipated him. "And may there be no moaning at the bar when I put out to sea . . ."

" 'Crossing the Bar' " Woodward said. He opened the scrapbook where bits of headlines told a vivid story. "German Resistance Stiffens After Initial Panic in Fight to Hold Bridges" . . . "Holland Corridor Tenuous. Allies Facing 120,000 Nazi Troops, Two Tank Divisions" . . . "Nazis Fiercely Defend Holland Bridges; Allied Tanks, Artillery Unable to Move Up." Then, finally, tragically, "British Pull Chutists Back Across Rhine; 1,200 Wounded Left Behind." "Their gallant fight," Woodward wrote in the *Herald Tribune* of September 29, "kept thousands of German troops occupied and prevented a large force of Hitler's elite troops from destroying entire British and American columns . . ."

In rustic Connecticut Woodward remembered the carnage. "The German intelligence had been too good and their reinforcements came up so quickly that even at the time I realized something had gone terribly wrong. I slept where I could, inside and out, ate cold food, and heard the German self-propelled 88s beating the hell out of our positions. It got so bad I simply could not get my dispatches out of Holland." After five days Woodward concluded that what he was doing mostly was risking his life. He came across a Jeep headed toward Belgium, jumped abroad, and flew back to London. "For the next week I pounded out stuff about the airborne invasion. My stories led the *Herald Tribune* for five consecutive days."

The overriding idea behind Operation Market Garden had been to conclude the European phase of World War II in 1944. But as the year wound down, a half million German troops were advancing through the Ardennes, on the German-Belgian border. This was the Battle of the Bulge, in which 19,000 American soldiers were killed. Operation Market Garden, preceding the Bulge, was premature, poorly planned, tragic for the Allies—and one hell of a story.

"I didn't like New York at all when I came back," Woodward said. "The people simply didn't understand the war. They thought we'd win easily, and when I differed, they didn't want to listen, even though I'd been there and heard the 88s and seen the corpses. I had to get away from the city, so I shipped out to the Pacific, and I ended up in a task force, aircraft carriers, cruisers, destroyers, just in time to run into some of the heaviest Japanese kamikaze attacks."

He favored two characters in the South Pacific war. One was John Lardner, covering the fighting for *The New Yorker* and *Newsweek*. The other was Captain Austin K. "Artie" Doyle, a native of Staten Island, who had played first base for the Annapolis varsity and was "the best naval officer" Woodward ever encountered.

"The battles were both terrible and spectacular," he said, "but there was a lot of down time as the ships moved about the Pacific. Heat and down time. I was carrying a lot of money and so was Lardner, and we fell to gambling, mostly dice, to kill the time. I don't remember if it was on Guam or in the hold of the carrier *Hornet* where I stopped rolling the dice long enough to offer Lardner a job. He was my first choice to be the *Trib* sports columnist after the war."

Lardner said tersely, not rudely. "Don't want to write every day."

"You won't have to," Woodward said. "I just need you to give us two columns a week."

Lardner did not intend to become a newspaperman again. "You can't afford me, Coach."

"For the two columns a week, I'll pay you $500. We'll syndicate you and we'll make the money back through syndication."

Lardner later told me he felt trapped. "But you know," John said, "there always seemed to be a small wolf hanging out at my kitchen door. The $500 a week had a nice cash register ring to it."

The men shook hands.

"So," Woodward said, after a healthy swig of his Connecticut 5-to-1 martini, "my two columnists would have been Lardner and Smith. Except for one thing. Double-Rubber overruled me. He said he would not authorize paying anybody $500 for two columns a week. I explained how syndication would make that back and more, but Cornish turned iron-headed. We won the war as you know, but I lost John Lardner."

I asked about the kamikazes. "Artie Doyle, the captain of the *Hornet,* said he had been reading my stuff for years, and he gave me the run of the ship. We'd arranged our destroyers in a perimeter, to protect the carrier, and I was on the bridge with Artie one day when a kamikaze broke through and headed right at us. All our five-inch guns opened up, but he kept coming. It didn't seem possible for some Japanese kid to fly through all the gunfire. It wasn't. But he was pretty damn close when his plane burst into flames and fell into the Pacific. Doyle stayed very calm. He told the lookouts to remain alert. He talked to his radar men. Kamikazes kept trying to get us for seventy-two straight hours. Four full days and nights. I took notes. Seventeen kamikazes got to take solo runs at us. Our gunners flamed every last one. Then, when it was safe again, Doyle got someone to requisition bats and gloves and a bunch of sailors gathered on the flight deck to play baseball.

"Rank had its privilege. Captain Doyle threw out the first pitch. He let me do that the next day. When we got further north, closer to Japan, he said, the weather would cool and the boys would switch to football. I could coach a team if I wanted, but this wasn't Amherst-Williams. The kamikazes kept trying to blow us up. Our Far Eastern football season never did get going."

"Called off," I said, "on account of war."

"When I got back, the old man [Ogden Reid] was shaky and Helen Reid asked what I wanted to do. I said that I would like to reorganize the sports section. I thought that would take three or four years, and then I expected Mrs. Reid would ask me to take over the Washington bureau. Instead she forgot about me. Or I thought she did until she popped up again and got me fired."

Woodward was coughing from time to time. His breathing had become heavy. But he rose to make a final round of drinks. "I have to drive," I said. "Could you make me just half a scotch on the rocks?"

"I don't know how to do that," Woodward said, "which isn't the question. The question is, Can you drink a half a scotch on the rocks?"

Bert Andrews, the man the Reids did install in Washington, was a strong, independent reporter until he fell in with a young member of the House Un-American Activities Committee, Richard M. Nixon. Under Nixon's sway, Andrews drifted to the right, keeping his growing closeness to Nixon and consequent loss of objectivity a turbulent secret. He evolved into a doctrinaire anti-Communist, like Nixon in his own early political years, and when Senator Joseph McCarthy and confreres trampled civil liberties, Andrews looked the other way.

"If," I said to Woodward in Brookfield Center, "you had gotten the Washington bureau, you would have undressed some red-baiting fanatics."

"I like to think so. I'd been under fire quite a bit during the war and Joe McCarthy's fake heroics—he was never in combat but he called himself 'Tail-Gunner Joe'—offended me more than I can say. Sure, I would have gone after him, and I would have gotten my staff to do the same, the way we went after the baseball rednecks. And I believe, I really do, I would have nailed McCarthy pretty quick. That would have been good for the country, but I also believe none of this would have changed my personal history very much. I would have ended up getting fired in Washington, instead of New York."

He suddenly saddened. "I've told you, I should have been managing editor." Woodward turned away. When he turned back, tears were rolling down his cheeks. "Wouldn't you think with all I've done they'd let an old man finish up in New York?"

He died at seventy-one, on November 29, 1965, of lung disease at a hospital in White Plains. *The New York Times* ran a splendid obituary, without a byline, and commented, "Those who held him in love, respect, or fear—it was difficult not to have strong feelings about this highly positive person—called him the Coach.

"This honorary title traced specifically to his preoccupation with football. . . . But by extension the nickname also reflected the generally high esteem in which he was held."

During the funeral service at St. James's Episcopal Church in New York, I thought that the *Times*'s publishing a warm, respectful obit about a man who had been so critical of the paper said something nice about the *Times*. It would have been nicer still if the *Times* had ever offered him a job.

A postlude came eighteen years later. One of the *Tribune*'s fine rewrite men, Kenneth Koyen, organized a dinner reunion of survivors from the regime of Whitie Reid. "No ad salesmen," he said. "No mapmakers. No new journalists. Just real newspaper people. Reporters." Fourteen of us met in a private room at the Williams Club and the ground rules specified that each person was to speak for three minutes, no longer. It pleased me to find Whitie Reid among my companions. Under Whitie my career had taken wing.

I thought then of what I had learned at the *Trib*. "To write English," in Stanley Woodward's phrase. The practical importance of such qualities as integrity and courage. To meet a deadline, then meet another and another. Woodward's own story proclaimed in large letters that big American institutions have little tolerance for nonconformists, however gifted they may be. All the more reason, therefore, not to conform.

I mentioned my struggles as a student and how the *Trib* became my university. I had many instructors. Woodward was dean. I looked down the table. Reid had aged well. If my Woodward reference bothered him, he concealed it. I said, "I'm glad you're here tonight, Whitie, so I can thank you."

Reid nodded and paused and blinked several times. At length he said, "Roger, we are all very proud of you." Eyes grew misty and we decided to make our reunion an annual event. That certainly would have been pleasant, but some people moved and others died. We never met again.

# CHAPTER 2

# The Captain

Here in my midtwenties I become the star baseball writer for
the New York *Herald Tribune* and achieve friendship with the
Dodger captain, a shortstop of profound kindness and great
nobility of character.

### Lines on My Father

*Down these deserted streets*
*toward the Grenada*
*where once he shared a room with a Pistol*
*Whose secret sign was a Louisville Slugger*
*at the bedroom door (meaning Annie was*
*naked beneath the sheets).*
*Down Atlantic and Flatbush where*
*he and Charlie Dressen after mixing Scotch and grasshoppers vomited in*
  *a shoe box*
*where in 1941 before death came knocking at the country's door,*
*he was carried on the shoulders of longshoremen.*
*I can still hear the shouts of freckle-faced Jewish*
*kids who broke Shabbat to celebrate in this musty shrine, with Hilda,*
  *Gladys, Happy*
*—to worship twenty-eight-year-old kids from Kentucky,*
  *from Compton, from Cairo via Pasadena, from Moonsocket and*
  *beyond; to boo Big Cat*

*Johnny Mize on fine summer days (oh to be old man Rickey*
*staying home on Sundays but pocketing the gate*
*at the Field of The Lord).*

*But February, 1992, I hear the cries of a father, too,*
*muffled by the filth and the eleventh inning*
*of potholes,*
*of beautiful ignorance, of*
*not knowing, or simply refusing.*
*He pauses long enough*
*to stare into the blackness of the coffee we share.*
*Together we enter the art of melted snow, city potholes*
*of blissful ignorance, of the forgotten known.*

*Of life, of death*

*Of a lonely art*
*my father leaves behind,*
*at a windswept corner of Flatbush, February, 1992.*

—MARK ALLEN REESE

If you have to explain a joke, the great comedian Fred Allen said, don't. Surely the same applies to poetry. The sorrow of Mark Reese's free-form poem springs from the sadness of the Borough of Brooklyn, from whom the Dodgers were ripped, and even more from the sort of generic sadness that comes at the changes time works on our surroundings, and our souls and bodies. That much is clear, but unless you were as intimately involved with the Brooklyn Dodgers as Pee Wee Reese and I once were, and Mark Reese would become, a skeleton key is in order.

The Granada was a semiseedy downtown Brooklyn hotel where the Dodgers placed their unmarried rookies. Reese joined the Dodgers along with another wonderful prospect, Harold Patrick "Pistol Pete" Reiser, who in 1941 led the National League in batting, total bases, runs scored, doubles, and triples. Red Barber, the celebrated broadcaster, called the two of them "the hallroom boys," as in a hall bedroom for youngsters still living with their parents. As the poem indicates, the two actually shared a suite at the Granada, where sometimes, in a tawdry setting, hormones took over. A grasshopper was and is a cocktail, in which are mixed Creme de Cacoa, cream, ice and Creme de Menthe. It is both green and sneaky. "Hilda, Gladys, and Happy" became popular characters at Ebbets Field. Hilda Chester was a baritone female fan who carried a cowbell, which she rang at appropriate moments, and inappropriate moments, as well. She liked to bellow at the slender Reese, "Pee Wee, have you had your glass of milk today?" Reese sometimes paused in mid-infield practice, spotted Chester in the stands—she favored a front-row seat in center field—and shouted back, "Yes, Hilda, I've had my glass of milk." Gladys Goodding served as ballpark organist, most notably the last time the Dodgers played in Brooklyn, which was on September 24, 1957, when she offered a stirring rendition of Chopin's Funeral March. This enraged the reigning monarch, Walter O'Malley, but Gladys had locked herself into the organist's booth behind a steel door and it would have taken a hand grenade to silence her. Except for guile, O'Malley walked about unarmed. Happy Felton, a onetime Broadway comic, was host for "The Knot Hole Gang" a pre- and postgame television show, featuring the Dodger "star of the day" and youngsters called "knotholers," after the time when outfield fences were crafted from wood and impecunious children watched big-league games through the knotholes.

The "kids" were ballplayers: Reese from Kentucky; Duke Snider, born in Compton, California; Jackie Robinson, born in Cairo, Georgia, but raised in Pasadena. Clem Labine was born in Woonsocket, Rhode Island, and here Mark is having a bit of fun, changing "Woon" to "Moon," which suggests a number of things.

"The lonely art" that Pee Wee left behind was playing shortstop, which he did about as well as shortstop can be played. At the time of the poem, 1992, he was approaching the age of seventy-five, and of course his old skills had vanished. Naturally that saddened him, but worse, the very stage on which he once performed, Pee Wee's great globe, had dissolved and left not a rack behind. Red Barber said more than once, "Everything happens at Ebbets Field." I think Barber's hyperbole here was acceptable. Great baseball happened at Ebbets Field, there were also some unusual comic moments, such as the proclamation one summer afternoon from the public address announcer: "Attention, please. A child has been found lost!"

I stood with Reese during the early 1990s when he saw the Ebbets Field site for the first time in thirty-five years. For a moment his face, still a Huck Finn kind of face, showed sharp dismay. Where was the right field wall, the stiff screen that rose above it, and the bulging scoreboard? What had become of the high opaque clubhouse windows fronting on a street, and the tiled rotunda with its repeating pattern of gilt crossed bats and golden baseballs? "Damn," he said quietly, looking at the faceless red brick apartment buildings that rose where the ballpark had stood. But he recovered quickly. "I'd have to say that these buildings look pretty nice. They're just not as nice as what was here before."

Mark Reese's use of the adjective "lonely" carries great importance. Baseball obviously is a team sport in which the actions of nine men are interlinked. But each individual stands alone, which means, if you are a shortstop, that all by yourself you face line drives, one-hoppers, spinning nubbers, and your own anxieties, in clear view of a boisterous and fickle public, as Pee Wee would confirm in the small hours of the morning after the Brooklyn Dodgers won the World Series for the first and only time.

Reese is best remembered today for one extraordinary, courageous, silent deed. The major leagues had become a bastion of American apartheid following the season of 1884 when a black athlete named Moses Fleetwood "Fleet" Walker caught forty-one games for the Toledo franchise of the then big-league American Association. (His brother Welday played five games in the Toledo outfield.)

Neither was Walker re-signed, nor was any black able to obtain a contract in what was called "organized baseball"—the major leagues and the minor leagues—for the following sixty-two years. Only one written document—from 1946—survives as physical evidence of this institutional and individual bigotry, but the cold fact is evidence enough: From the late nineteenth century onward, whites-only became a big-league rule, as commanding as the one that says three strikes define an out. Jackie Robinson joined the Dodgers just before opening day in 1947. That led to the strike threat that Woodward exposed, but racism was hydra-headed.

If we do have to play with him, some other ballplayers thought, we'll make him so damn miserable he'll quit. Maybe we can make him fall apart. Pitchers threw at Robinson; despite his agility he was hit by rocketing fastballs ten or fifteen times a year, about once every two weeks all season long. A number of opposing players tried to spike him, particularly in his rookie season when he played first base and was a stationary target for base runners. Enos Slaughter, the Cardinal outfielder out of North Carolina, and Joe Garagiola, the catcher and broadcaster out of a section of St. Louis called Dago Hill, both spiked him on the left foot. Perhaps most punishing of all were the harsh, repetitive volleys of bench jockeying. They called him Snowflake and Jungle Bunny and worse.

Robinson possessed a stinging tongue, and he could hold his own, one on one, with any bench jockey in the game. But before signing Robinson to a contract, Branch Rickey exacted a promise. In the beginning, anyway, Robinson was not to respond in kind. A man disinclined toward understatement, Rickey cited as an acceptable role model Jesus Christ. When Robinson asked if Rickey wanted someone without the courage to fight back, Rickey's response shook down thunder. "No. I want somebody with the courage *not* to fight back." Robinson acceded: He would turn the other cheek, and his fiery personality remained screened, at least until August 24, 1948, when he was first tossed from a game for yapping at an umpire.

The year 1947 was different from what had gone before. Baseball's Cotton Curtain was coming down. Robinson played for Brooklyn. Then, later that season, came Larry Doby and Luke Easter in Cleveland and Hank Thompson with the St. Louis Browns. Four black faces among four hundred. It was a start that carried an undeniable message beyond numbers. Integration was a wave of the future in baseball and in America at large. As Leo Durocher told Dodger players in spring training that season when they were circulating a petition to have Robinson barred from joining the Brooklyn club: "This fellow [Robinson] is a great player and he's gonna put money in your pockets and mine. But he's only the first, boys, only the first! There's many more colored ballplayers coming right behind him and they're hungry. They're scratching and diving. Unless you wake up, these colored players are gonna run you right out of the park. . . ."

Like the St. Louis strike threat, the Brooklyn petition died, but during the early months of Robinson's silent rookie season, racist taunting swelled. To this day surviving Dodger players talk about the verbal assaults on Robinson in tones of horror and looks of distaste. "Bench jockeying was one thing," says an old outfielder named Gene Hermanski. "You lived with it and you did a little yourself. But this was worse than bench jockeying. The stuff they shouted at Robinson was"—he searches for a word—"disgusting."

Apparently the needling reached a crescendo on the Dodgers' first trip to Cincinnati, a border town separated from the old Confederacy only by the murky waters of the Ohio River. Reese was raised downriver, in Louisville, Kentucky. ("Absolute segregation," he said.) He played amateur and minor-league ball in Louisville and developed an enthusiastic following, particularly after he made the major leagues in 1940 when he was twenty-one years old. Whenever the Dodgers traveled to play the Reds after that, some of Reese's old ball-playing friends from the segregated sandlots of Kentucky made the 85-mile drive up the river valley to watch him work at Crosley Field.

The Dodgers opened in Cincinnati on May 13, 1947, and as the team moved out for infield practice, the taunts began. Some shouts came from the stands, some from the Cincinnati dugout, where the rangy and intimidating Ewell Blackwell, six foot six inches of venom, made more noise than anyone else. Robinson stood at first base, catching hell. But in a situation that might have tried the patience of a Gandhi, he kept his pledge and did not respond. Suddenly and spontaneously, Reese raised a hand and stopped the practice. Then he walked from shortstop to first base and put an arm around the broad shoulders of Jackie Robinson. He stood there and looked into the dugout and into the stands, staring into the torrents of hate, a slim white Southerner who wore number 1 and just happened to have an arm draped in friendship around a sturdy black man who wore number 42. Reese did not say a word. The deed was beyond words. "After Pee Wee came over like that," Robinson told me years afterward, "I never felt alone on a baseball field again."

"With malice toward none; with charity for all; with firmness in the right, as God gives us to see the right . . ." The words, of course, are those of another Kentucky native, Abraham Lincoln. The character that comes to mind is Harold Henry Reese, who died in the summer of 1999 at the age of eighty-one. Summing up near the end, when he was battling cancer, Reese said, "I didn't plan any of this, to be a spokesman for integration. People in my own family, my mother back in Kentucky, thought I had no business playing baseball with a Negro. But somehow I didn't see it that way. I thought if the colored guy could help the team, he deserved the chance to try. I'm not a philosopher, but I suppose I was trying to make the world a little better. That's what you're supposed to do with your life, isn't it?" I can't imagine more eloquence from a dying man.

Even before his championing of Robinson, Reese's arrival in Brooklyn was a dramatic turn for everyone with a sense of the borough's baseball history. Reese appeared after decades of gawky mediocrity at Ebbets Field, where good teams were uncommon and great rookies all but unknown. Mighty-muscled Lou Gehrig put on a Yankee uniform in 1923, before his twentieth birthday. Mel Ott, a stumpy slugger, cracked the New York Giant lineup at the age of sixteen in 1926. He would lead the National League in home runs five times. By contrast one typical Brooklyn "rookie" was Johnny Cooney, who spent several years pitching for the Boston Braves (34 victories, 44 losses) before becoming the Dodgers' starting center fielder in 1936, around the time of his thirty-fifth birthday. He could run down fly balls but in his three seasons as an Ebbets Field regular, across 370 games, Cooney did not hit a single home run. There was no Brooklyn dynasty, no consistently dominant team, no perennial contender across the half century between the 1890s and the outbreak of World War II. Brooklyn's major-league history traces from the 1880s, soon after the National League was organized, and in 1890 the Brooklyn Bridegrooms won the pennant by six games. (The 1890 nickname proceeded from the weddings of several players in 1889.) The team later became the Superbas, then the Robins, after a portly, profane manager called "Uncle" Wilbert Robinson, before emerging in the early 1930s as the Dodgers, supposedly because Brooklyn streets were so lined with steel tracks that only a trolley dodger could survive. There is a nice four-syllable beat to the name Brooklyn Dodgers that is lost in the later and laborious Los Angeles Dodgers. But the nickname Dodgers, like the nickname Bridegrooms, is partly comical and certainly fails to suggest a ball club charged with testosterone and menace. There never was a team called, say, the Brooklyn Tigers. The image of Brooklyn baseball abroad in the early twentieth century was something mild and somewhat humorous: newlyweds playing for a fat manager and dodging trolley cars on the way home from another losing day at the park.

My knowledge of early Brooklyn came (and comes) not primarily from formal histories, of which there are a few, but from stories and photo albums handed down through my family, which had settled in Brooklyn eighty years before I was born. I've seen my great-grandmother seated in Victorian splendor in a horse-drawn carriage, leaving on a summer weekend trip to Coney Island, where she remembered staying at the Elephant Hotel, a structure actually built in the shape of an elephant. That may have contributed to a venerable joke: "How do you get down off an elephant? You take the trunk line down."

I've seen other relatives, in suits and ties and derbies, attacking food at a family picnic beside a replica of an ancient Greek temple on the banks of the sixty-one-acre lake in Prospect Park. The people look comfortable and well fed. Having made grand and perilous journeys to Brooklyn from Alsace starting in 1848, they seemed content afterward to stay within the confines of their new native grounds.

In my childhood our basic family reference work was the twenty-nine-volumes of the eleventh edition of the *Encyclopaedia Britannica,* published by the Cambridge University Press in 1910 and 1911, and still regarded by some scholars as the finest of encyclopediae. Of course you find nothing within its 30,000 pages on tetracycline, Albert Einstein, or thermonuclear bombs, but the entry on Dr. Samuel Johnson was prepared by the noted Victorian poet Thomas Babington Macauley. I still have enjoyable times reading the article on dreadnoughts, those old battlewagons that ruled the seas, and assimilating the extended piece on chess. Recently I cracked volume four, which runs from Bisharin, a nomad tribe of African Arabs, to Calgary, to see what the chancellor, masters, and scholars of Cambridge had to say about Brooklyn along about 1910.

The entry, which is unsigned, describes Brooklyn as "formerly a city of New York state, U.S.A., but since 1898 a borough of New York City. . . . Population in 1900: 1,166,582, of which only 310,501, or 26% were native born of native white parents. . . . Most of the streets are from

60 to 100 ft. wide. . . . On Wallabout Bay, at the bend of the East river to the westward, is the New York navy yard, the principal navy yard of the United States, established in 1801 and commonly but incorrectly called the Brooklyn navy yard. A naval hospital, having accommodations for 500 patients, is to the east. . . . Greenwood cemetery in Brooklyn is one of the most beautiful cemeteries in the United States. Among the principal monuments are those erected to Roger Williams, Samuel F. B. Morse, De Witt Clinton and Horace Greeley." The article does not mention a Brooklyn baseball team, but does include a crusher to Brooklyn egos: "For a considerable portion of its inhabitants Brooklyn is only a place of residence, their business interests being in the borough of Manhattan; hence Brooklyn has been called 'the city of homes' and 'the dormitory of New York.'" That touched a continuing problem for Brooklyn psyches. We thought we lived in a hometown, not a dormitory.

Back in volume three the old Britannica devotes almost four pages to "base-ball" in an interesting piece, pointing out that from the 1840s onward organized teams, "called the Excelsior, Putnam, Atlantic and Eckford clubs," played the game in Brooklyn. That's a lot of early baseball and probably suggests why my father, born on Clinton Street in 1901, was so native to the game.

Gordon Kahn's ballpark memories illumined a compelling history. I heard of Zack Wheat, called Buck, an outfielder who played in Brooklyn for eighteen years and hit .300 or better thirteen times. My father smiled when he spoke of George Napoleon "Nap" Rucker, a left-hander famed for his change of pace, who won twenty-two games in 1911. He positively glowed telling me about Clarence Arthur "Dazzy" Vance, an intimidating fastball pitcher who led the National League in strikeouts seven times during the 1920s. My father had been a college third baseman; he knew the game and told his stories well. Before he and I could talk seriously about the great and terrible events that coincided with my childhood—the Depression, the rise of Japanese militarists, Stalin's terror, the ascent of the Nazis—we talked Dodger baseball almost as equals. Did I think Johnny Cooney's backhand grab in right center was a better play than George Watkins's leaping grab against the right-field wall? my father asked. "Yes, because Cooney had to run a longer distance."

"Not a bad answer. Not a bad answer at all."

In such conversations with my green-eyed, mustached, deep-voiced father, the game became a magic casement opening on to the adult world and its wonders. Some archly describe baseball as a children's game, but big-league baseball was and is strictly for grown-ups. I don't know about other places, but when I was seven or eight, Brooklyn baseball was a serious, if somewhat sorry, business, at least to Brooklynites.

I played the old ballplayers' names within my head, Zack Wheat, Buck Wheat, standing in to hit left-handed, waggling his back leg; Nap Rucker with the mystifying slow ball; the Old Dazzler, who pitched wearing a long-sleeved undershirt, whatever the weather. Vance cut the right sleeve in several places at the cuff so that his pitches came out of flaps of white cotton. White baseball against white cotton. That made it hard to pick up the ball early, which you have to do to get your bat around on a major-league fastball. In 1924, Vance struck out 262 hitters, 104 more than the great Walter Johnson of the Washington Senators. (Strikeouts came harder in those distant days, when most batters were slap hitters, intent on making contact with the pitch.)

Sometimes my father recalled 1916, when Brooklyn won a pennant. Wheat led the league in total bases. A utility outfielder named Casey Stengel batted .279 with eight homers. But the World Series that followed is best remembered for a fourteen-inning game in which a twenty-two-year-old Red Sox left-hander named George beat Brooklyn 2 to 1. That was Babe Ruth, who won twenty-three times during the regular season and finished with an earned run average of 1.75, best in the American League. The Red Sox won that series, four games to one.

After the disruption of World War I and during the unfolding scandal of the fixed 1919 Series, Brooklyn won another pennant in 1920 and took on the Cleveland Indians, in a best five out of nine World Series. On October 10 in Cleveland, with the Indians leading the fifth game, 7 to 0, Clarence Mitchell, a Dodger pitcher, came to bat with Pete Kilduff on second base and Otto Miller on first. No one was out, but only briefly. Mitchell smacked a line drive up the middle that Bill Wambsganns, the Cleveland second baseman, snagged. He stepped on second, doubling Kilduff, and tagged out Miller, who was running with his head down and, it would seem, with his eyes closed. This remains both the only unassisted triple play in World Series history and the October benchmark for dreadful baserunning. *The Baseball Encyclopedia* describes the game as memorable and "strange." Cleveland won it, 8 to 1, and took the series, five games to two.

As my father recounted the Wambsganns episode, I was brought squarely up against a defining question. Why had Brooklyn never won a World Series? My father considered carefully and said, "That's quite a long and involved story." Then, rather than impose the kind of abstract baseball analysis that even today I find tedious, he began to tell me about the ultimate old Dodger, a tangle of skill and incompetence, ego and obscenity, named Floyd Caves Herman, sometimes called "the other Babe."

Babe Herman, a wide-eared, six-foot four-inch native of Buffalo, was described by the redoubtable Rogers Hornsby as "the perfect freeswinger." He batted .381 for Brooklyn in 1929 and .393 in 1930, with 241 hits, and 143 runs scored, which still stand as Dodger records. He hit for the cycle—single, double, triple, homer in the same game—no fewer than three times. But once he dropped his bat, Herman made tracks for trouble. It has been written that Babe Herman once tripled into a triple play. That's a canard. But on August 15, 1926, Herman did double into a double play.

Taking on the Boston Braves at Ebbets Field, the Dodgers loaded the bases with catcher Hank DeBerry on third, Dazzy Vance on second, and Chick Fewster, an outfielder, on first. Herman lashed a stinging drive against the right-field wall. DeBerry scored. Vance, concerned that the ball might be caught, broke late and stopped a few strides past third base. This confused Fewster, who was running on Vance's heels, and between second and third he paused to think things over. Herman, charging like a locomotive, ran past Fewster and was automatically out for passing the runner ahead of him. Herman ignored the umpire's call. He kept going and slid into third, just as Vance was also sliding in, but from the opposite direction. The Boston third baseman, not knowing who was out, began to tag Herman, who was already dead, and Vance, who was quite safe on third base. Then he chased Fewster, who would have been safe at second, had he halted there. But Fewster panicked, and ran past the base and into right field.

Since the Babe had safely passed second base on his hard line drive, he was credited with a double. But he was out for passing Fewster, who was in turn out after being tagged in the outfield (and would have been out without the tag for leaving the base path). Considering this implausible play at leisure, one concludes that probably Fewster and Vance were as much at fault as Herman, but Babe put the blame squarely on Vance, saying, "He shudda run, like me." The pitcher responded with a witticism that showed familiarity with the prose of Washington Irving. Vance called Herman "the headless horseman of Ebbets Field."

In 1935, three seasons after Herman left the Dodgers for points west, the Brooklyn front office engaged Casey Stengel as manager. Later in Stengel's career he earned a reputation as a great tactician. But the Stengel who came to Brooklyn as a manager in 1934 was famous mostly as a funny fellow, and, as Stanley Woodward suggested, an amusing drinking companion. My father told me that once, when Stengel was being hooted by a Brooklyn crowd, he doffed his baseball cap and out flew a sparrow.

"How did he get the bird under the cap?"

My father suppressed a grin under his mustache and said, "He didn't say." In later years, when I asked Stengel the same question, he ducked amiably. "Kid, I don't want to talk about the fucking sparrow no more." I don't suppose any of us will ever know.

In three years Stengel brought the Dodgers home sixth, fifth, and seventh; he would be sixty years old before he managed a team into the World Series. Particularly in the bleak Depression years sportswriters enjoyed writing humorous and coincidentally disparaging stories about the Dodgers. One Eddie Murphy of the New York *Sun* wrote from spring training, "Overconfidence may cost the Dodgers fifth place." John Lardner anointed Ebbets Field "the mother temple of daffiness in the national game." The general sense within the borough was different. At least we *had* a major-league team. Maybe we were only a borough, not a city, and a dormitory borough at that, but we did have a major-league team. Think of all the places that didn't. Miami, Minneapolis, San Francisco, and Seattle, for example. My father more than once said with pride that Brooklyn "is a good baseball town." It wasn't Paris. Nobody wrote a song called "April in Brooklyn." But we lived in a good baseball town. In 1930, during the heyday of Herman, the team drew 1,097,329 fans, the second-highest total in the National League. During the Depression the attendance figure slipped below half a million for four consecutive seasons, pushing the Dodgers toward bankruptcy, but my father said again and again, "If they had a decent team, they'd draw another million." This was strictly inside-Brooklyn stuff; attracting a million fans to Ebbets Field had become a matter of local pride. But few sportswriters lived in Brooklyn or looked at things in our provincial Brooklyn way. They fastened on to the daffiness theme and would not let go. The Daffy Dodgers, they wrote and wrote. They must have liked the alliteration.

Brooklyn has since developed twenty-first-century chic. Such neighborhoods as Brooklyn Heights and Park Slope have become fashionable, and such institutions as the Brooklyn Museum and the Botanic Garden are widely admired. But outsiders regarded the Brooklyn of my boyhood as a backwater, a sort of East Coast Topeka, possessed of only three significant assets: the Navy Yard, quiet in peacetime; the comic-opera Dodgers and Coney Island, with its roller coasters bearing such names as the Cyclone, the Thunderbolt, the Mile Sky Chaser, and the Rocky Road to Dublin. There were two amusement parks, one of which, Luna Park, had captivated the great Russian author, Maxim Gorky, but long after his visit burned to the ground in 1949, possibly to collect insurance for the owners. That left Steeplechase, the Funny Place, an enormous, glassed-in structure, spreading between Surf Avenue and the Boardwalk. A combination ticket, priced at fifty-five cents, got you on every ride. You entered Steeplechase through slowly rotating barrels that knocked many off their feet. You found a giant slide that dumped you onto a large deck with spinning disks that hurled you into a padded railing. One of the walkways, seemingly innocent, led to a stage where a clown harassed unsuspecting women. As they threw up their hands in self-defense, jets of air blew up their skirts. Some of my Froebel Academy classmates and I were ogling in the Steeplechase theater one Saturday afternoon when a movie actress named Arlene Judge smiled slightly and kept her hands high while her skirt blew upward, revealing sheer underpants and the dark triangle within. Squired by a playboy named Bob Topping, she was slumming in Coney Island. A grizzled man behind us cried out hoarsely, "Attaway, girlie! Show us what ya got."

Our pleasant shock at seeing so much of a Hollywood star immediately gave way to panic. We were gathered in a den of sin. "Let's get out of here," one of my classmates said, "before some teacher spots us."

In my memory Brooklyn was simultaneously naive and wonderful and one hell of a great place in which to grow up.

Far from Brooklyn, in Louisville, summer of 1939, Pee Wee Reese was appalled to hear that the Dodgers had bought his contract. The terms of the purchase attested to his promise. The Triple-A Louisville Colonels received $35,000, which the Dodgers borrowed from the Brooklyn Trust Company, and four players to be named later. Each would be valued at $10,000. This $75,000 deal was the biggest in the history of both Louisville and Brooklyn baseball and one of the half dozen biggest deals up to that time. (When the Yankees brought Joe DiMaggio from the San Francisco Seals in 1935, the full price was only $25,000.) "I wanted to make the majors," Reese told me, long afterward, "but not in Brooklyn. *Never* in Brooklyn. I read the papers. The writers called the Dodgers 'The Daffiness Boys' and I didn't want to go daffy."

Actually, the Boston Red Sox had taken over a cash-short Louisville franchise the year before, supposedly to bring Reese into their organization. Why let him go? "Manager Joe Cronin of the Red Sox very shrewdly put his okay on the deal whereby the Boston-owned Louisville club sold shortstop Reese to Brooklyn for $75,000," wrote Shirley Povich in his *Washington Post* column of July 23, 1939. "Because if there was anybody in the Red Sox farm system who was a threat to Cronin's shortstop job with the Red Sox, it was Reese." Cronin not only played shortstop at Fenway Park, he managed the Sox from 1935 through 1947. He won only one pennant; his solid hitting made his managing job more secure. If he were bounced from the starting group, he might also be released as manager. The Reese deal was good for Cronin and wonderful for Brooklyn, but even in the Red Sox's unmatched history of godawful decisions—selling Babe Ruth in 1920, turning down Jackie Robinson in 1945, spurning Willie Mays in 1949—peddling Reese ranks with the dumbest. If the Red Sox actually had fielded a team with Reese, Robinson, and Mays, in the period around 1950, the term "Yankee Dynasty" would have fallen into disuse.

★ ★ ★

Harold Henry Reese was born a long way from Brooklyn on a small farm in Meade County outside of Louisville, on July 23, 1918, as American forces were helping bring World War I to its conclusion. Soon afterward his father, Carl, sold the acreage and moved into Louisville where he found work as a detective for the Louisville and Nashville Railroad. Reese remembered his father as a dark-haired, intense man with a fondness for bourbon whiskey. Once when I asked if his mother worked, Reese said, "She had a full-time job—keeping my father sober."

Carl Reese endorsed the prevailing Kentucky brutalization of blacks. Reese recalled that when he was about ten years old, his father walked him to a tree on which a stout horizontal branch stretched 12 feet above the ground. "When a nigger gets uppity," the father said, "this is where we string him up. We hang him high. That's why we call this the Hanging Tree."

Reese was fair-haired, a pale, thin boy, gifted with extraordinary hand-eye coordination. The Louisville *Courier Journal* sponsored an annual marbles tournament, and at the age of twelve Reese finished second. As Reese remembered it, the large marble, which you propelled with a thumb, was "the shooter." The smaller marbles, the ones you tried to hit, were "pee wees." Marbles, not size, spawned the nickname with its euphonious repetition of the long "e." Pee Wee Reese. Three spaced syllables. That was how he signed autographs till the end of his days.

When Reese enrolled at duPont Manual High School, he did not look like a professional baseball prospect although eventually he made the varsity as an infielder. He was very fast and possessed a strong throwing arm, but, he said, "I didn't weigh much more than a hundred pounds when I graduated." Professional baseball, major-league baseball, was only a shore dimly seen. Given the times, late Depression, and his prospects, Reese decided he had to find a job. He didn't think of college. Few working class boys considered college during the 1930s. Filling family larders was the priority. He became a lineman for the Louisville telephone company and in his spare time played sandlot ball for the New Covenant Presbyterian Church. "The job was hard work," he told me, "climbing up and down telephone poles all day long, but I put on a lot of body strength. That was the best thing about the telephone company job. It made me stronger." Growth patterns vary; Reese surged in late adolescence. Eventually he stood five feet nine and weighed a solid 160 pounds. Beer and soda cans in the 1940s were made of steel not tin or aluminum. When others chided him about his lack of physical strength, Reese liked to assume a deadpan look, while silently crushing a steel can with one hand.

The New Covenant team, with its slight, strong-handed shortstop, won the Louisville church championship in 1937. The prize was a trip to New York City where the Yankees and the Giants met in the World Series. With Lou Gehrig, Joe DiMaggio and Tony ("Poosh 'Em Up") Lazzeri, this was a powerful Yankee team; the Yankees won handily, four games to one. The Giants' only victory came in game four when the great left-handed master of the screwball, Carl Hubbell, threw a six-hitter and defeated the Yankees, 7 to 3. For Reese this was a week full of firsts. He had never before seen a subway, or a concrete and steel ballpark or playing fields so vast. Dead center field at the Polo Grounds stretched 480 feet distant from home plate. The deepest point in the Yankee Stadium outfield was 466 feet away. "I noticed the power hitting, too," he said. "That series Gehrig, DiMaggio, and Lazzeri all hit home runs. I remember thinking these fellers looked pretty strong."

"Did you imagine yourself out there?" I asked.

"Absolutely not. If you had told me in 1937 I'd be playing in a World Series four years later, I would have thought you'd had too much to drink."

A sportswriter subsequently asked William "Cap" Neal, general manager of the Colonels, Louisville's entry in the American Association, about "the kid shortstop in the church league, name of Reese."

"I'm not interested," Neal said. "He's too small and he can't hit." Neal stayed adamant, but at length, after watching Reese play shortstop on a half dozen sandlots, he reconsidered. He signed Reese to a 1938 contract and gave him a bonus check for $200. Actually, Neal signed Reese's mother, Emma. At eighteen Pee Wee was still a minor, and the contract had to be signed by his legal guardian.

"You're kinda small," Neal said, "and the pitching in our league is a helluva lot better than that amateur stuff you've been seeing. But do your best. Maybe we can work you into the lineup in two or three years."

"I've watched your team, Mr. Neal," Reese said. "Right now I can play better infield than anyone you've got." An injury to a veteran got him into the lineup early in the '38 season. He started 139 games for Louisville that year and 149 games a season later. In 1939 he led the American Association in stolen bases and triples and batted .279, fine for a terrific fielding shortstop.

He retained a sharp recollection of the day he left the telephone company to go to spring training with the Colonels. The foreman said, "I wouldn't be so quick to jump at a baseball contract. Think this over before you quit. The phone company will always be here."

"I'm young, sir," Reese said. "I believe I can afford to take a chance." Years later, after he had been inducted into the Hall of Fame, Reese told me the story with quiet relish. He paused before concluding, in Cooperstown, "Where that foreman is today, I do not know."

Mostly dormant since the unassisted triple play shattered them in 1920, the Dodgers began to stir in 1938 with the arrival of the new general manager, Leland Stanford "Larry" MacPhail, who, in a shrewd if manic rush, brought the splendid broadcaster Red Barber to Brooklyn, installed lights at Ebbets Field, and talked the Brooklyn Trust Company, which held a mortgage on the ballpark, into giving him a blank check. The Brooklyn National League Baseball Club, Inc., owed $800,000 to the bank, but was paying neither principal nor interest. If the bank financed him, MacPhail said, he could put together a good team that would make some money and pay its debts. The bank president, George V. McLaughlin, went along with MacPhail. "I had no choice," he said. "If I foreclosed on Ebbets Field, which the state bank examiners wanted me to do, we would have lost half our depositors."

MacPhail outfitted the team in shiny satin uniforms for night games and experimented with yellow baseballs. He hired Babe Ruth to coach at first base in 1938, and Ruth, then forty-three, entertained everyone by walloping medium-speed batting practice pitches over the forty-foot-high screen atop the right-field wall. MacPhail bought Dolph Camilli, a powerful first baseman, from the Phillies (for a minor-leaguer and $45,000) and traded four players to the St. Louis Cardinals for Lippy Leo Durocher, a slick, light-hitting shortstop whose normal speaking volume was a bellow. The '38 Dodgers, managed by dour Burleigh

Grimes, finished seventh, but with Durocher, Camilli, Babe Ruth, and a nifty Jewish center fielder named Goody Rosen, it was a lively seventh.

Grimes was through. We all knew that; the whole Froebel Academy baseball varsity knew that. But who would manage the Dodgers in 1939? Leo Durocher, a shrewd pool-hall hustler and a ferocious baseball man, or Babe, the Great Bambino, whose fame and bacchanalian behavior were, so to speak, monuments of the Republic? MacPhail went for Durocher, whom Ruth had dismissed as "the All-American out."

"We may have finished seventh, but this ain't no fucking seventh-place club," the Lip said, with his customary elegance. Rejected in Brooklyn, George Herman Ruth, the greatest ballplayer who ever lived, retired to his Riverside Drive apartment. He cried for hours.

Durocher's Dodgers finished third in 1939, the season before Reese arrived. Years later Durocher told me that when he first saw Reese in spring training at Clearwater, Florida, in 1940, he said to himself, "Leo, you can rest your ailing tootsies." MacPhail dissented. Everyone knew, he insisted, that Durocher was the premier fielding shortstop in the game.

"Larry. That was six years ago. I'm thirty-four."

"You can play another two or three years."

"Sure, I *could*. I could also see balls going by me by a yard that I used to get like nothing. We're talking about shortstop, something I know a little bit about, Larry. Reese would be in front of those balls waiting. What we got here is a diamond that you found in the wilderness. What we got to do is polish the diamond, and he is going to be as good a shortstop as they ever heard of in the major leagues."

"I'm paying *you* to play shortstop."

"Reese is going to be the Dodger shortstop!"

"If you're not out there at shortstop tomorrow, you're fired!"

According to Durocher, it went on like that for three years, and the only time he played shortstop was when Reese was hurt. "That kept me busy in his rookie year."

Reese had to catch up with a new world in a hurry, and not everything came easily. At Wrigley Field in June a journeyman right-hander named Jake Mooty threw a fastball into his skull. It was a warm day, and most of the bleacher crowd sat without jackets. Reese lost sight of the baseball against a backdrop of white shirts. There were no batting helmets then, and Reese suffered a severe concussion, with intense headaches and nausea plaguing him during the time he spent at Illinois Masonic Hospital. He missed three weeks. His rookie season came to an end on August 15 in Brooklyn when, sliding hard into second base, he fractured a bone in his left heel. The reviving Dodgers finished third and drew tantalizingly close to a million fans: 955,668. Brooklyn was indeed a good baseball town. Although Ebbets Field, with an announced capacity of 31,902, was one of the smaller big-league ballparks, that was the second-highest total in the majors.

MacPhail finished redesigning the Dodgers the following May when he acquired the all-star second baseman, Billy Herman from the Chicago Cubs for two journeymen and $65,000 of the Brooklyn Trust Company's money. The Dodgers won the 1941 pennant, their first since 1920, edging a strong Cardinal team, by 2½ games. Reese played in 152 games (out of 154) and fielded like a brilliant youngster. He made great plays and led all National League shortstops in errors. "He misplays some chances," my father said, "but most of the time they come on balls that other shortstops don't reach."

That season, the last season before the Japanese assaulted Pearl Harbor, the Dodgers drew 1,214,910 fans, the highest total in baseball. Pretty good for a borough, we thought. Pretty darned good for a dormitory. It was difficult not to gloat, particularly with the New York Giants, Manhattan's darlings, finishing fifth. Whipped by the impassioned *Brooklyn Eagle,* urged toward hysteria by the soft-voiced agitating of Red Barber, Brooklyn celebrated its first pennant in twenty-one years with a raucous parade up Flatbush Avenue to Grand Army Plaza and Brooklyn's own Arc de Triomphe, the Soldiers' and Sailors' monument. The *Eagle* reported that a million people, half the borough's population, including infants and ancients, watched the ballplayers roll through the streets in open cars. I remember someone holding up a sign that read: "Pee Wee Reese for President." It is difficult now to summon up the Brooklyn pride that rose in another century; difficult, but not impossible. Essentially we natives felt that there was the world out there where you could find yourself a peck of trouble. And then there was Brooklyn, First Place U.S.A., the isle of happiness.

But victory did not brighten the air for long. In a few final spasms of daffiness, the Dodgers managed to lose the World Series to the Yankees, dropping two of the games in implausible ways. Red Ruffing outpitched Curt Davis and the Yankees won game one at Yankee Stadium. A day later Whitlow Wyatt, Brooklyn's ace, squared the series with a six-hitter. He also grazed the chin of Joe DiMaggio with a fastball, prompting DiMaggio, who usually suppressed emotion on a ball field, to curse the pitcher. Wyatt beckoned from the mound, inviting DiMaggio to brawl. That was not done in the American League to a New York Yankee, least of all to the leader of the Yankees, St. Joe. But this was one pugnacious Dodger team, a gang you damn well wanted on your side in case the scene at Flynn's Bar & Grill turned ugly. There was no physical combat at Yankee Stadium. Umpires stepped in before Wyatt and DiMaggio could tangle. "But my pitcher showed some fucking guts," Durocher said. "We ain't gonna be bullied by The Big Dago or nobody else."

When the series resumed at Ebbets Field, "Fat Freddie" Fitzsimmons, a rotund and rugged forty-year-old knuckleballer, shut out the Yankees into the seventh inning of game three. Then Marius Russo, the Yankee starter, walloped a wicked liner up the middle. The ball crashed into Fitzsimmons left knee and caromed high. Reese came in a few steps and made the catch. Fred Fitzsimmons hobbled and swore and could not continue. Durocher rushed his best relief pitcher, Hugh Casey, into the game, but neglected to see that Casey warmed up properly. The Yankees scored two runs off a cold Casey and won the game, 2 to 1. "My fucking fault," Durocher said. "I shoulda made sure Hughie heated up." In what might have been Fitzsimmons's finest hour, the old warrior lay on a training table, one leg under mounds of ice, wincing and continuing to swear.

The next day the Dodgers carried a 4-to-3 lead into the ninth inning; a victory would have tied the Series. Casey, now warm and loose, retired the first two Yankees. With two strikes on Tommy Henrich, he broke off a mighty curve. Henrich swung and missed. Strike three. But incredibly Mickey Owen, the Dodger catcher, failed to move with the pitch. Instead of getting his body behind the ball and blocking it, he made an amateurish backhand stab. The ball skipped past him, and Henrich ended up safely at first. The Dodgers had let the final out of the game get away. A deluge of runs followed; the Yankees won, 7 to 4. Tommy Holmes wrote in his *Brooklyn Eagle,* "The condemned man got up from the electric chair and walked away." The Yankees clinched the series a day later with a comparatively easy 3-to-1 victory. Flukes, everybody said. Fluking line drive hit Fitzsimmons. Fluking big curve fooled the catcher. Without the flukes, we all agreed, the Dodgers would have taken the World Series. Damn flukes, we said. The best team didn't win.

The 1942 Dodgers won 104 games but finished second to a Cardinal team that won 106. Reese led the league in double plays and total chances for a shortstop, but he continued to encounter spells when he made too many errors. During one loose stretch, fans behind the Dodger dugout began to ride him. "Hey, scatter-arm. Hey, fumble-fingers. Don't drop your glove." According to at least one of the fans, Reese looked up and shouted, "Why don't you Jews shut up!" On July 31 a spectator named S. L. Satin wrote baseball commissioner Kenesaw Mountain Landis, who worked out of Chicago, and lodged a complaint. Landis forwarded a copy of Satin's letter to the Dodger offices at 215 Montague Street and demanded an explanation. Although staunchly antiblack, Landis did not condone anti-Semitism.

Using Dodger stationary, Reese responded on August 13, saying that he remembered the incident very well. "The fans," he wrote Landis, "abused me terribly using most insulting and profane language. I took these people's [sic] insults and riding until I could not stand it any more. I did holler at them to shut up. I did not use the expression 'Jew.'"

To me, at least, the denial is not convincing. In the 1940s, specifically before revelations of the Holocaust, casual anti-Semitism was widely accepted in America. People said a sharp bargainer "Jewed me down." Some said to Jews, "If you had a nose full of nickels, you'd be a millionaire." Dizzy Dean thought it was clever to call Hank Greenberg "Mo." I first heard the word "kike" on a sandlot ball field. That was unpleasant, but it was the way things were.

Further, Reese himself, growing up in Louisville in the days when the Ku Klux Klan still paraded, emerged from a decidedly redneck background. The S. L. Satin incident in Brooklyn, like the hanging tree in Louisville, is a landmark. With the years Reese grew and triumphed over his background; the kind and compassionate man I met in 1951 had passed his thirty-third birthday. By then he was enjoying Passover meals at the home of Louis Effrat, a sportswriter with *The New York Times.* His closest friend away from baseball was a Jewish pop music agent named Julie Sterns. The Dodger he admired most was Jackie Robinson., The Pee Wee Reese that I remember, in George Washington's stirring phrase, gave bigotry no sanction. But it took profound introspection and many years of effort to ascend that peak.

In September 1951 the *Herald Tribune* dispatched me to cover a football game between New York University and Princeton. The orange-and-black Princeton squad won by five or six touchdowns; it was not the sort of game to hold one's interest. That night the Dodgers, then virtually tied with the Giants for first place, would be playing the Phillies at Shibe Park in what the sportswriters called a must-win situation. The year before, the Dodgers had lost the pennant on the final day of the season; now the Giants had charged up from a 13½-game deficit and were threatening to overtake them. That afternoon the Giants had won in Boston, securing a midday half-game lead.

I caught a train from Princeton to the North Philadelphia station and arrived at Shibe Park at game time. "What are you doing here?" said Harold Rosenthal, the *Herald Tribune*'s beat man assigned to the Dodgers.

"I thought I'd write a dressing-room story."

"Good idea," Rosenthal said. "Get down there after the game and get back up here real quick. Maybe you'll have some quotes that I can use in the lead. But be careful. Things are tense as hell around here. Be sure you don't set anybody off. Talk to Reese, got it? He's the shortstop. Tell him what you need. He'll help you out."

"Even if the Dodgers lose?"

"You don't know Reese. He'll help you out no matter what."

The Dodgers did not lose. An Associated Press reporter nicely summarized the game:

The thoroughly aroused Brooklyn Dodgers crushed the Phillies, 5–0, tonight behind Don Newcombe's fiery fast ball and climbed back into a tie with the New York Giants for the National League lead. Thus Brooklyn and New York go into the final day of the season each with 95 victories and 58 defeats.

Newcombe, achieving his 20th victory of the season, set the Phillies down with seven hits. He received sensational fielding support from Jackie Robinson and Billy Cox as well as 10 hits by his teammates including a two run homer by Andy Pafko off Phillies' ace, Robin Roberts.

I was twenty-three years old, younger than any starting Dodger, and this was the first major-league game I had ever covered. Baseball writers were the aristocrats of the sporting press, and they zealously guarded their sanctum. I felt nervous sitting in a big-league press box and even more nervous about entering a major-league locker room, especially after the Dodgers had played such a fabulous game. Although I followed Rosenthal's instructions, my nerves continued to vibrate. During my heedless days in that prim Brooklyn prep, through the crowded stretches at a noisy high school, and finally in those forlorn periods at the cold urban university where I stumbled over alpha and omega, one constant held: From April to October I rooted for Pee Wee Reese. I did not invent that franchise. Thousands, probably millions, also rooted for Reese, who would play 2,071 major-league games in uniforms supplied to him by the Brooklyn Dodgers. Now, in the raging intensity of a knotted pennant race, I was to meet him for the first time face-to-face. As I introduced myself, my voice changed from baritone to tenor tremolo.

We shook hands and Reese said, "I'll be glad to help you, but you don't want to hang around me."

"Why not, Mr. Reese?"

An easy smile and laughter in the eyes. "Because," Reese said, "I'm not good copy."

"What a wonderful ball game," I said.

"Yes, it was." He looked up. "Jack, come over here!" Robinson did. "This new feller is Roger Kahn from the *Herald Tribune*. Tell him how come you played such a helluva game."

Robinson grinned and he, too, shook my hand. Forget the pomp of press cards and my position as a crack young staffer at the wondrous *Trib*. Within, I was a Brooklyn kid. I had just shaken hands with Pee Wee Reese and Jackie Robinson. That may be as much of heaven as I shall know on earth.

The following spring Rosenthal decided to quit covering the Dodgers. "It's probably the best job on the paper," he told me over and over, torn between relief and despair. "With characters like Reese and Robinson and Duke Snider this team is one great ongoing story. But the travel is eating me up. In this job I spend half my life on the road. I'm not cut out to be an itinerant worker."

"You aren't exactly harvesting lettuce," I said.

"Don't be so fucking smart," Rosenthal snapped. He was unhappy.

Assigning me to the Dodgers, Bob Cooke said simply, "Just write what you see." That turned out not to be simple at all, but having learned a few lessons from Woodward, Cooke did not send out his people with a long set of instructions. A bad reporter seldom can be helped; a good reporter learns how to find his way. I joined the team at a Miami hotel called the McAllister, becoming the *Trib*'s Dodger beat man at twenty-four, still younger than anyone around, except the batboy. Even the number-three radio broadcaster, Vince Scully, was a few years older than I, or said he was. That has since changed. In recent years Scully seems to have shaved numbers off his official age. He now lives on the West Coast, where that sort of thing is widely known as "the Zsa Zsa Gabor margin of error."

The Dodgers' great effort in Philadelphia had faded. What everyone remembered that spring, and nobody mentioned, was the game of October 3, 1951, when Bobby Thomson hit his famous ninth-inning home run off Ralph Branca at the Polo Grounds and won the play-off and the pennant for the Giants. During the 1948 season Durocher had quit managing the Dodgers and taken over the Giants, which linked him to Benedict Arnold, as most Brooklyn people saw matters. Durocher's unfettered jubilation at winning the play-off did not make the Dodger defeat easier to take. Further, this Brooklyn team had also lost the 1950 pennant (to the Phillies) on the last day of the season. No major-league team in history had ever stumbled quite so abysmally in consecutive final acts. After the seasons of '50 and '51, the Dodger issue became not daffiness but something else. Many questioned the team's collective courage. No one doubted the talent of the Dodger ball club that I was assigned to cover in March 1952. The gut issue was . . . well . . . the gut issue was guts. "I wonder if as a group they aren't like that old Dodger pitcher, Red Evans," said the *Eagle*'s Tommy Holmes. "When Evans first came up in 1939, he lost some close ones, 2 to 1, 3 to 2. But later on it turned out that if he had to lose 'em 14 to 13, he could do that, too." By the time Red Evans was dispatched to Louisville as part payment for Reese, his Brooklyn record stood at 1 and 8.

As I came gradually to realize during the 1952 season, the Dodgers had something to prove, and it transcended the game of baseball. Their personal courage was on the line, their character, their manhood. No one felt these challenges more profoundly than the Brooklyn captain, Pee Wee Reese." When you lose pennants like that," he said, "and all those World Series, it makes you wonder what sort of person you really are."

Our friendship did not burst forth fully formed. He was ten years older than I, rather a large gap between young men. I was a bit in awe of him, and Reese, beneath the charm and wit, was somewhat shy. On top of that, he was self-conscious about his lack of a college education.

The Dodgers barnstormed north from Florida, playing a fifteen-game exhibition series with the Boston Braves and drawing large crowds, who came principally to see Jackie Robinson. Mobile on Monday; New Orleans on Tuesday; Montgomery on Wednesday, Nashville, Chattanooga, Knoxville and—what an unfortunate name for a segregated Southern town—Lynchburg. Why did all those Southern cooks put ham fat in the string beans? And what the hell was a chitlin? Never mind. *Glory, glory,* this integrated team kept marching on through a South that was defiantly apartheid, and just by playing ball games, black and white together, it made a powerful statement.

Reese and I had drinks in Pullman dining cars on one or two occasions. He said he was not comfortable talking about himself and proceeded to ask me thoughtful questions. Wasn't I awfully young to have the job I had with a major New York newspaper?

Yes, I was.

Had I always wanted to be a writer?

"No, Pee Wee. My first dream was to have your job. I didn't decide to become a writer until I was nine years old, or maybe eleven."

"But my job," he said, "is harder than you may think. I read in the papers 'Reese settled under a routine pop fly.' You've played some ball. Look at me carefully next time I'm under a pop fly. The play isn't routine at all. Every cord in my neck is sticking out. That routine pop-up is ten stories high."

"Coming down," I said, "an aspirin tablet turns into a mortar shell."

Reese grinned. "Pretty much."

"Better you then me," I said. He laughed. I was a reporter and he was a ballplayer, but this was not an interview. It was something much more valuable: a conversation. Reese had been playing professional baseball for fifteen seasons, he told me, "and I have spike scars on my shins to prove it."

"Are the games still fun?" I said.

"Not really. It's work. I don't enjoy playing under pressure, or the night games. I like the baseball life, meeting new people like you. Making friends. But I don't like baseball too much during working hours."

I took that in slowly, and as I did, he asked where and how I had studied writing. "The most interesting study was last summer, at a conference at Bread Loaf in Vermont and the guiding character was Robert Frost."

"Do you know Robert Frost?"

"I've met him."

"What's your favorite Robert Frost poem?" Reese asked. "Do you know one you can recite?"

"Here's a short one," I said.

> *The way a crow*
> *Shook down on me*
> *The dust of snow*
> *From a hemlock tree*
>
> *Has given my heart*
> *A change of mood*
> *And saved some part*
> *Of a day I had rued.*

Reese sat silent. The train was rushing through rural Tennessee. "That's very beautiful," he said. "It must really be something to be able to write that beautifully." Then, "Who is the best sportswriter on a newspaper?"

"Right now I'd say Red Smith."

"Why?"

"It begins with his command of the language," I said. "He says he tries to show a decent respect for the mother tongue, by which he means English."

"Do you know," Reese said, "why people say Shakespeare was the greatest writer who ever lived?" We talked about that for some time, Reese listening hungrily to what I remembered from the Shakespeare commentary of James Joyce and Ernest Jones, the Welsh psychotherapist who was Freud's colleague. At the same time, I was aswarm with questions about playing shortstop in the major leagues and about Reese's response to the integration of baseball. But I contained myself.

That was the beginning. Afterward, circumstance and certain skills, talents and curiosity joined us in a nurturing friendship that endured for a half century. Whatever Reese became—sportscaster, business executive, multimillionaire (and he would be all of these)—I always saw him as a shortstop, gliding to his left, leaping to his right, slim, powerful, and balletic as he pivoted beside Jackie Robinson at the center of the double play that was itself at the center of baseball integration. As I told him, on several occasions, shortstop, big-league shortstop, was something I once had wanted to be, like Reese a dancer in the wind (and dirt and brawls). After our friendship ended—in the only way it could—I came to believe that in rooting for Reese I had also been rooting for myself, or at least a fantasized version of myself. With his innate grace and unpretentious nobility toward Jackie Robinson, Reese enlarged my understanding of what it was to be a major-league ballplayer and what it was to be a man.

Our friendship flowered in the hurly-burly of the road, with shared tables in dining cars and hotel coffee shops, and afterward the ball games, the great ball games, and then the baseball bars with waitresses who grew more beautiful with every drink.

"My husband plays trumpet in a band," the tawny Cincinnati blonde was saying, "and right now the band's away. I'm kinda lonely."

"I can't believe this, Pee Wee. That beautiful girl is trying to pick us up."

"Us? Is 'us' the right word, Rog?"

"The road," one sour baseball writer told me, "will make a bum of

the best of 'em, and, kid, you ain't the best." But it didn't make of bum
of either Reese or me. A lot of America back then was the road, the
train whistles on a hot summer night, the towns flashing by, all the
Winesburgs outside your Pullman window, the girls whom you would
never see by daylight. That is a bit to handle when you are twenty-four
and have expense money in your wallet. Pee Wee, no prude, suggested
how I might conduct myself on the road, more by example than by
preaching. But one night near closing time at the Victoria Club, an East
St. Louis piano bar, he struck my arm and said, "Rog, you don't really
need another drink." That was a point of profound importance, particularly for a writer. Most of the writers I knew who took that extra
drink, and another and another, died young. Gwen, the girl at the piano,
was wearing a deeply low-cut gown. She said she'd play any song I
wanted if only I would lay a five-dollar bill between her breasts.

"Day game tomorrow," Reese said, and he hustled me toward a cab.

"Gwen was damn good-looking," I said, feeling annoyed.

"Next trip," Reese said. "If she still looks good to you then, go
ahead. Right now it's plumb too late to fall into trouble. Can I tell you
something?"

"You already have."

"Add this. You can't take 'em *all* to bed. Nobody can."


Reese's Brooklyn playing years, 1940 through 1957, the last season in the
picaresque history of the Brooklyn Dodgers, were interspersed with humor, with casual deeds of kindness and illumined by his concern for others. One night at Ebbets Field the late Joan Kahn, my first wife, was
sitting in a photographers' booth when a foul bounced out of the upper
deck into a metal support that held up the huge lenses, called Big Berthas,
on the old-fashioned press cameras. The ball spun backward into Joan's
face and broke her nose. Ushers helped her to a first-aid room. Walter
O'Malley, the buccaneer who owned the Dodgers, immediately sent me a
scrawled message. "Don't bother to sue. Courts have held we don't have
to protect that location. Should you sue me, you will lose." If O'Malley
felt concern for an injured spectator, he masked it well.

Reese's message in the clubhouse was different. "How's your wife
getting home?"

"I'll drive her, but I have to write my story first."

"Take your time with the story," Reese said. "I'll drive Joan home." When I finally arrived at my apartment, he was applying soothing talk and an ice pack to a patient who was in pain but delighted by the company.

The next spring at Vero Beach Reese said, "Why don't you go out to left field and shag a few?" When I reached the outfield, Gil Hodges was batting. He slashed a nasty line drive over Reese's head and the ball came bounding toward me looking like a hand grenade. Who else was on the field? Reese, of course, Robinson, Duke Snider, just to mention the Hall of Famers. If there is a God, I thought, please don't let this one go through the wickets. I moved up slowly, dropped down to one knee. The ball plunked into my glove. *Whew.* The shortstop called my name. "Yes, captain?"

"You're supposed to pick up the ball afore it stops."

With his open manner, Reese said things few others dared. Once Robinson was raging against the steady run of knockdown pitches he had to face. "Jack," Reese said, "some guys are th'owing at you because you're black and that's a terrible thing. But there are other guys, Jack, who are th'owing at you because they plain don't like you." Robinson blinked. No one but Reese talked to him that way. Then Robinson nodded and said, "You've got a point."

His admiration for Robinson was profound and unself-conscious. In a sense it began on a troopship bringing Reese home to America after his navy service during World II. A petty officer told him that short-wave radio had broadcast the news that the Brooklyn organization had signed a black man.

"Is that a fact?" Reese said.

"Pee Wee," the petty officer said in a teasing, singsong way, "he's a shortstop."

"Oh, shit," Reese said.

Across a brace of nights, Reese lay in a bunk, measuring his situation and himself. He'd won the Dodger job at shortstop. It belonged to him. "Except suppose he beats me out. Suppose he does. I go back to Louisville. The people say, 'Reese, you weren't man enough to protect your job from a nigger." In the bunk only one response seemed right. "Fuck 'em." "I don't know this Robinson," Reese told himself, "but I can imagine how he feels. I mean, if they said to me, 'Reese you got to play in the colored guys' league,' how would I feel? Scared. The only white. Lonely. But I'm a good shortstop, and that's what I'd want 'em to see. Not my color. Just that I can play the game. And that's how I *got* to look at Robinson. If he's man enough to take my job, I'm not gonna like it, but, dammit, black or white, he deserves it."

By the time Reese and I became friends, Robinson was established at second base. He never had a big-league shortstop's throwing arm. He and Reese played cards together, went to racetracks together, and even shadowboxed together. "The first thing I think about Jackie," Reese told me, "is that he is such a great ballplayer. The next thing I think is that I don't know how he did what he did. I mean, he took a pretty good beating the first couple of years, and the better I've gotten to know him and what he's really like, the more amazed I get that he could have done it at all. He changed his personality completely to do what he did, changed it so completely that when I look back, I just don't believe it. What Jackie did, all that suffering in silence, wasn't merely amazing. When you consider what he's really like, it was impossible."

At length the New York baseball writers voted Reese their Good Guy Award, which he would receive at a formal banquet in the Grand Ballroom of the Waldorf-Astoria. A few days before, he telephoned me from Louisville and said that he was nervous about making a speech before a large crowd. Maybe I could meet him at the hotel in the afternoon and go over the speech he was putting together." I need your help, but I'm getting some help here, too, from a friend who knows the classics." This is the speech Reese presented to me (and delivered to an audience of two thousand.) "Gentlemen. If I possessed the oratorical fire of Demosthenes or the linguistic elasticity of Branch Rickey, I could wow you with superlatives. But, frankly, fellers, I ain't got it. Thank you very much."

The Dodgers would win seven pennants during Reese's tenure at shortstop, six after Robinson joined him in the starting lineup. For many years Reese made his summer home in a quiet mews called Barlow Terrace in the Bay Ridge section of Brooklyn, overlooking the entrance to New York Harbor. Other Dodgers—Carl Erskine, Duke Snider—

moved into the same neighborhood and mixed pleasantly with the community, going to movies, shopping for groceries, sending their children to a local pediatrician. Soft-spoken though he was, Reese was the leader, and his popularity in Brooklyn became boundless. "In all my Brooklyn years," he told me, "I couldn't buy a sweater. I'd try, but whoever owned the story would not accept my money. They'd always say, 'Pee Wee, take the sweater as my gift.'"

In 1954 he batted over .300 for the first and only time. He was a lifetime .269 hitter, but dangerous. He seemed to hit premier pitchers as well as he hit journeymen. "I don't know why. Maybe I bear down more."

Finally, in the summer of 1955, the Dodgers decided to stage Pee Wee Reese Appreciation Night on July 23, his thirty-seventh birthday. A short, fast-talking Dodger promotion man, Irving Rudd, took charge of the arrangements. "We were afraid of nights," Rudd began a swift emotional narrative, "because we'd had some bad experiences with hustlers. I mean guys telling us they were ready with a big night for some player, grabbing all the publicity, and then giving him a second-hand Mickey Mouse watch. But the newspaper guys pressed us on Pee Wee, so I moved in.

"First thing that happened was Pee Wee came to me and said he was making pretty good money and he didn't want people struggling on fifty bucks a week contributing anything to him. So I fixed that. I didn't allow any public contributions, just stuff from merchants who could afford it.

"Boy, what a haul. And what a night. Around 33,000 people showed up and that was the only sellout at Ebbets Field all year. We got a wire from the president [Eisenhower] who couldn't make it because he was in Geneva. We got gifts. My God, we got gifts.

"Now I suppose you're curious about the car. A lot of auto dealers wanted to give Pee Wee a car but they wanted it to be exclusive. So I set up a lottery, with five or six cars on hand and the keys to all of them in a box, and Barbara, Pee Wee's daughter, is supposed to reach in and grab.

"Well, there was a Chrysler and a Cadillac, expensive cars, and there was a Chevrolet, a good car but selling for a grand less. Barbara grabs and she comes up with the Chevy key and people started booing. Everybody got on me for not rigging it so Pee Wee gets the Chrysler or the

Caddy. But that woulda been larceny and Barbara was only twelve and what am I supposed to do, teach a twelve-year-old kid larceny?"

On the field before the next day's game Reese summoned Irving Rudd and said, "Why don't you get a suit that doesn't look fifteen years old?" Afterward Rudd picked up the story: "He shoved something in my hand. It was a $150 gift certificate from Wallach's [an upscale men's clothing store]. Pee Wee wouldn't take it back." (In the 1950s you could buy a fine suit for $150; today, of course, that gets you a fine necktie.)

Reese was playing shortstop at Yankee Stadium on October 4, 1955, when the Brooklyn Dodgers won their only World Series. Fittingly, the final out came on Elston Howard's grounder to short. Some said Reese choked and threw the baseball into the dirt and only Gil Hodges's great pickup saved him and Brooklyn from yet another daffy defeat. Nonsense. The throw was shin high, an easy catch for a big-league first baseman.

Late that night Reese and I ended up toasting the universe at the vanished bar on West Fifty-seventh Street called Whyte's, where a few years later George Cornish reconnected with Stanley Woodward. Pee Wee's face was shining, a child's face on Christmas morning. "Can I ask you something?" I said. "Two out in the ninth. You've played on five losing Series teams. You're one out from winning a Series. Howard's up. What are you thinking?"

"I'm thinking," said the bravest shortstop I've ever known, 'I hope he doesn't hit the ball to me.'"

After Reese left baseball in 1960, he called me and said, "NBC wants me to be a broadcaster [with Dizzy Dean] on the *Game of the Week*. What do you think?"

"Grab it. You can't miss."

"How can you say I can't miss? You know how I speak. Sometimes I say 'throwed' for 'threw.' Stuff like that. This is network TV. Every English teacher in the country will get on my case."

"Just be yourself and everybody, even the English teachers, will love you. My mother was an English teacher and she loves you."

"And if everybody doesn't?"

"Then I'll owe you a bottle of scotch."

"I like J&B." Reese said. He went on and made a great success of broadcasting. I never had to buy the bottle.

We saw each other frequently over the years afterward, and in the late 1980s we planned to lunch, with J&B, at a restaurant Reese liked in Venice, Florida. I was covering spring training. Reese, then vice president for sales at Hillerich and Bradsby, the company that manufactures Louisville Slugger bats, was vacationing in a condominium he had bought beside the Gulf of Mexico. At the last minute he called. "We can't have lunch today," The tremolo I sounded in 1951 had moved into Reese's voice. "I have to go the Mayo Clinic. I've got cancer."

Our days wound down as he fought a brave, quiet fight with death, almost always holding on to his humanity and humor. "Hey, Rog," he said one day. "I cannot believe that Pee Wee Reese is seventy-five years old."

"Hey, Harold, I cannot believe that Roger Kahn is sixty-five years old."

The captain paused, but only briefly. Then he said, "We were talking about *me*."

Surgery at Mayo seemed to defeat the first cancer, which appeared in the prostate gland, but later there was cancer in a lung. That spread to the bones. Before long Reese was ill beyond saving. As he wasted away I remember thinking this was the sort of death that should have befallen Josef Goebbels, not Pee Wee Reese.

Near the end Mark Reese sent me a letter of terrible beauty. "The prognosis," Mark wrote, "is not good. The cancer has settled in the brain. Pee Wee is often delirious, sometimes delusional. The other day he stared at me with a blank look and said, 'All my life I've pondered sleep.' This echoed in my mind throughout the day. . . .

"That night I sat down to dinner with my father for what would more than likely the last time. I thought of all the other times I had sat down to dinner, just another family sitting at the table to break bread and share the events of the day. I thought of the dinner discussions, some heated, some mundane. I thought of all the times he missed dinner because he was on the road or a flight was late or a game went into extra innings. Regardless, I know my old man was there or at least coming home.

"But at this dinner, though he was there, I knew he never would return. From his wheelchair he seemed to study my every move, as if to ask, 'Who is this stranger invading my home?' I couldn't get my breath.

After excusing myself to go into the den, I felt as if the life were being drained from my body. As Turgenev said, 'A boy doesn't become a man until he loses his father.' Maybe this is that process, a kneeing blow to the gut.

"So I sat on the floor in the den trying to regain my breath and composure. It was then that I looked at all the photos of my father that adorned the walls. There he was in all his glory, sliding into second base, standing at the edge of the dugout with Jackie Robinson, fielding a ground ball. The most important element was the one I took for granted. It graced the pictures. It was his smile. It then dawned on me that my father had a key, a key to the secret of life.

"He knew how to enjoy life, and never to question a single second of it. I used to press him and ask why he was not confronting the meaning, if any, of our state of being. Wasn't there a chance it was all nothingness? Dad would look at me and shake his head because he knew he possessed the key. Life is here for us to enjoy. If you look deeply enough, you see that in his smile.

"That night I returned to the dinner table. When I sat down beside Dad, we both smiled. Dad looked at me once again with the eyes of the knowing, as if to relish this moment with his son, a moment of being alive, of being awake, even as we both pondered sleep."

Reese died in high summer, on August 14, 1999, a good day to play a little hardball. He had just passed his eighty-first birthday, and soon a sculptor was fashioning a statue of him that stands in front of Parkway Field in Louisville. That is a fine thing, but it is even finer to think, as I do, that he still is with us. I know he survives in my mind and in my heart. Anywhere a white and a black work side to side in friendship, Pee Wee is there. Where one finds humanity and kindness and humor and love, the captain is surely there, as well.

For all the torment that besets America, there is something profoundly right with a country that can produce a Pee Wee Reese.

# CHAPTER 3

# The Poet

Here, in a time period from my twenties into my early thirties,
I learn some things about what it is to be a writer.

In my own baseball world I was a pretty good hitter. I don't mean that
I could have done anything with major-league pitching. Except for an
infinitesimally small fraction of mankind, *nobody* hits major-league
pitching. But far from Fenway and the Hall of Fame my bat won games
for *Esquire* magazine in the New York Literary League and I managed
thoroughly to ruin one summer for a Simon and Schuster editor who
thought he could find an avocation on a fast-pitch softball mound, hard
by the dunes and bikinied temptations of East Hampton. I hit that man
so hard that at length every time I came to bat against him, I had to sup-
press a laugh. But now I stood in Bread Loaf, where I had come to study
writing, and the pitcher gazing down on me was no less a right-hander
than Robert Frost. "Ol' Potato Face," we called him. "Ol' Potato Face,"
but never loud enough so he could hear.

The white hair was tousled and he was perspiring under the August
Vermont sun. He had learned somehow that I was a sportswriter, and
the word "sport" intensified his desire to get me out.

"Ready?" he called.

"Yes, sir." I certainly was ready, but mostly I felt concerned. Frost was seventy-six years old, fifty-three years my senior, and if I happened to hit a line drive through the pitcher's box, I might silence America's most eloquent voice. I adjusted my stance so that I faced the third baseman and with great care chopped Frost's first pitch, which was high, harmless, and profoundly hittable, toward one of Pearl Buck's little embryo novelists at third. He got the ball over to first. I had made a triumphant out. Frost looked pleased and prepared to face the next hitter, a bespectacled graduate assistant who said that she had never hit a ball before. (Nor did she then.)

Beginning with the day when I encountered Keats, the sonnet that begins "When I have fears that I may cease to be," I came to regard poetry as the most exalted form of writing in the English language. And the most difficult as well. I have read poetry by such prose masters as Hemingway and Joyce, and their poems disappoint. The lute song was too delicate for both.

Embracing poetry is hardly unique to me. Two of the most gifted sportswriters ever, Red Smith and John Lardner, were informal poetry scholars. Smith could quote long passages from Robert Browning, a poet difficult to memorize because his rhythms are irregular. Lardner enjoyed a game in which the players tried to stump each other by quoting lines from a poem that one was challenged to identify. Doggerel and wildly popular poems were off-limits. Lardner's particular favorite almost always stumped newcomers, who had come to the bar at the Artist and Writers Restaurant, where these games took place, expecting to hear talk about Sugar Ray Robinson or Casey Stengel. They sometimes did. Lardner's favorite poem for the quiz game begins:

> The glories of our blood and state
>    Are shadows, not substantial things;
> There is no armor against fate;
>    Death lays his icy hand on kings:
>      Sceptre and crown
>      Must tumble down,
> And in the earth be equal made
> With the poor crooked scythe and spade.

The author, at age two, with his mother, Olga Kahn, Cornell 1923.

Big, bespectacled Stanley Woodward, "The Coach,"
the great sports editor at the New York *Herald Tribune*.

Sports columnist Red Smith, who idolized Woodward,
during Smith's halcyon years at the *Herald Tribune* in the 1950s.

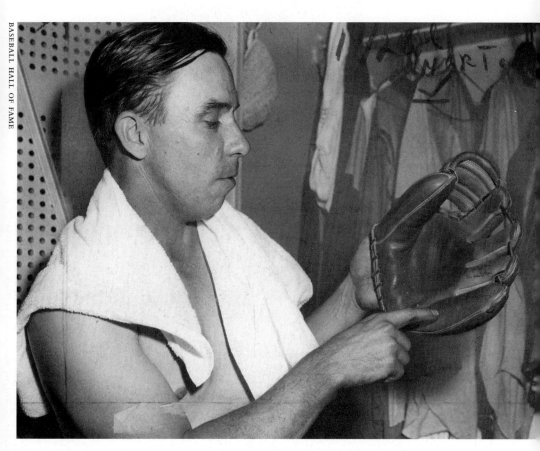

Hall of Famer Harold "Pee Wee" Reese, Brooklyn Dodger captain and shortstop, considers a constant Ebbets Field companion, his glove.

Jackie at the bat: Robinson ready to launch one during spring training.

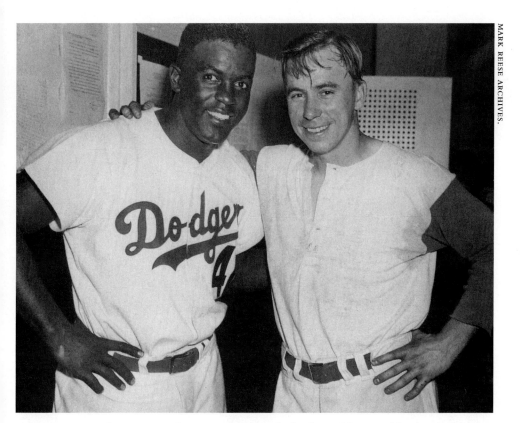

Companions and co-stars: Robinson and Reese, the leaders of the Brooklyn baseball pack.

Robert Frost in a thoughtful moment.

Roger L. Kahn, at age seven, trying to launch one.

Young Roger and Alissa perched on a tree in Martha's Vineyard, 1971.
Years afterward, Alissa graduated with honors from
the Rhode Island School of Design.

Young Roger's mother, Alice, getting ready for a sail with Gordon, off Barbados in 1972.

The author and Olga in the summer of 1973.

Roger L., star quarterback at Harvey School, completes a pass in a late 1970s football game.

Alice, Roger, and Olga after the game.

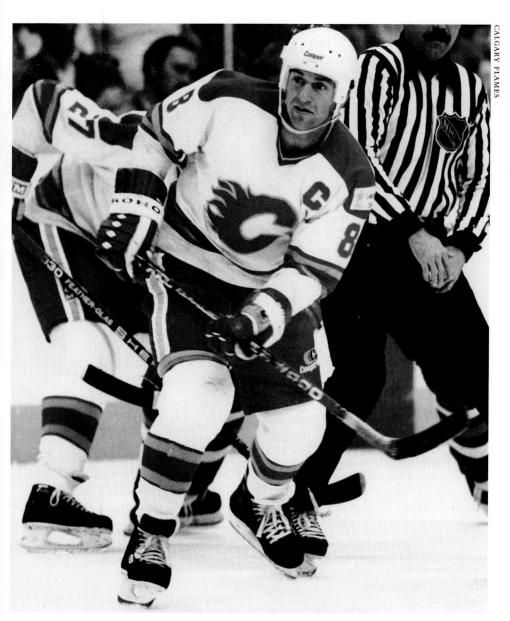

Doug Risebrough, young Roger's favorite hockey coach,
during his tenure as captain of the Calgary Flames.

Ace Los Angeles Dodger right-hander, Orel Hershiser,
whose kindness to young Roger is well remembered.

Roger L., in a proud moment at hockey camp in Canada.

KAHN ARCHIVES

The author and his wife, Katharine Johnson Kahn, in a recent photo taken at the net.

Those lines were written by James Shirley, 1596–1666, not widely known these days, but once renowned as "the last of the Elizabethans." What many writers particularly love in poetry is the beautiful sound. A great poem makes beautiful sounds, as surely as does the *Moonlight* Sonata. After that one admires the precision. A sonnet runs fourteen lines, not thirteen. Iambic pentameter decrees ten beats to the line, not nine or eleven. Beyond and amid such considerations is the magic, beautifully described by Marianne Moore when she wrote that poetry "can present for inspection imaginary gardens with real toads in them." (Miss Moore, who died at the age of eighty-five in 1971, lived in Brooklyn for over thirty-five years but became a Yankee fan.)

In the last summer before I began covering the Dodgers, I spent my two-week *Herald Tribune* vacation at the Bread Loaf Writers' Conference, which was conducted on the grounds of Middlebury College in the Green Mountains of Vermont. At Bread Loaf there was neither television nor radio, just hours of talk about the craft. The journalist Lincoln Barnett, in charge of the nonfiction sessions that summer, told us that he had obtained a successful interview with Bing Crosby, a difficult man, because he let Crosby know that he was familiar with the works of Benjamin Franklin. In preliminary research Barnett learned that Crosby admired Franklin. "When I'm writing a profile for *Life,*" Barnett said, "I shamelessly use every device I can find. I need the money."

*Life* also had asked him during the 1940s to write a 3,000-word profile of Albert Einstein "Obviously," he said, "capturing the most complex man on earth in 3,000 words was impossible and just as obviously, given my financial situation, I leapt at the assignment." Barnett felt that before he called on Einstein in Princeton, he had to understand the universe as Einstein envisioned it. That led him to such questions as "Is the universe shaped like a saddle?" It seems to me that if the universe is limitless, it cannot be said to have any shape at all. But that does not fly with every physicist, or at least it didn't fly with Dr. Einstein. At length Barnett got his assignment modified. He would not write 3,000 words about Einstein. Instead he would do a 3,000-word profile of the universe. That also proved daunting and, as some asked mischievously, what would he do for an encore? Barnett elected to write a book called *The Universe and Dr. Einstein* (still in print) and let the magazine editors carve out a 3,000 word slice. (After we became friends I learned that he had a wife and a mistress, situated three hundred miles apart. He loved them both, but supporting the double life was what created Barnett's financial situation. The captain's paradise is costly.)

The poet May Sarton said at Bread Loaf that writers should not be embarrassed about producing short stories for "the woman at the sink," by which she meant the millions of subscribers to slick women's magazines. But if the stories were to sell, she went on, they would have to be "sensitive, perceptive, and aware." Sarton repeated that phrase daily, and it came to lend humor to some of the transitory romances that arise during writers' conferences, in Vermont near an outdoor trysting place called Texas Falls.

HE:   I want to sleep with you.

SHE:   Are you *sensitive*?

HE:   Yes.

SHE:   And *perceptive*?

HE:   I'm very perceptive.

SHE:   And *aware*?

HE:   Dammit, get undressed.

William Sloane, a prominent publisher, said that if we were going to insist on trying to compose novels, he had a thing or two to tell us. He was tired of reading submissions "about boys who just aren't very good at games." Aside from that we had damn well better begin our novels with something in motion, a rocketing express train, a speeding car, a running man, something, anything, in motion, even the wind. When Sloane took questions, I said, out of my twenty-three years of wisdom, that there was nothing in motion when Dickens began *A Tale of Two Cities,* "It was the best of times, it was the worst of times." Sloane probably had heard that before. "As soon as you can write as well as Dickens," he said, "you may begin your novels any way you wish. For now start with something in motion . . ."

To be sure, Frost was the star, and he seemed to enjoy being asked if in his own young days he had attended writers' conferences. The question made him laugh. Then he responded, "There weren't any." Some wondered if Frost really approved of writers' conferences, which is what he intended for some to wonder. He liked mysteries and ambivalence.

One night, and one night only, Frost read poems to a small group of Bread Loaf people and some elder ladies from the nearby village of Ripton. This was an informal country read. Finishing "The Road Not Taken," Frost looked up and said, "It's so much clearer in my mind." Later, when pages stuck in his book, he said quite audibly, "Son of a bitch." That drew a collective gasp from the Ripton ladies, who were all wearing long, dark dresses and who all seemed to have the same surname, Dragon. Frost liked to say, "I let a dragon run my farm." He had a dry voice, a sandpaper voice, that somehow worked to make his poems more compelling. I don't think I fully measured his lyricism until that long-ago summer night when he read beside the mountains. Then I heard wondrous sounds:

*She is as in a field a silken tent . . .*

And the quatrain:

*Love at the lips was touch*
*As sweet as I could bear;*
*And once that seemed too much;*
*I lived on air.*

There was no reception afterward. Frost was not much for easy intimacy, but he agreed to take a few questions at the lectern. One young writer asked, brashly and thickly, what a particular poem meant.

"It means what it says."

"I'm not sure I really understand."

"Would you like me to state it in worse English?" Frost did not like being crowded.

A young woman said of another poem, "I know what it meant to me, but I don't know what it means to you."

"Maybe I don't want you to," Frost said.

Except for his intensity on the softball field, where he desperately wanted to get everybody out, he remained distant, though physically close. I thought he was entitled to his remove. By rather a large margin, Frost was the best damn writer in the place.

After I had covered the Dodgers in 1952, when they won a pennant and lost a seven-game World Series to the Yankees, I enrolled in a private poetry course conducted by Kimon Friar, a small, wiry man, who was born in Turkey to an American father and a Greek mother. Friar had been director of the Poetry Center at the Ninety-second Street YMCA where he encouraged famous poets and gifted amateurs to read their works from the stage of a small theater. He conducted the course in his small Upper East Side apartment, urging students to write poetry and lecturing on contemporary verse forms. Working with Friar I discovered quickly that I was no more of a threat to Keats than I was to Reese. More important, Friar opened a world wholly different from Byron, Shelley, and Keats (that "trio of lit'ry treats"). I learned to read and understand the great poets who were publishing new forms of verse in the middle of the twentieth century—E. E. Cummings, T. S. Eliot, Ezra Pound, Wallace Stevens, and Dylan Thomas. Frost's work was more approachable than that of the others, but only superficially so.

All these artists, except Pound, came to the Ninety-second Street Y to read, and I went there to listen. Most of the readings were wonderful. Eliot severe, clipped, sounded very British for a native of St. Louis. Cummings's thin, clear voice displayed a mastery of timing. One highlight was the appearance of Thomas, who, my father said, had the voice of a Welsh organ. Dylan read with great beauty at the start, beginning sonorously with the lines, "I see the boys of summer in their ruin." He was sipping a clear liquid that from a distance appeared to be water. It was not. The liquid was gin, tepid gin, which Thomas drank without ice. Eight or ten poems along, his diction began to slip, and soon he was wasting his dramatic gifts on a slurred verison of a randy chestnut, "Getting Fanny's Bun." That was simultaneously disappointing and sad.

Thomas was actually an Un-Frost: soused where the New Englander drank sparingly, public and personal where Frost preferred reserve, and boastful of his sexual conquests of everyone from coeds to Katherine Anne Porter, an attractive author out of Texas, whose works include the novel *Ship of Fools*. Thomas's wife, Caitlin, complained angrily about his infidelities while she was left behind in Wales "in a bloody bog."

Thomas had begun making extended visits to the United States when he was thirty-five. His readings quickly became popular, and the Caedmon recordings of the readings sold extravagantly. Thomas relished fame and even notoriety but, for whatever reasons, he could handle neither. (He might have benefited from some coaching by Pee Wee Reese.) After yet one more extended drinking bout in 1953 at his favorite American haunt, the White Horse Tavern in Greenwich Village, he lost consciousness. He never revived and died a few days later in St. Vincent's Hospital. Someone carried an obituary to me from a teletype into the sports department of the *Herald Tribune*.

I said to Harold Rosenthal, "Damn. Dylan Thomas died."

"How old?" Rosenthal said.

"Thirty-nine."

"Don't feel upset," Rosenthal said. "Thirty-nine is good for a poet."

Ring Lardner Sr. wrote once that there was nothing more depressing than an old baseball writer. He saw them at the ballparks, lugging heavy typewriters up endless ramps to a press box where they would see a game today very much like the game they saw yesterday. After three years of covering baseball, which meant watching 180 games a season, counting spring training and the World Series, I started losing focus. Someone would say at a party, "Who won today?"

"The Dodgers, 5 to 3. Wait. Sorry. That was yesterday. Today they lost, 3 to 1."

Bob Cooke, generally annoyed at my championing Robinson and integration, switched me to the New York Giants in 1954. Blacks on the Giants included Willie Mays, but the team was passive on racism, refusing to argue with the hotel the ball club used as spring training headquarters in Phoenix when the hotel manager would not allow Mays to register. The Giants sent Mays off to reside with a black family, and officials told sportswriters that they were doing this because a young person—Willie was twenty-three—would be happier living in a family setting. We actually believed them. In the late 1990s, when I last saw Mays, he was still fuming at "not being allowed to stay with my own teammates."

Durocher dominated the Giants scene, manipulating sportswriters by lending money to a man from the *Times* who was a neurotic gambler and buying whiskey for an alcoholic who worked for the *New York Post*. If either criticized his managing, Durocher warned, he would carry tales to their editors. A superficially charming and profoundly unpleasant character, Durocher drew a sweetheart press. My 1955 run-in with him was the specific that led to my leaving the *Herald Tribune*, but I suppose I had been looking for some way to make a graceful exit, anyway. I did not intend to become an old baseball writer, and Labor Day doubleheaders at Forbes Field in Pittsburgh had lost their allure. "The trouble with Pittsburgh," said Dick Young of the *Daily News*, "is that all the pretty girls in town are pregnant."

I became sports editor of *Newsweek* in 1956 and lingered for four years, a period enriched by my friendship with John Lardner, Ring's oldest son, who wrote a weekly column there and contributed to various other magazines. John was a wonderful stylist and an impressive thinker on topics as diverse as boxing, politics, the press, television, baseball, and the famous circus gorilla Gargantua. "I saw a good deal of Gargantua," he wrote when the big ape died. "We had little to say to each other, both being of a reserved, introspective turn of mind, but whenever I watched him tear an automobile tire in two, I mused on the folly of man and his vaulting ambitions."

The *Newsweek* of the late 1950s would be terra incognita to the journalists of today. Anti-Semitism bubbled at the top. When assigning my colleague, Jack O'Brien, to write a story about a Florida real estate boom, the publisher, Malcolm Muir, said, "Give us a good piece, Jack, and be sure you nail those Miami Beach Jews." John Denson, the man who would later force Woodward into retirement, was the editor, and although we usually got along, he liked to tell me, "Remember, Kahn, no niggers in the sports section."

"It's *my* sports section, Mr. Denson."

"Yes, but it's *my* magazine."

We struck a compromise. I could write about blacks as often as I chose, but no pictures would accompany those stories. During my entire tenure *Newsweek* never ran a photograph of Jackie Robinson, Jim

Brown, Willie Mays, Hank Aaron, or Floyd Patterson, the heavyweight champion.

Except for a few so-called soft sections, education and music, women were not permitted to write. They were employed as fact-checkers, responsible for keeping the magazine free of errors. If you had been trained as a newspapermen, intent on getting things right on your own, the magazine system seemed odd. You could leave any sort of factual gap in your piece and it was up to the researcher to find the fact. Otto Friedrich tore apart this approach in an essay called, "There Are 00 Trees in Russia." Had Friedrich, an assistant foreign editor, actually typed that sentence, the research women of the Foreign News Department would have been required to find out how many trees were growing in the Soviet Union even though, and this was Otto's point, that number was impossible to establish.

Romances, or anyway sexual encounters, between researchers and writers were more the rule than the exception. AIDs did not exist back then, nor did the concept of sexual harassment. (In fairness to both sides, the women sought affairs and even one-night stands almost as enthusiastically as did the men.) "Never underestimate the importance of lunch with martinis," said Frank Gibney, the senior editor who had hired me at John Lardner's urging. "Lunch is an indispensable preliminary."

Some called Newsweek "the Fun House," and, as in a small town, there were few secrets. It amused me at morning staff conferences to watch the eye-play between an editor and a researcher as they sedately presented a story idea, just hours after they had whooped the night away in a king-size bed at the New Weston Hotel across the street. The Newsweek editorial staff averaged two or three divorces a year.

Denson brought in the energetic Gordon Manning, who promptly (as they like to say at news magazines) asked me to write a cover story on Stan Musial, the best hitter in the National League and probably in baseball. Manning had done a bit of research. "Musial comes from a Pennsylvania mill town called Donora," he said. "Pick up the Cardinals in Pittsburgh and then go back to Donora with Musial and visit his mother. You know. 'Hundred-thousand-dollar star still visits Mom back home.'"

In Pittsburgh Musial said he was visiting Donora the next day to talk with children at a hospital and, yes, to visit his mother. I was welcome to join him if I agreed not to write about the trip. "My mother was with us in St. Louis, but she and my wife had different ideas about running the house, so Mom decided to go back to Donora, where her old friends were. She picked her own apartment. It's over a store. No matter how you write the story, it going to come out all across the country, 'Stan Musial's Mother Lives over a Store.'"

I didn't argue. "I've got to come up with something else, Stan. Can you give me something else?"

"I think I can."

Three nights later in a Pullman club car bound for New York, I asked Musial if he was a guess hitter. "I don't guess," he said. "I know." With great care he explained that every pitcher's assortment of pitches moved at different speeds. That is to say, there were standard speeds, each different, for fastballs, breaking balls, and changeups. Musial had committed to memory the speed of each delivery in the repertoire of every opposing pitcher, roughly 210 different pitches from 70 different arms. When he batted, he concentrated so that in the first thirty feet of the baseball's flight, he picked up its velocity. Then, knowing who the pitcher was and that particular pitcher's assortment, he determined what sort of pitch was coming when the baseball was still thirty feet away. That told him how the ball would move as it approached home plate. All this happened in less than two-fifths of a second. To do what Musial did was nothing less than a phenomenal accomplishment. Musial batted .300 or better in twenty of his twenty-two seasons with the Cardinals. He didn't need steroids. He had a mind.

I wrote the cover story with great enthusiasm, but Manning reacted angrily. "Where's Musial's mother?" he said. "Nobody cares about this shit," I told him that if he didn't want the story I would sell it somewhere else. I would also resign and tell John Denson why I was quitting. Manning backed down, muttering, and he continued to mutter until Red Smith wrote a syndicated column saying my story (and Musial's) was the most interesting piece on hitting he had ever read. I did not resign just then, but after John Lardner died of an agonizing coronary in the spring of 1960, there seemed no point in loitering at the Fun House, and I left. Nobody except Schaap, eager to replace me, and John

Denson, who offered me a $5,000 raise, seemed to care much, and I was not offered the Lardner column. According to an executive editor, James Cannon, that was because "the Muirs do not like Jews." Some time afterward, when the foreign editor's chair became vacant, the Muirs refused to promote Otto Friedrich, the most brilliant staffer at the magazine. Malcolm Muir Jr. said Friedrich "lacked panache." Otto showed panache and more across the 1960s when he became the last and finest managing editor in the long history of *The Saturday Evening Post*.

Running *Newsweek*'s tiny sports section usually occupied three days a week. By agreement I could spend my spare time freelancing. During the years at *Newsweek* I published roughly forty articles in periodicals, ranging from *The New York Times Magazine* to the Phi Beta Kappa publication, *The American Scholar,* to *The Saturday Evening Post*. I titled an *Esquire* article on Babe Ruth "A Look Behind a Legend," and it won the E. P. Dutton Prize as best sports magazine article of 1959, an award determined by a jury of eminent journalists to whom stories were submitted anonymously. After a lot of research—questionnaires to every surviving Ruth teammate as a starter—I set down the big man as he really was, with the booze, the babes, the insensitivity, the excess, as well as the howitzer home runs. Quentin Reynolds, a famous World War II correspondent, wrote an appreciation that ran two pages longer than my story. Though subsequently I received the Dutton prize five more times, none thrilled me like winning the first one. In writing about Ruth, I was creating innovative sports journalism, hard-edged but not cruel, making a hero mortal but scarcely ordinary. (That approach was critical to *The Boys of Summer,* and it reverberates today in such splendid works as Jonathan Eig's biography of Lou Gehrig, *Luckiest Man.*) Sadly, the Dutton competition ended during the 1980s. The anonymity of the submissions guaranteed that stories were judged on merit, without journalistic logrolling or, just as common in the writing craft, backstabbing. Nothing comparably prestigious or fair exists today.

In 1960, as a prizewinning journalist, with the press box and the news magazine behind me and my thirty-third birthday looming, it was time, I thought, to begin writing books. As with Musial's belting a long one, the process was more difficult than it appeared. I was getting divorced, always expensive for a man under the old ground rules of New

York State. An agent offered me some quick cash to rewrite a doctor's diet book and after that to collaborate with Mickey Rooney on the little actor's life story. The diet book took a month and in time reaped $90,000. I took to saying, "I've established my base rate: one million, eighty thousand dollars a year." Not all my acquaintances in journalism were amused. Some were struggling to make $90,000 a decade.

A great many things were happening all at once. Except for my father, Gordon Jacques Kahn, who died when I was twenty-five, John Lardner was the first close friend I lost to death. He never reached the age of fifty. That made me angry, and, as happens, moments of anger fed hours of depression. John had shared his fierce pride in being a writer and some of that rubbed off. He was an important part of what would be called today my "support structure." He planted the seed for a book—he was too ill to undertake it himself—about the remarkable life and the rambunctious times of the great heavyweight William Harrison "Jack" Dempsey. Real writing, serious writing, consumes years. Not so much the composing, the typing, but thinking through what you want to say. I called the Jack Dempsey book *A Flame of Pure Fire,* Lardner's term for Dempsey stalking an opponent in the ring. I finished it thirty-eight years after John died. I know a bit about gestation periods. Harcourt published the book in 1999. Commenting in *The New York Review of Books,* Joyce Carol Oates, herself the author of *On Boxing,* called *A Flame of Pure Fire* "exemplary."

Writing from the heart and gut and succeeding makes life sweet. But that is not what I was doing in 1960. I seemed to be writing from, and for, the wallet. I had not quit the story conferences and king-size beds of *Newsweek* to become a hack, but, and I knew this better than anyone else, my books in progress were the very sort of potboilers I scorned. To some degree I was influenced by the money, and in Rooney's case by what I thought would be an inside look at Hollywood, including Rooney's first wife, the black-haired, sultry actress Ava Gardner. A story going around, which Rooney denied, held that one night he turned to Gardner in the quiet of the bedroom and said, "What do you say to a little fuck?"

According to the story Gardner answered, "Hello, Little Fuck."

★ ★ ★

*The Saturday Evening Post,* then entering the climactic years of its Norman Rockwell period, was a splendid writers' market, paying generously, treating its contributors with respect, and publishing, week after week, a pedestrian magazine. It was selling six-and-a-half million copies every issue with a formula that had evolved over a century. Straightforward articles that glorified the American businessman combined with feel-good fiction. The editor in chief, Ben Hibbs, was a native of a village called Pretty Prairie, Kansas. "There are thousands of Pretty Prairies throughout this land," Hibbs wrote, "and herein lies my faith in America. I don't mean to say that there are not plenty of fine and patriotic people in our great cities, and within the ranks of organized labor. I merely say that, in the country and the country towns there is still a stability of life and thought, which is our greatest bulwark in a time of crisis." Rockwell described Hibbs as "easygoing and quiet but with iron in his soul."

When Otto Friedrich took over the magazine, he found in inventory a novel Hibbs had purchased for $50,000 from a master of pulp named Clarence Budington Kelland. It was called *Impersonation* and, Friedrich said, the opening sentence belonged to the ages: "Garland Lee owed much of her glamorous success to the fact that she looked like the wholesome girl next door." Friedrich did not find any Hemingway in inventory. The *Post* had never published Hemingway; indeed, in 1938 its editors rejected the great short story *The Snows of Kilimanjaro.* (Esquire then bought it for $500.)

During my *Newsweek* years I sold six nonfiction pieces to the *Post,* the rate moving from $1,250 to $1,750. All the stories had to be eighteen pages long. Shorter and they'd come back with a request for more. Longer and they'd come back with a request for cuts. Hitting eighteen pages on the nose every time in the days before computer paging tricks was difficult but not impossible. You could always adjust typewriter margins. The *Post*'s editors intended to sustain an approach that had worked well for a long time, and writers came to know what the editors wanted. In the words of Al Hirshberg, the Boston journalist who collaborated with Jimmy Piersall on *Fear Strikes Out,* "To sell the *Post* you write a nice bright piece. Then you dull it up a little."

Over a pleasant lunch I told Irv Goodman, the editor in charge of the *Post's* New York office, "I've written a bunch of stories you people wanted. Now I'd like to do one that I want." So-called visits, or conversation pieces, were popular with Hibbs. A visit with Bing Crosby, a visit with Arthur Godfrey, and a visit with Lucille Ball, in which we learned that Lucy herself, famous as she was, personally met the bus that brought her little daughter home from school. What piffle.

I told Goodman a conversation piece could very well work, even with someone who had something of substance to say. That would be, as I later called the story, "A Visit with Robert Frost." The go-ahead from Hibbs and his senior associates, who worked in Philadelphia, arrived with one ukase: Not too much poetry, please. The *Post's* editors believed "our loyal readers aren't into the study of contemporary poetry." Frost qualified as a story subject not as a poet but as an American Original, like Walt Disney or Gary Cooper, or Rockwell, or Hibbs. I would go forth on the finest assignment of my life under a dictum that said: Don't write about what the subject does. Stay away from the quintessence of an extraordinary life. Set down Frost, but kindly skip his poetry.

I certainly was not going to do that, but . . . what *would* I do? The thought of sitting alone and conversing with the great poet, then eighty-six, was simultaneously stimulating and alarming. This was hardly comparable to interviewing Mickey Mantle, where, when things went wrong, you could properly assume that the ballplayer was suffering from a hangover. If the Frost interview went poorly, there would be no one to blame but myself.

I had read all of Frost's work and memorized a good deal. I had observed at least one touch of his nature during my days at Bread Loaf. As I have mentioned, he didn't like to be crowded, but I laboriously began to prepare a list of questions for him. One or two popped up for myself. Was I going to see Frost on behalf of *The Saturday Evening Post*? That was the justification. But, more deeply, wasn't I going to see him for private reasons of my own? What I wanted to say was something like this, "Rob, I'm feeling shaky with this divorce and all the solitude that goes with it and I miss my kid and I don't understand why I keep agreeing to write potboilers. I'm trying to figure out how to make a satisfactory life and write things that I can respect. Sort of like you. But how do I do that, Rob?"

That was exactly what *not* to say. If I had, the interview would have been one of the shortest in the annals. Actually, I never called him Rob. We became friendly, but it was always, and appropriately, considering the age gap, "Mr. Frost."

I decided against using a tape recorder. Electronics and the Green Mountains struck me as a poor mix. Given Frost's eloquence, I wanted to capture him verbatim, so I packed my old press box portable, with scraps of Polo Grounds peanut shells still lurking in the keys. Kathleen Morrison, a forceful and attractive New England lady, married to Theodore Morrison, the director of the Bread Loaf conference, said she would set up a typing table in Frost's cabin. "It's a bit of trouble, but I'll do it," she said. "You know, don't you, that the only reason Frost is seeing you at all is because you are a Bread Loaf boy? He doesn't usually grant interviews."

I drove my car, a Citroën described in sales literature as "tortoise shell," French auto-speak for tan, to Williamstown for a pre-Frost evening at the then reasonably bucolic Williams Inn. Before retiring I read some of his poems, "Acquainted with the Night," "Reluctance," and the one that begins "Tree at my window, window tree." The Williams Inn had provided a tree at my window. Then I read "Sand Dunes" and went to sleep.

I arrived at the Homer Noble farm, near Ripton, on September 2, 1960. This was Frost's summer headquarters. Kay and Ted Morrison lived in a large farmhouse near the two-lane blacktop road. A horse barn lay off to one side. Frost resided by himself in a cabin on the shoulder of a steep hill. It had been a pleasant summer. The corn was tall.

"You sure you didn't bring one of those tape recorders?" Kay said.

"No. As I said, I thought I'd type while he talked."

"Good. He does not like tape recorders. He feels they make things permanent whether he means them to be permanent or not."

"When you finish," Ted Morrison said, "I hope you can join us for martinis."

Frost was wearing blue slacks, a gray sweater, and a white shirt, open at the collar. Under white hair, his face was weathered and wrinkled and wholly attractive. Ol' Potato Face, maybe, but a beautiful potato. His mien was serious, with a suggestion of humor in the deep-set green eyes. He was, to be sure, the man who had written in serious merriment:

*I never dared be radical when young,*
*For fear it would make me conservative when old.*

He was not tall, perhaps five foot eight, but his build was sturdy and suggested a man who was no stranger to the plough. He did not offer a formal hello. Instead he said, "Did Lefty Tyler ever pitch in a World Series?" That was Frost's way of saying he remembered who I was, and that he knew I had been writing about baseball. My late father helped with the response. I had heard often from him about the "Miracle Braves" of 1914 who were last on July 4, but rallied to win a pennant and sweep the World Series from the Philadelphia Athletics. The Braves did it, my father said, with three pitchers, Dick "Baldy" Rudolph, Bill James, and George "Lefty" Tyler, the one native New Englander in the group. Tyler hailed from Derry, New Hampshire; Frost once taught at Pinkerton Academy there.

"Tyler pitched a strong game in the 1914 Series, Mr. Frost, but it went into extra innings and he didn't get a decision."

Kay listened without interest. She helped set up my typewriter on a small table and said, "Now I'm going to leave you two and Lefty Tyler." We settled into Adirondack chairs facing one another across the little typewriter table and there I was, in a small, pleasant cabin seated beside a stranger named Robert Frost. The Reese tremolo returned to my voice, "What have you been doing lately?"

"I'm never doing anything lately. If I wrote novels or epic poems I could tell you what I've been doing, but I don't, so I can't."

Silence.

"You, um, lecture."

"Lecture. That's your word not mine. I talk and then I read. Never wrote out a lecture in my life."

Clearly it was proceeding badly. An inner voice said, *You are disgracing yourself!* I wanted to flee. Forget Frost. Write "A Visit with Casey Stengel." "An Evening with Frank Sinatra." "A Morning with Richard Nixon." *Anything.* This is embarrassing. But a blessed spirit from years past, my mother's great creed, held me, and I heard myself saying, "Before I go, Mr. Frost, I wanted to tell you that three lines of yours have meant a great deal to me." In a poem, "*Bereft*," Frost is alone in his cabin as a storm approaches. Alarmed, he hurries through the door. "Out in the porch's sagging floor, / Leaves got up in a coil and hissed, / Blindly struck at my knee and missed."

I said, "Leaves as a snake. What an image!" Frost's chill demeanor fled. He said, half to himself, "You saw that, did you? Usually they only see what the anthologizers want them to see. But you saw that, did you? Very good." His leaned forward, poked his left fist gently into my ribs, and we were men together. We talked long after that and we talked often, and I guard my memories of Frost as a treasure beyond price, which indeed they are.

He said, "You're a journalist. You write sports?"

"Yes, mostly. I write other things as well."

"Of course," Frost said, smiling. "We all have to lead more than one life. Poets, sculptors, lead two or three lives at the very least." He paused. "I don't have to ask where you're from," he said. "New York. I can tell by the way you speak, just as you can tell that I'm from New England by the way I speak."

More comfortable now, I returned to my first question. "I guess I didn't put it well, but I was simply wondering what you have been doing recently."

"I never am doing anything really," Frost said. "I can't talk about my plans until I see how my plans work out. If I were writing a novel or an epic I could tell you what I've been doing, but I don't write novels or epics.

"I don't have any routine. I don't have any hours. I don't have any desk. I never wrote out a lecture in my life. I never wrote a review, a word of criticism. I've possibly written a dozen essays, but you couldn't call mine a literary life." Frost chuckled and gestured at the typewriter. "You use that thing pretty well."

"Thanks," I said.

"Never learned to type myself," said Robert Frost.

Some, but not all of our conversation, appeared in the article I wrote, one that has been anthologized many times, usually with my consent, sometimes not. A number of readers may be familiar with a few of the things Frost had to say. But coming to the conclusion of this chapter, one will, I think, see Frost and hear his words in a new and quite shattering way.

Staying in the present at the cabin, I asked a global question. "Khrushchev and Castro and Kennedy. What do you think about what the *world*'s been doing lately?"

"I wonder," Frost said, "if God hasn't looked down and turned away and said, 'Boys, this isn't for me. You go ahead and fight it out with knives and bombs.'"

As you may have gathered, or are about to learn, Frost ran a conversation as a good pitcher runs a baseball game, never delivering quite what you expect. There were semihumorous answers to serious questions and serious answers to semihumorous questions, Frost was a master of the conversational change of pace.

"The world," he said, earnest now, "is being offered a choice between two kinds of democracy. Our is a very ancient political growth, beginning at one end of the Mediterranean Sea and coming westward, tried in Athens, tried in Italy, tried in England, tried in France, coming westward all the way to us. A very long growth, a growth through trial and error, but always with the idea that there is some sort of wisdom in the mob. 'Demos' is the ancient Greek word for mob. Put a marker where the growth begins at the eastern end of the Mediterranean, and there's never been a glimmer of democracy south of there. Over east, in Asia, there have been interesting ideas, but none bothered by a belief in the wisdom of the mob.

"Our democracy is like our bill of fare. That came westward, too, with wheat and so on, adding foods by trial and error and luck. I think, when corn comes in good and fresh, what would I have done if Columbus hadn't discovered America." Again the change of pace.

"What is this Russian democracy [under Stalin and Khrushchev]? Ours, I say, is like our bill of fare, kills a few people every year probably, but most of us learn to live with it. The Russian democracy is like a doctor's prescription. Take it whether you want to take it or not. I have pretty strong confidence that our kind of democracy is better than the trumped-up kind. I'm pretty sure we're going to win. I'm on our side anyway."

Two years earlier, in 1958, the Russian Jewish poet and novelist, Boris Pasternak, author of *Doctor Zhivago,* won the Nobel Prize for literature. But Khrushchev and his henchmen blocked the path to Stockholm and Pasternak could not accept the honor and the cash that went with it [214,559 Swedish kronor or $31,499.15, perhaps a quarter of a million dollars today]. An ad-hoc group asked Frost to issue a personal protest. "I couldn't do that," he said. "I understood who he was and what he wanted. He could have used certain means to get out and get the Nobel money, but he didn't want to. He had done what he wanted. He'd made his criticism. He lived in a little artists' colony outside of Moscow; that was where he wanted to live. He was a Russian, and he had made his criticism of Russia and now he wanted to be left alone. I had to respect that. I'm a nationalist myself."

Frost placed one hand before his eyes, and when he spoke again, his voice was soft. "Unfinished business," he said. "I'm very much in favor of unfinished business. Some of them aren't, but every single heading in the newspaper represents a whole lot of things that have got to stay unfinished, that can't be finished. Us and Russia, that might take a couple of hundred years before it's finished. That's one of the hard things about dying, wondering how the unfinished business will come out.

"Oh, you could go crazy with too much unfinished business. You'd feel unfulfilled. You make a finished article out of this, and I make a finished poem. But talk about anyone's career. That has got to be suspended and thought about a great deal, and you're not saying much about it till you see how it comes out. You suspend judgment and go to bed."

Outside, beyond the window, a lawn stretched down the hill. To the far left rose the corn. To the right a brown field lay, newly turned by the plough. Beyond the valley mountains rose, deep green. "Three things have followed me," Frost said. "Writing, teach a little, and farming. The three strands of my life."

"About writing," I said.

"A boy called on me the other day and said, 'I'm a poet,'" Frost went on. "I said; 'That's a praise word. Wait until somebody else called me that.' " Frost laughed a little now. It had been a long and lonely time until many people called Robert Frost a poet.

"I started by the ocean," Frost said. "San Francisco. My father was a newspaperman there. He went to Harvard, finished first in his class, but he never talked about that. Once he got West he put the East behind him, never mentioned it, drank enough for three generations of Frosts, died young. My mother was born in Scotland, raised in Ohio."

"Did you grow up amid books?" I said.

"Didn't you, didn't you?" Frost said, his voice almost a chant. "Oh, I never got the library habit much. I have an interest in books, but you couldn't call me a terribly bookish man."

There were two bookcases in Frost's living room, and on the window seat beside our chairs books rested in three small stacks. His recent reading ranged from Latin poetry to a work on modern architecture. But the room was not overrun with books. The average prep school English teacher lives among more books than did Frost.

"We came to southern New Hampshire after my father died," Frost said. "I escaped school until I was twelve. I'd try it for a week and then the doctor would take me out. They never knew what was the matter, but I seemed to be ailing. I got so I never wanted to see school. The first time I liked it was in New Hampshire. I liked the noon hour and the recess. I didn't want to miss what went on then, and so I became interested in the rest of it, the studies.

"It was a little country school. There was no grading. I could go as fast as I wanted, and I made up the whole eight years in a year and a half without realizing I was doing it. Then they sent me down to Lawrence [Massachusetts] to live with my grandfather and go to high school where my father had gone. In high school I had only Greek, Latin, and mathematics. I began to write in my second year, but not for any teacher. There were no English teachers, but we had an active school magazine. I must have been reading Prescott's *Conquest of Mexico*, because my first poem was a ballad about the night the Indians fought Cortez. [Frost called the poem "La Noche Triste," and it appeared in the *Lawrence High School Bulletin* of April 1890.] People say, 'You were interested in the way children are interested in cops and robbers.' But it wasn't that way at all. I was interested in Indians because of the wrongs done to them. I was wishing the Indians would win all the battles.

"Dartmouth was my chief college," he said, "the first one I ran away from. I ran from Harvard later, but Dartmouth first. In a little library at Dartmouth I saw a magazine, and on the front page there was a poem. There was an editorial about the poem, so evidently that magazine was in favor of poetry. I send them a poem, 'My Butterfly.' It's in the big collection."

"My Butterfly" is a poignant lyric in which Frost sees a butterfly "in airy dalliance, / Precipitate to love." Soon afterward he comes upon the butterfly near the house, broken-winged and dead. Frost wrote in sorrow:

> Save only me
> There is none left to mourn thee in the fields.

"After I sent that to the magazine, they bought it [for $15] so easily that I thought I could make a living this way. But I didn't keep selling 'em as fast as that. The magazine was called *The New York Independent*, and after they bought the poem they asked that when I sent them more, would I please spell the name of the magazine correctly.

"When I told Grandfather Frost I wanted to be a poet, he wasn't pleased. He was an old-line Democrat, the devil take the hindmost, and here I was, making good grades, and wanting, he thought, to waste my life. 'I give you one year to make it, Rob,' he said. I put on an auctioneer's voice. 'I'm offered one, give me twenty, give me twenty, give me twenty,' I said. My grandfather never brought up poetry again."

Frost married Elinor White, his covaledictorian at Lawrence High, in 1895, and set about rearing a family and dividing his life among poetry, teaching, and farming. "I had to find other means than poems," he said. "They didn't sell fast enough, and I didn't send my poems out much. Oh, I wanted them to want my poems. Some say, 'Do you write for yourself entirely?' 'You mean into the wastebasket?' I say. But I had pride there. I hated rejection slips. I had to be very careful of my pride. 'Love me little, love me long.' Did you hear that? Were you brought up on that? 'Love me little, love me long.'" Frost smiled. "But not too little."

He placed a hand before his eyes again. "One of the most sociable virtues or vices is that you don't want to feel queer. You don't want to be too much like the others, but you don't want to be clear out in nowhere. 'She mocked 'em and she shocked 'em and she said she didn't care.' You like to mock 'em and to shock 'em, but you really do care.

"You are always with your sorrows and your cares. What's a poem for if not to share them with others? But I don't like poems that are too crudely personal. Where can you be personal and not in bad taste? In poetry, but you have to be careful. If anybody tries to make you say more—they have to stop where you stop."

Sometimes Frost chose to tell me more about certain poems than was generally known, revealing their interplay with episodes and even tragedies in his personal life. He had a stirring phrase for life. He called life "the trial by existence." He told me the things he did perhaps as friend to friend, perhaps as writer to writer, perhaps both. The ruling condition was gently put, but firm: I was not to share the private insights he provided with the general public and—least of all—with any critics. Some of what he had to say was quite intimate. For decades I kept my counsel, but now, so many years afterward, I think, that when we get there, I can say more in this book than I have before. Frost died almost half a century ago, but in a way I saw him just last summer when I visited his grave. His stone is sheltered by maples (and a birch or two) in a pretty country churchyard at Bennington, Vermont. Standing above the stone, I heard his voice resound again in the carved epitaph he had composed for himself. "I had a lover's quarrel with the world."

Atop the steep hill in Ripton where we were talking long ago on that mild September day, Frost sat back, comfortable after a while, and his comfort reached out to me, and I felt calm and profoundly happy that, to put this on the simplest level, he and I were getting along. The closeness came quickly. He surely sensed my admiration for his work. "We have all sorts of ways to hold people," Frost said. "Hold them and hold them off. Do you know what the sun does with the planets? It holds them and it holds them off. The planets don't fall away from the sun and they don't fall into it. That's one of the marvels. Attraction and repulsion. You have that with poetry and you have that with friendships."

For a time in his youth, guarding his pride, developing his art, Frost expected to work as a New England farmer for the rest of his life, "But people asked me out to read," he said, "and that kind of checked that. Then, when I was teaching in the academies, it would be eating me all up, taking me away frm poetry too much. Whenever it got like that, I'd run away.

"I didn't have any foundation to help me, but I had a tiny little bit of money saved up, and I went to England. Not for the literary life. I didn't want that. But we could live cheaper there. The six of us [Elinor and four children] went to England and we stayed for three years for thirty-six hundred dollars, fare and everything. We lived poor, but we had a little garden, and we got something out of it, and we had some chickens. We lived very much like peasants. I was thirty-seven years old, and I'd never offered a book. My poems were scattered in magazines, but not much. Then one day I thought I'd show a little bunch of poems. I left them with a small publisher, and three days later I signed the contract. Funny, it had never occurred to me to try a book here. *A Boy's Will,* that was the book."

Or perhaps that is not funny at all. "My Butterfly" appeared in 1894. Eleven years later Frost published "The Tuft of Flowers" in *The Derry Enterprise.* That poem, which became enormously popular at readings, describes solitary mowing in a field after someone else has worked adjacent land, also alone. Encountering the other man, Frost says "in brotherly speech:"

> *"Men work together" I told him from the heart,*
> *"Whether they work together or apart."*

"Into My Own," the poem that gives this book its title, ran in *The New England Magazine* in May of 1909. Each of these Frost poems is extraordinary and obviously none was rejected per se. But neither did a publisher, any one of the dozens of American publishers then doing business, seize on them after they appeared in periodicals. Nor did any publisher, recognizing the gifts of the artist, offer him a contract for a book of poetry or even encouragement toward that end. This was another sort of rejection, as troubling to a man of Frost's sensitivity as a flat turndown. His work was printed, and after that nothing happened. Don

Marquis, a gifted journalist, once wrote in the magazine *The Sun Dial*: "Publishing a volume of verse in America is like dropping a rose petal down the Grand Canyon and waiting for the echo."

The dreadful silence Frost faced in the United States was a factor in his transatlantic move. He rented a cottage in Beaconsfield, twenty miles north of London, and in October of 1912, when he was thirty-eight years old, he took "a bunch of verses" to the London firm of David Nutt and Company, which published them on April 1, 1913. The title, *A Boy's Will*, came from Longfellow, who wrote in "My Lost Youth,"

> *A boy's will is the wind's will*
> *And the thoughts of youth are long, long thoughts.*

"I went to England mostly unpublished," he said, "but after I got my book published, they wanted me to join the literary life and asked me to a group that was run by Ezra Pound.

"Economy. That was what Pound said he wanted. I write a poem and give it to you; you write it in fewer words. Six people sitting around a room, writing poems in fewer words. Pound said, 'Got a poem on you, Frost?' I pointed to my head. 'Up here.' I wrote it out and picked up a magazine.

> *Ah, when to the heart of man*
> *Was it ever less than a treason*
> *To go with the drift of things,*
> *To yield with a grace to reason,*
> *And bow and accept the end*
> *Of a love or a season?*

"Pound came back in a little while. 'Don't have too much on you, Frost. Took you forty words. Best I could do was thirty-three.'

" 'Yes,' I told him, 'and destroyed my rhyme and destroyed my meter and probably destroyed my sense.' " Frost leaned forward and jabbed an elbow into my ribs. "That settled Pound's hash," he said. "He never tried to tell me how to write poetry again."

Frost was fiercely proud of his art long before American presidents or academics knew that the art existed, and he kept his pride very much as it was through all his years. He rejected Pound's advice, but because Frost was, as he put it, "for poetry," he never rejected Pound, even in the face of notably outrageous behavior. During the early 1930s Pound moved from England to Rapallo, Italy, and became an enthusiastic supporter of Benito Mussolini, "the Sawdust Caesar." During World War II Pound spoke on Italian State Radio, denouncing America's entry into the war and peppering his comments with anti-Semitism. He did this amid the killing of a million and a quarter European children who were murdered only because they were Jewish. After the defeat of the Fascists, Pound was brought back to the United States and charged with treason. Found unfit for trial by reason of insanity, he was committed to St. Elizabeth's Hospital in Washington, D.C. There psychiatrists noted a disturbance they categorized as "grandiosity of ideas and beliefs." Some felt the doctors, quite limited themselves, were misinterpreting Pound's ingrained conceit and developed flamboyance. Whatever, Pound, not the psychiatrists, was under lock and key.

While controversy rumbled, Frost visited Pound in the hospital, then summoned Sherman Adams, a New Englander who was White House chief of staff under Dwight Eisenhower. Disdaining talk on the clinical issue, Frost told Adams that Pound should be freed for one fundamental reason. "It's wrong to imprison poets." Adams listened and talked to Eisenhower. Pound was released soon afterward and returned to Italy where in a 1967 interview with Allen Ginsberg he apologized for "my stupid, suburban anti-Semitism."

But immediately after being released from St. Elizabeth's, Pound was making no apologies. Instead he began writing unpleasant letters. "Scatological," Frost said. "He keeps using the word 'shit.'"

From Frost the word shocked. My mouth fell.

"But that's not the worst thing," Frost said. "The worst is what he's doing to [T. S.] Eliot. He writes Eliot and says, 'I was wrong about you. You are not a good poet.'"

It was in the British Isles that the profoundly American Robert Frost first found literary understanding and significant praise. William Butler Yeats, the bard of Ireland, said that *A Boy's Will* "contains the best poetry written in America for a long time." A year or so later David Nutt issued a collection that Frost called *North of Boston*. The first two poems in *North of Boston* are "Mending Wall" and "The Death of the Hired Man," both now recognized as classics. An English contemporary of Frost's, a journalist and poet named Edward Thomas, wrote of *North of Boston,* "These poems are revolutionary because they lack the exaggeration of rhetoric." Someone showed *North of Boston* to the wife of Henry Holt, the American publisher. Mrs. Holt was mightily impressed, and presently Holt and Company agreed to issue the book in the United States. Mr. Holt seemed less convinced of Frost's artistry than was Yeats, Edward Thomas, or Mrs. Holt. Or anyway unconvinced of Frost in the American marketplace. Holt's first printing of *North of Boston* numbered 150 copies. There has never been a day since when Frost's poetry has been out of print.

Once a collection of his work appeared in the United States, Frost felt comfortable returning to his homeland. He still had to work at farming and teaching. He was forty years old before he gained wide American recognition, and he was almost fifty before his volume *New Hampshire* won him his first Pulitzer Prize. "But I always knew," he said to me. "Even as a boy by the Pacific I knew a day would come when they would want to read my poems." It struck me, as I sat in the little living room that Frost had gone from obscurity to great fame making relatively few changes in his way of life. The Vermont cabin was as simple as the house where he dwelled when there was no choice but to live simply. One difference was that by the time of our first talk in 1960, a sizable portion of the world was trying to beat a path to the woods and up to Frost's front door.

"You have to be careful of idolizers," he said. "Emerson calls an unwanted visitor a devastator of the day. It's a cranky Yankee poem, but I suppose he was pestered all the time by people who wanted to go deeper into him than he could go himself, and, goodness, he was such an artist they should very well have left it where he did. They think, the idolizers, that you've injured them. Whether they injured you or not, the idolizers always think you've injured them.

"How much do you need someone who always thinks you're a hero? How much do you need being thought a hero all the time? People say,

'I got over this. I got over that.' They are a lot of fools, the people who say you get over your loves and your heroes. I never do. I don't change very much."

"Has your method of writing changed?"

"If I'm not in shape so I can strike it out, like a good golf stroke or a good swing of the bat, there's not much I can do. Oh, you get so that some days you can play a beautiful game, but there are always days when you can't. Those days, I can't redo them. They're done. Down the sink.

"What some seem to do is worry a thing into shape and have others worry with them. Not to say I don't have the distress of failure, but the worry way isn't for me. There are the days you can and the days you can't, and both are training toward the future days you can. Do you know the story about how the bear is born?"

I didn't

"The bear is born shapeless, says the story, and the mother licks it into shape. That's the way it is with some people's writing. They revise and revise until all that's left is a finely polished revision. No good piece is worried into shape. A child is unfortunate that needs to be reshaped just after it's born. Is a poet made? A poet might be through all the years of trial and error, but any good poem is not made. It's born complete."

In many of Frost's poems, loneliness is a strong theme. Elinor died in 1938, and by 1960 three of his five children were dead. Surely thinking of myself, I asked how he could come to terms with solitude.

"In the big newspaper office," Frost said, "where everyone sits alongside the other and writes—I couldn't do that. Even reading. I've got to be totally absorbed when I read. Where there are other people reading, too. I don't feel very happy.

"Alone you take all your traits as if you were bringing 'em to market. You bring them from the quiet of the garden. But the garden is not the marketplace. That's a big trouble to some: how you mix living with people with not living with people, how you mix the garden with the marketplace.

"I like the quiet here, but I like to have a big audience for my talks, to have a few turned away. I like to feel all that warmth in the room. At Kansas City once they told me, 'You see that hazy look down the end of the hall. That's whiskers. Them's beatniks.' They came and I wish 'em

well, but I do like some form in the things I read." Or, as Frost put it in
his poem "Pertinax":

> *Let chaos storm!*
> *Let cloud shapes swarm!*
> *I wait for form.*

(Publius Helvius Pertinax, was emperor of Rome in the year 193.
He attempted to curb the random excesses of the Praetorian Guard—
the storm troopers of antiquity—and restore order and form to Imperial Rome. Members of the Praetorian Guard murdered him. Soldiers
then placed Pertinax's severed head on a lance and held it high as they
paraded about the streets. The reign of Pertinax had lasted for three
months.)

In Vermont the late afternoon sun brightened a field beyond the window. "Used to play softball out past there," Frost said. "You remember,
don't you? You remember that I pitched. Nothing flatters me more than
to have it assumed that I could write prose—unless it be to have it assumed that I once pitched a baseball with distinction. They don't let me
do all the things I want to any more, but if we had a ball, I'd pitch to
you a little, and I'd surprise you." He grinned.

"You still like sports?"

"Oh, yes. You get a certain glory out of being translated, but no, no,
it doesn't work. So much is lost. There are other arts that are international. High jumping. Boxing. They understood Jack Dempsey's left
hook quite readily in French and German. Nothing was lost. But with
poetry, I sometimes tell 'em, 'Poetry is what's lost in the translation.'

"I follow baseball. I'm a New Englander, so I root for the Red Sox,
but I don't really like the way the Red Sox play. Too much in the manner of Boston gentlemen."

"How do you like your baseball played, Mr. Frost?"

"Spike 'em as you go around the bases."

Then we were serious again and I asked about another strong theme
in Frost's work, the theme of God. "Don't make me out to be a religious
man," Frost said. "Don't make me out to be a man who has all the

answers. I don't go around preaching God. I'm not a minister. I'm always pleased when I see people comfortable with these things. There's a rabbi near here, a friend of mine, who preaches in Cincinnati in the winter. He talks at the Methodist church here sometimes and tells the people in Cincinnati that he's a summer Methodist.

"People have wondered about him at the Methodist church. One lady was troubled and said to me, 'How do they differ from us?'

" 'What you got there on that table?' I said.

" 'That's a Bible,' she said.

"I didn't say any more.

" 'Oh,' she said. 'The Old Testament. Why can't you have a Jew in church?' she said, and she understood."

Frost's voice was strong. "There's a good deal of God in everything you do," he said. "It's like climbing up a ladder, and the ladder rests on nothing, and you climb higher and higher and you feel there must be God at the top. It can't be unsupported up there. I'd be afraid, though, of any one religion being the whole thing in our country, because there would probably come a day when they would take me down to the cellar and torture me—just for my own good."

He smiled briefly. "There is more religion outside church than in," Frost said, "more love outside marriage than in, more poetry outside verse than in. Everyone knows there is more love outside the institutions than in, and yet I'm kind of an institutional man."

We turned back to poetry then. "They ask me if I have a favorite," Frost said, "but if a mother has a favorite child, she has to hide it from herself, so I can't tell you if I have a favorite, no."

"Is there one basic point to all fine poetry?"

"What language?"

"English."

"The phrase," Frost said, slowly, clearly. "And what do I mean by a phrase? A clutch of words that gives you a clutch at the heart."

I took that in gradually, and while I did, Frost went on for a bit. "You hear from some that certain poems are for the young, not for the old. I don't believe that's so. Any poem I ever cared for I still care for. Do you get over things?"

"I'm not sure."

"Anything I ever thought I still think. They are a lot of fools, the ones who say you get over things, your old loves, your old poems. I never do . . ."

*The Saturday Evening Post* published "A Visit with Robert Frost" in its issue of November 1960 and drew a response that neither I, nor perhaps even Frost, anticipated. More than four hundred letters came to the magazine, variously thanking me and Frost. Some clipped the article and asked if I would autograph it. One reader in Dawson, Georgia, wrote, "I shall forever be grateful to the two of you for reawakening dreams, dreams that a busy country doctor thought he had no time for."

One writes—at least I write—not simply for ambition and bread and fame, but to make a difference; as Pee Wee Reese put it, "to make the world a little better." The poet Stanley Kunitz commented that the body of one's work "is not an expression of the desire for praise, or recognition, or prizes, but the deepest manifestation of your gratitude for the gift of life." When interviewers ask, "In a sentence or two, can you sum up what Robert Frost has meant to you," I am struck dumb. I know the meaning begins with exquisite gratitude for his friendship, for his sharing with me the gift of life.

The following spring Kay Morrison telephoned and said, "Frost wants to see you." This time I brought along my son Gordon, who, at the age of four, was eighty-three years younger than Frost. As I approached the cabin, Frost came to the door, smiling, and said, "I didn't read all of your article. I get tired of myself. But I'm glad you came up, so I could thank you for writing it."

After a while Gordon went out to play in the cornfield. "You know," Frost said, when we were alone, "in all the years I taught at Amherst I never said a poem to my class."

"Why not, Mr. Frost?"

"They never asked."

"I'm asking."

"You're only saying that because you feel you have to."

"No, sir. And I don't have to. It would be wonderful if you would say a poem to me."

He sat back and spoke two stanzas from the poem "Sand Dunes."

> *Sea waves are green and wet*
> *But up from where they die,*
> *Rise others vaster yet,*
> *And these are brown and dry.*
>
> *They are the sea made land*
> *To come at the fisher town,*
> *And bury in solid sand*
> *The men she could not drown.*

Both us paused for thought. I considered the sound of his words, his voice, the immediacy of his phrases and the transcendent rhythm in his work. "Could you ever teach rhythm?" I said.

"No," he said, touching an ear. "It's either there or not."

"That pleases me," I said, "because Gordon is four and he listens to Elizabethan lyrics even though he doesn't understand the words."

"Four years old and responds to rhythm, you say?"

"Yes."

"Of course," Frost said, "because his heart beats and he's seen the waves."

When it was time to go, I gathered the child, hiked him onto my shoulder and started down the steep hill, Frost ran to the porch calling, "The boy, the boy. I have to say good-bye to the boy." I turned and then the boy stared in wonder at Frost, at a face that had survived so many winters. He put out a small unwrinkled hand and began to stroke Frost's cheek. Frost leaned closer and looked at the boy with a gaze I read as love.

Down the hill I heard Frost cry after me, "Come back again, if you'd care to." Because trivialities crowded my time, I never did.

Robert Frost died on January 29, 1963, a month short of his eighty-ninth birthday. Some time after that Clay Blair, running a new and more vigorous *Saturday Evening Post,* handed me bound galleys of Frost's letters to his old friend Louis Untermeyer, a minor poet but a highly successful editor of verse anthologies. "'Holt is publishing the book," Blair said. "They want $10,000 for magazine rights. I'll pay it if you'll agree to edit the letters for me."

Frost had told me, almost casually, about the suicide of his only son, Carol, who shot himself during the autumn of 1940. "How did you survive?" I asked. Frost said only six words. "I lived wild for a time." He wrote to Untermeyer: "I took the wrong way with him. I tried many ways and every single one of them was wrong. Some thing in me is still asking for the chance to try one more. There's where the greatest pain is located." Frost then offered these lines:

> To prayer I think I go,
> I go to prayer—
> Along a darkened corridor of woe . . .

I could not realize that Frost's tragedy with Carol foreshadowed a disaster that lurked ahead for me, amid life's windblown leaves that coil like snakes . . .

# CHAPTER 4

# The Pioneer

Here I find myself a part of what was called "The Negro Revolution," alongside its early leader and constant champion, a surprisingly conservative man.

In the late winter of 1953 Jackie Robinson hired me to help him start a monthly magazine for blacks called *Our Sports*. This was before such concepts as black power had taken wide hold, and the magazine, like Robinson at the time, focused on integration. I would write a bylined column in alternate issues and help Robinson prepare his own column, which was to appear every month. "I can only get you $150—that's $150 a month, not a week," Robinson said. "I wish it could be more. But I'd like to work with you, and I hope you'd like to work with me."

I remember my acceptance speech verbatim. "That would be great, Jack." And it was. Working closely in hotel rooms and Pullman cars and coffee shops, we formed a splendid intimacy, which was not without moments of civil but distinct disagreement. Supposedly, the theme of our pieces was baseball, but as we traveled the country sharing both the intensity of a pennant race and the intensity of journalism, we touched on money, lust, and diverse aspects of the human condition. Black-white sex interested Jack a great deal, particularly the clichéd and racist notion that big, black bucks (like Jackie Robinson) were preoccupied with getting white women naked and into bed. "First of all," Robinson said, "did you know Ted Williams, big, white Ted Williams, chased a beautiful black girl all over Havana, trying to nail her? And he struck out."

"I did not know that. How do you know it?"

"Sources," Robinson said. "What you writers call sources. And here's something else. More white women want to go to bed with me than I have time for."

"Congratulations," I said.

Over a quick smile Robinson said, "Eat your heart out." He was a ferociously competitive character and needling, sometimes across the lines of taste and sense, was one symptom.

Nineteen years later, when Robinson died, his friend and physician, Arthur C. Logan, asked me to deliver one of the eulogies at the Riverside Church, which rises near both Columbia University and Harlem, a dominating structure on Riverside Drive, built with Rockefeller money and modeled after the thirteenth-century Gothic cathedral in Chartres, France. The funeral would begin there at high noon on October 27, 1972. After that the carillon would play, or specifically, a carillonneur named Dionisio Lind would play the Laura Spelman Rockefeller Memorial Carillon.

The day before, as Arthur Logan and I sat in the living room of the Robinson home at 103 Cascade Road in North Stamford, Connecticut, this gentle and tormented physician spoke in sorrowful tones. Rachel, Robinson's widow, was not your basic, cheerleading baseball wife. Intelligent and ambitious, she had completed postgraduate studies and become director of psychiatric nursing at the hospital affiliated with Yale Medical School. For some years she had been commuting north to New Haven while Jack was commuting south to New York. Their lives were largely separate, which is not to say without love.

An odd assortment milled about the room, dominated by a massive gray stone fireplace. Someone was playing a sitar. A few other men, with long hair, talked urgently, and one could overhear Freudian jargon. Probably Rachel's friends from the Yale psychiatric commune. I wondered how many, or how few, of these people gathered to comfort a widow had ever seen Jackie Robinson play ball.

"It's for the best," Logan said, "His diabetes was so virulent we couldn't do very much to slow its course. Then there were blood pressure problems, and that on top of the diabetes created a nasty situation. He was suffering from all kinds of internal hemorrhaging. In months or a year we would have had to amputate his legs, his circulation was getting that bad. Can you imagine Jackie Robinson blind and without legs in a wheel-chair? Death isn't always the worst thing."

Arthur began quietly to weep. When he recovered, he said that Jackie would have wanted me to speak at his funeral, leaving me flat-tered and touched and worrying about how on earth I would get a eu-logy into shape, a eulogy for a great man, on such short notice.

But that was not to be. Logan called me later and said that a promi-nent cleric at Riverside Church had informed him that only ordained ministers could speak from the pulpit; the Reverend Jesse Jackson, who barely knew Robinson, got the call. In the huge cathedral, Jackson deliv-ered a big farewell that was sonorous and impersonal. He said Robinson had taken a stumbling block and turned it into a stepping-stone. As the choir of the Canaan Baptist Church of Christ began singing in the back-ground, Jackson's voice rose. He said that in the end Jackie Robinson had gotten tired. Then Jackson dropped his voice dramatically. "So he stole home."

That played well, but as I was leaving the church, I was collared by a small, intense publicity man named Irving Rudd, the same character who had organized Pee Wee Reese Night at Ebbets Field. "Can I buy you a drink?" he said.

"Sure. I don't much feel like going out to the cemetery."

Inside a Broadway bar called the West End, Rudd said, "It was a nice service, except that guy Jackson's ending spoiled it. Stole home, my ass. I knew Jackie, maybe not as good as you, but enough to know that Jack-son was just blowing smoke. If there is a heaven, Jackie's up there right now, but he isn't figuring he's safe at home. He's torn his cap off and he's saying to the Big Umpire in the Sky, 'That was one lousy call. I was only fifty-three years old.'"

In ensuing days I wondered some about my exclusion from the pulpit. Robinson had been overjoyed at the success of *The Boys of Summer*, which was the number-one nonfiction bestseller during the last summer of his life. That led to some unusual dialogue after my telephone rang one July day. Jack began, in the ballpark language we used to use, "You son of a bitch."

"Why am I a son of a bitch, Robinson?

The tenor voice sounded vigorous. "Your damn book has my telephone ringing all the time. I get no peace. Some of them called me an Uncle Tom for working for white bosses. Now they're finding out I wasn't an Uncle Tom. And that's all because of you and your damn book."

"You're welcome, Jack. How are you?"

"Not bad for an old man going blind."

That took away my breath. I must have gasped. "No, I'm fine, really," Robinson said. "People have read me sections of your book. I always knew you had something like that in you."

Now, with Jack gone, I found myself barred from a pulpit where he would be celebrated. I don't think he would have liked that much. To understand Robinson, one does well to recognize that not only did he fight prejudice against blacks, but also he detested prejudice of any sort. All forms of bigotry and, most particularly anti-Semitism, stirred the white heat of his rage, and I thought, perhaps unfairly, perhaps not, that my Jewish last name, more than any lack of ordination, led the cleric to redline me away from the pulpit of the Rockefeller church.

The most visible Rockefeller at the time, Nelson, was a friend of Robinson's and a so-called political moderate. Or anyway so-called by the Goldwater crowd in the all-white hard-right wing of the Republican Party. But Nelson the Moderate had immoderate tendencies. He once ordered the destruction of a mural being painted in the main lobby of Rockefeller Center by the great Mexican artist Diego Rivera. The mural favorably depicted such Communists as V. I. Lenin (and also offered a nice portrait of Abraham Lincoln). When Rivera refused to expunge Lenin, Nelson is said to have appeared in the lobby accompanied by armed guards, paid off Rivera, and had him dragged away. Rockefeller's goons then hacked the mural to bits. Nothing, not a fragment, survives. Diego Rivera was indeed a Communist, but Rockefeller knew that when he hired him. I am afraid that, unlike Jackie Robinson, Nelson the Moderate at heart was not an ecumenical man. That he had an extended affair with an Israeli-born beauty does not alter my view. Lust will trump bias every time. Such were my thoughts as I tried to

come to terms with Robinson's death, an adjustment made more difficult by our renewed closeness in the summer of 1972.

He had recently been championing the cause of Latin baseball players and in midseason he agreed to accept an award from an agency of the
Puerto Rican government. The setting would be that great tourist trap
of a restaurant, Mama Leone's, which had become a hangout for sporting types. You walked into a great hall, decorated with virginal, alabaster
nudes, and then settled into a northern Italian, western-Broadway version of a Lucullan orgy, from oversized shrimp lying dormant in a
creamy sauce, through spicy minestrone softened by grated Parmesan
cheese, then on to a huge mix of meats and pasta and winding down
weightily with biscuit tortoni and espresso. "We are eating," some of the
sportswriters said, in those cold war days, "as though the Russians were
in the Bronx and marching south."

Jack asked me to serve as master of ceremonies. When I met him at
an upstairs room, reserved for a preluncheon private party, his eyes
looked startling. The irises were bloodred. The pupils appeared totally
blank. Diabetes had robbed focus from these eyes, which once could
damn near count the stitches on a hundred-mile-an-hour fastball. After
a lifetime in which he neither drank nor smoked, Robinson now was
sipping a screwdriver. "The doctors think whiskey will help my circulation, but I can't stand the taste of the stuff. This"—he indicated his mix-
ture of orange juice and vodka—"tastes less like a drink than anything
else I could find."

A wiry, weathered man approached. Clyde Sukeforth, seventy, the former big-league catcher who scouted Robinson for Branch Rickey years
before, had driven down from his home in Waldoboro, Maine. Sukeforth
liked what he saw in the young Robinson, and the two went on to form
a steadfast friendship. "Jack," I said, "here's Sukey." He blinked, unseeing.
I turned him gently toward Sukeforth, but they were standing nose to
nose before Robinson was able to recognize someone he had known for a
quarter century. Then he smiled and made a pleasant greeting.

After some speeches, the Puerto Rican delegation presented Robinson with a set of golf clubs, some luggage, and certificates good for "an
all-expenses-paid two-week five-star vacation for you and Mrs. Robinson on our island."

"Thank you," Jackie called from his seat at a table some thirty feet from the dais.

"As a final gift to Jackie Robinson," I said, "we are not going to ask him to make a speech."

Later he said, "You were great but you should have let me talk."

"I was concerned about your making it to the dais. It was up some rickety steps. You might have stumbled and fallen down."

Robinson thought briefly. "I guess that's true," said the best base runner I ever saw.

He asked me to visit quite a few times, and I'd find him alone in the big Cascade Road house. We'd drink some coffee and he'd ask me to open and read aloud his mail. One morning I read a notice from a bank in Stamford that said he was two or thee months behind in his mortgage payments. "You know I'm having a pretty good stretch," I said. "Can I help you out?"

"No," he said, quickly, firmly. "I've always made money and I always will."

A few days later a television producer optioned documentary rights to *The Boys of Summer* and included in the package permission fees of $5,000 to each of the six ballplayers whose stories he intended to use. Robinson signed cheerfully. He was on the telephone again soon afterward. "I know this documentary means more to you than just a fee," he said, "because it will sell a lot more books. I don't want to mess that up. But can I have your permission to ask for more than $5,000?"

"Sure. I imagine you can get more than the other fellers."

"I don't want that," Robinson said. "I want to ask for more money for the others, too. We were teammates. We all should get the same. I just want your okay to ask for more for everybody."

I told Jack I thought that was damn decent. The producer, less impressed, turned him down. Robinson, uncomplaining, went along with the original deal on a *Boys of Summer* documentary: $5,000 for one and all. (That documentary never was made, largely because the producer's marriage disintegrated. He informed me he was putting *The Boys of Summer* on hold so he could shoot another "even more important" documentary which he intended to call *Divorce Around the World*. If that show ever played the networks, I missed it.)

Within days of Robinson's death, I received a registered letter from a white-glove New York law firm, The lawyers were representing Rachel Robinson, and the letter rescinded permission for me to use Robinson's story in the documentary. The tone was imperious, even threatening, and since I was not producing, directing, or writing the proposed documentary, the letter seemed misdirected.

But I understand that emotions run strong for those we loved who are gone, and I have no intention of criticizing the character, integrity, or courage of Rachel Isum Robinson, a woman who heroically endured racial prejudice and who lost both her firstborn son and her husband within a period of sixteen months.

Joan Hodges, Gil Hodges's widow, recalls a day in spring training when Jackie Robinson approached her in Dodgertown, the team's base in Vero Beach, Florida, and mentioned that Rachel felt ill. The Dodgers had a road game scheduled, and Jack asked Joan Hodges if she would look after Rachel while he was away. A warmhearted Italian girl from Brooklyn, Joan ministered to Rachel for several days. "Would you believe," Joan says, "that some of the other Dodger wives were critical of me? They didn't believe it was right for a white woman to look after a lady who was black."

Rachel herself mentions a traumatic Florida episode of her own. Dodgertown was organized as a self-contained base; beyond the practice fields, sliding pits, and pitching machines, there were tennis courts, a golf course, a swimming pool, and a formal dining room for team executives and sportswriters in which tuxedoed black waiters served splendid dinners. But it was predominantly a men's club. There was no beauty parlor on the grounds, and when Rachel wanted to have her hair done, she discovered that no hair stylist in all-white Vero Beach would accommodate a black woman. Just north of Vero lay a ramshackle black community called Gifford, which is where Rachel had to go to be coiffed. She called for a taxi. No Vero Beach cab would carry a black. "So," she says, "I walked the seven miles to Gifford with little Jackie, who was still quite small, beside me." Then Rachel had to walk back. Finally, on the long road leading from downtown Vero Beach to Dodgertown, a jitney stopped. It was carrying the black waiters who would work the dinner shift. "That's how Little Jack and I finally returned," she says, "riding in this little bus with the waiters. A lot of cars with white drivers had passed us on the road. None of them offered us a lift."

Robinson had Branch Rickey, and then Pee Wee Reese, during his ordeal, and, for part of the time anyway, he had me. Across long periods—when the Dodgers were on the road—Rachel was alone, except for her children, who were small. That she sustained herself as well as she did is remarkable.

The Jackie Robinson I remember was fierce and tender, full of energy and passion, gentle with children, somewhat paranoid with white adults, tight with a dollar, and a man who grew intellectually every year of his brief life. He'd had some education when he exploded into the apartheid world of major-league baseball, but he was neither very sophisticated nor particularly cultured. The child of a vagrant father and a devout, churchgoing domestic worker, who almost always voted Republican because the Emancipator had been Republican, Robinson remained a Republican all his life, preferring Eisenhower to Stevenson, Nixon to Kennedy, and emphatically, near the close of his life, Nixon to McGovern.

The appearance of a black athlete on a big-league field seemed radical to many Americans in 1947, when the major leagues had been all-white for sixty-three seasons. Robinson's play—the exuberant baserunning (nineteen steals of home), the clutch line drives, the bunts timed and placed perfectly, and his combative ways with rivals, umpires, and sportswriters also suggested from afar a radical nature. But close-up Robinson was decidedly, in Robert Frost's phrase, an institutional man.

It is difficult for many young people in the twenty-first century to imagine a time when the major-league and the minor-league playing fields were closed to blacks, from the triple-tiered eminence of Yankee Stadium down to the last wooden bush-league ballpark that lay hard by the little community of Oblivion, U.S.A. Moses "Fleet" Walker and his brother Welday were blacks who played for Toledo of the then big-league American Association in 1884. In 1885 their contracts were not renewed. Supposedly, the leader of the racist movement in baseball was Adrian Constantine "Cap" Anson from Marshalltown, Iowa, an intimidating six-footer who played first base for the Chicago Cubs and managed the team from 1879 through 1897. He once batted .399, and the teams he managed won five pennants. This most vociferous of baseball's racists was elected to the Hall of Fame in 1939 by the Baseball Writers Association of America, an organization of newspaper sportswriters that has an exclusive on the voting rights. There is no record of his racism troubling voters.

Anson's harsh views were hardly unique; early baseball was a cauldron of bigotry. John McGraw, the noted early manager of the New York Giants, denigrated Latin players as "a bunch of coffee-colored Cubans." In his book *Pitching in a Pinch,* Christy Mathewson, a college man and a devout Christian, referred to Chicago catcher Johnny Kling as "the Jew." (Recently found records indicate that Kling actually was a Lutheran.)

Ring Lardner was a fine journalist whose gifts crested in short stories. In the issue dated July 31, 1915, *The Saturday Evening Post* published his wondrous fable "Alibi Ike." Here, as was his wont, Lardner uses as narrator a fictive big-league ballplayer who is an oaf, not like you or me, of course, but somewhat reminiscent of the man next door. When the story begins, the oaf is talking:

"His right name was Francis X. Farrell and I guess the X stood for 'Excuse me.' Because he never pulled a play, good or bad, on or off the field without apologizin' for it.

"'Alibi Ike' was the name Carey wished on him the first day he reported down South. Of course we all cut the 'Alibi' part of it right away.

"He ast me one time, he says:

"'Why do you all call me Ike for? I ain't no Yid.'"

That quickly Lardner shoves us face forward against the boorishness, bigotry, and vulgarity that have been as much a part of big-league baseball as the double play. Virginia Woolf, not to my knowledge a hardball fan, commented that Ring Lardner's stories let us "gaze into the depths of a society."

Certainly the American press, as much as organized baseball, was mired in the depths of racism. Major newspapers accepted monochromatic baseball as the way things were, while practicing a similar apartheid in their own hiring policies. No mainstream New York newspaper employed a black sportswriter until 1959, twelve years after Robinson's Brooklyn debut. Then the *Times* hired Bob Teague. Even the Yankees, who resisted integration, had signed a black player, Elston Howard, four years earlier. Those few blacks, from the so-called Negro newspapers, who did make their way into press boxes were restricted to the rear row. Back of the bus, back of the press box. They also were subjected to ridicule. One black reporter (for a black New York newspaper) had a prominent forehead. Some of my press-box colleagues made fun of him. They called him Abner Doubledome.

A leading exception to the historic editorial passivity on racism was commentary in *The Daily Worker,* the official newspaper of the Communist Party of the United States. Lester Rodney started a sports section in the *Worker* in 1936. (We spoke in the spring of 2005; at the age of ninety-four Rodney remained vigorous and an enthusiastic tennis player.)

"It's amazing," he said, "that you didn't find one word in the great papers of the time about the great pastime not allowing people in because of the pigment of their skin. Our goal in the sports section of the *Worker* was immediately to tell the baseball brass that there were black players who were of big-league star caliber." Specifically, the *Worker* mentioned the storied pitcher Satchel Paige and the great slugger and catcher Josh Gibson. "We circulated a petition to the fans," Rodney said. "We asked if they'd be willing to have their teams sign a qualified Negro. We gathered about 1.5 million signatures from people who said yes. Finally I got Leo Durocher to tell me, "Hell, I'd sign some of these guys in a minute if I got the okay from the big shots.""

Awkward though the ideologues of the religious right may find it today, and perhaps some centrists as well, the Communist Party was a leader in focusing attention on the bigotry of organized baseball. Indeed, the sports section of *The Daily Worker* did a better job of exposing intolerance than did the *New York Post* or *The New York Times.*

My idealized press, or media, would not simply report but lead in enlightened ways. Fortunately, I early encountered one leader, of indeterminate politics, who was impassioned and outspoken. My Brooklyn prep school was entirely white, which of course led to an all-white boys' baseball varsity. The other prep teams we played also were all-white. That might have seemed, as it did to many, the natural way of things. The ballplayers we played with and against were white; the big-leaguers that we watched and often idolized were white. So were the umpires, the coaches, the managers, the ticket takers, and the men who peddled beer, hot dogs, and scorecards. But just about the time I started secondary school in 1940, I began listening to a weekly radio sports show out of Los Angeles. The broadcaster, Sam Balter, had been a guard on the United States basketball team that won a gold medal in the Berlin Olympics of 1936. This was the same Olympics in which Jackie Robinson's brother, Mack, won a silver medal in the 200-meter dash. (When Balter died at the age of eighty-eight in 1998, obituaries mentioned that the championship basketball game was played outdoors in the rain with a soccer ball. There was no mention of how the Nazis reacted to the outstanding performance of Balter, who was Jewish.)

"The Inside of Sports with Sam Balter" combined news and editorializing. Remarkable for the time, the show consistently challenged baseball's right to advertise itself as the national pastime. Balter explained: "It is not that at all when the rulers of the game deliberately exclude hundreds of qualified athletes solely because of the color of their skin. Baseball will truly be our national pastime *only* when it opens its gates to all Americans—including Negroes!" Balter had a great microphone presence. Under the prodding of his broadcasts I lost my own passivity, ceased to be color-blind and came to know in my bones, long before Robinson arrived in Brooklyn, that baseball's racist policy was dead wrong.

Whenever that rare white newspaperman, Shirley Povich of *The Washington Post* or Dave Egan of the *Boston Record,* raised the issue of baseball segregation, the commissioner, Kenesaw Mountain Landis, offered a ready response: "Negroes are not barred from organized baseball by the commissioner and no rule forbids their entry." This was duplicitous. There was a rule, of course, although unwritten. The late Bill Veeck told me that when he was running the Milwaukee Brewers of the minor-league American Association in 1940, he decided to sign "three or four Negro ballplayers." As soon as word reached Landis's office, the commissioner reacted. "Landis had a simple message for me," Veeck said. "He would invalidate any contract I made with a black player and, for conduct detrimental to the game, he would bar me from organized baseball for the rest of my life." Landis died in 1944. Three years later Veeck, then president of the Cleveland Indians, integrated the American League by signing the outfielder Larry Doby. In another era, 1978, Veeck hired Doby to manage the Chicago White Sox.

It was the prevailing racist climate that made Branch Rickey demand that Robinson not fight bigots with his fists. In an unpublished manuscript that Rachel Robinson donated to the Library of Congress, Robinson writes of one particularly appalling incident. "We were having a card game on a train. High Casey [he of the missed third strike], a Southern-born relief pitcher, startled everyone by declaring, 'Back home, when we used to need some good luck, we'd just reach out and rub an old nigger woman's head.'

"For a moment I sat in the tense silence. Mr. Rickey, I was saying to myself. I'm sorry, Mr. Rickey, but here goes the *real* Jackie Robinson. No red-blooded Negro lets a white man insult him like this.

"The next second I heard the echo of that rumbling voice in Brooklyn. '. . . courage enough *not* to fight back . . .' In a blinding flash which cut though my anger, I saw headlines about a brawl that would give voice to everyone who opposed integration in baseball and humiliation to those who fought for it.

Quietly I told the man holding the cards to deal."

My family and Jackie Robinson first intersected through the radio program *Information, Please,* which my father helped found during the late 1930s. Quiz programs were becoming popular, and *Information, Please* elevated the format to a fairly intellectual level. A erudite master of ceremonies, Clifton Fadiman, a critic and essayist, asked questions of a panel of "experts" that included a renowned columnist, Franklin P. Adams, a classically cultured *New York Times* sportswriter, John Kieran, and the eccentric, acerbic musical vagabond Oscar Levant. The program began with the crow of a rooster and an announcer declaiming: "Wake up, America! It's time to stump the experts!" After introductory comments, Fadiman began asking questions that had been submitted by listeners. If your question was used, you won a modest little prize. If your question actually stumped the experts, you were awarded a complete set of the *Encyclopaedia Britannica.* My father's role was to edit questions and make a final selection of the twelve to fifteen that were used every week.

His job tended to extend into our apartment in the Grand Army Plaza section of Brooklyn and to our summer home upstate. "Can anyone give me," my father would say at dinner, "three lines of poetry containing the word 'light'?"

My mother might offer Milton's "When I consider how my light is spent . . ."

Kidding a bit, I could put in, "Dawn's early . . . Darn, what is the next word, Dad?"

My father enjoyed spicing the dinner quizzes with humor. Here he cited a comment from *The Merchant of Venice*: "A light wife doth make a heavy husband."

We ranged from literature to sports to science to music, leading my mother to tell me one afternoon, "Your father is a typical American. He likes baseball and Beethoven." (I am not certain Mother's view of the typical American was entirely accurate.)

Through each thirty-nine-week radio season a variety of guests signed on so that Fadiman was always addressing the questions to a panel of four. Conversation among the panelists often sparkled. One— unfortunately I forget *which* one—who was appearing while suffering from gum miseries observed, in a wonderful play on *King Lear*, "How sharper than a serpent's child it is to have a thankless tooth."

During the presidential race of 1940, Wendell Willkie, the Republican nominee, used a guest appearance on *Information, Please* as part of his campaign. He was charming and energetic and turned out to be an authority on the Reconstruction Era in the South. The actor Ray Miland, noted for his performance as an alcoholic author in *The Lost Weekend,* had studied hydraulic engineering at Oxford University. Another actor, George Sanders, famously urbane and possessed of an upper-class British accent, was born in Russia and had dreamed of singing opera. Pert Jan Struther, author of the immensely popular wartime English novel *Mrs. Miniver,* charmed the nation and my father with her poise and style. Dorothy Parker, the celebrated Algonquin wit, sounded dour, the result, my father suggested, of a hangover. Politicians, scientists, journalists, ingenues, psychiatrists, novelists, and hustlers all vied for a guest spot on *Information, Please,* which offered half an hour of fame and $1,000. "Our fundamental requirement," my father said, "is intelligence. Wit helps, but intelligence comes first. If a guest isn't smart enough to answer any questions, we end up paying for half an hour of silence."

"I could handle that, Dad," I said. He turned away.

Jackie Robinson was chosen to be a guest expert in 1947 and a few days before the show he appeared for a briefing in my father's office at 444 Madison Avenue. No guest went on the program "cold." During the briefings my father tried to elicit what he called "the guest's other areas of knowledge." He then had questions selected away from the guest's obvious specialty toward another topic in the guest's ken. Miland got a few on hydraulics; Sanders got one or two on opera. No one ever was told the questions in advance. Part of the program's excitement was its spontaneity. But this was show business, not an abstract seminar, and it was important—to the producers and to the ratings—for everyone to talk.

By the time Robinson met my father he had become a celebrity. Before Pearl Harbor he was a crack running back at UCLA. The California sportswriters called him "Lightning Jack." After signing with Branch Rickey, Robinson played the 1946 season with the Montreal Royals in the International League. He stole 40 bases, led the league in runs scored, batted .349, and paced his team to victory in the Little World Series, which matched the winner of the International League pennant against the top team in the American Association. Robinson hit .400 in the Little World Series. Montreal won the seventh game, 2 to 0, the same score by which the Brooklyn Dodgers would win the seventh game of the 1955 World Series. In the family-sanctioned biography *Jackie Robinson,* Professor Arnold Rampersad offers an account of what followed the victory in Montreal:

> Hustling to leave the ball park in time to catch a plane, Jack made the mistake of stepping back onto the field before he could shower and change. Deliriously happy Montreal fans snatched him up in celebration. . . . Hugging and kissing Robinson, slapping him on the back, they carried him on their shoulders in triumph. . . . When Robinson reappeared outside in street clothes, a large part of the crowd was still waiting. They stormed around him. Knowing exactly what he had accomplished over the season, they sang in tribute, *"Il a gagne ses epaulettes"*—He has earned his stripes. In the [Pittsburgh] *Courier* [a prominent black newspaper] Sam Maltin wrote memorably of the astonishing scene. "It was probably the only day in his-

tory in history that a black man ran from a white mob with love instead of lynching on its mind.

Clearly Robinson was accustomed to attention before my father invited him to Madison Avenue in the late spring of 1947. After some baseball talk—Robinson praised the breaking stuff of Boston Braves right-hander Johnny Sain—my father asked about Robinson's interests beyond sports.

"A little history, Mr. Kahn. I've read up quite a bit on Abraham Lincoln."

Asking a pioneering black man questions about Lincoln seemed too obvious, my father thought, and even patronizing. He mentioned that Jack had attended UCLA.

"When I was at UCLA," Robinson said, "in order to keep my scholarship I had to play football, basketball, and baseball and run track. I competed on four varsity teams and I had to practice with four varsity teams. Class work? I got C's and I was lucky to get them."

On the ensuing radio program, Robinson answered parts of three or four questions. As a guest expert he proved acceptable, but no more than that. But he seemed to be, my father reported, "an awfully decent person," and Dad and I made many trips to Ebbets Field to root for the Dodgers, as we always had, and now also to root for Robinson and the cause of integration.

However tense things grew between us, before the halcyon days at the *Herald Tribune,* my father and I could relax together at the ballpark. We felt an immunity there from tension, stress, and even time. No one caught cold at Ebbets Field, or had his telephone service cut off for nonpayment. You didn't worry about midterm exams at the ballpark or how you would like to shape your life. The world was a diamond, green and brown and white, and your entire future was the next inning. No one aged at Ebbets Field; nobody died. The hot dog salesmen never changed. The crowds always looked the same. Identical cops worked there every day. The same children loitered around the green in the middle of a city that was not a city but a borough.

Ebbets Field was a community ballpark, set among apartment houses, frame buildings, and garages. The apartment building where my family lived during the 1940s rose only eight blocks distant, and as my father and I proceeded to a ball game on foot, we walked a bit on Eastern Parkway, the Brooklyn boulevard styled after the Champs Elysées. Then, turning south on Washington Avenue, we could see flags flapping from the roof of the old ballpark, which was not a superdome or a stadium but a ballpark, gray and dun-colored and sooty. There was nothing glossy about the place. If it was too small a home base for what was becoming a dominant major-league team, it also remained marvelously intimate. The other New York City ballparks, Yankee Stadium in the Bronx and the Polo Grounds in upper Manhattan, had vastly greater seating capacity. To some the architecture of Ebbets Field suggested a gross, pretentious warehouse, and every August the grass began to die. Then work crews had to spray the outfield with green paint. There weren't enough seats, and the parking was impossible, and, worst of all, the place had been designed in the days when a baseball possessed all the resiliency of a rolled sock. Later the lively ball would leap from bats, and pitchers working there developed sore arms, Jell-O hearts, shell shock. No one, at least no one sober, ever compared Ebbets Field to the Acropolis. Yet to my father and me (and to Pee Wee Reese and Jackie Robinson) gray, sooty, dun-colored, undersized Ebbets Field was a shrine. None of us actually said that. It would have sounded pompous. We never *had* to say it. We felt it.

When Dad and I saw the flags, we quickened our pace because the flapping flags meant ball game today. Dad knew the game well, if not with the astounding professional expertise I encountered later in Reese and Robinson and Musial and Casey Stengel and Warren Spahn and Leo Mazzone, the great pitching coach. For many years I deferred to Dad's baseball knowledge. After all, he had played college ball and I had not. He told me why a high fastball—"the high, hard one"—is so tough to hit and why a wide, slow-breaking curve—"the roundhouse"—doesn't often work in the big leagues. I learned that outfielders should keep throws low so a cutoff man can intercept them and catch a runner trying for an extra base, and that the corner infielders, at first and third, should shade toward the foul lines whenever a double would be particularly damaging. This was not simplistic Baseball 101, but something like an advanced intermediate course, and enjoyable for both instructor and student.

It seemed that nothing changed over the years at Ebbets Field except,

except that now, in the late 1940s, something had changed—and most visibly. The home team, the Dodgers, wore white, and the players' skins had always been white, and the umpires had always been white, and so had the managers and the coaches and the ground crews who swept the infield, so that at game time no spike marks remained in the dirt. The ticket takers were white men, like the candy butchers and the peddlers of Cracker Jack and sarsparilla, but suddenly here, in 1947, with Hitler and Mussolini newly dead, this big athletic fellow, number 42, out there strutting his stuff on the ball field, was a departure. Jackie Robinson was a very dark-skinned black man. There was nothing uncertain in his shade. The color was uncompromising ebony. Looking at his black, muscled arms coming out of the home-white shirt sleeves, taking that in jolted your consciousness and made you realize, in a shocking instant, and long afterward, that all the baseball heroes who had gone before, Ruth and Cobb, Mathewson and Gehrig, Walter Johnson and Dizzy Dean and Hank Greenberg, had been white men. Robinson's color brought you to a stop. Had his color been lighter, the impact of his presence would have been less.

The character of Robinson's play was like nothing else anyone had seen, at least since the high times of Ty Cobb. In fact "Bojangles" Bill Robinson, the great black dancer, called Jack "Ty Cobb in Technicolor." Branch Rickey said, "The single word I use to describe Jackie is adventure. The man is all adventure on a ball field." Robinson was powerful, of course, but not naturally a home-run hitter. He held the bat high, motionless and high, and when the pitch came in, he swung down on the ball. This gave his drives a backspin that made the line drives climb the air 350 feet away. "Catching those drives," an outfielder said, "is like trying to catch a 3-iron shot in golf. The damn ball keeps climbing away from you." Robinson walked in a pigeon-toed gait, which gave no hint of his bursting speed, any more than stolen-base figures suggest his prowess as a base runner. Robinson never stole more than thirty-seven bases in a season, but he knew when to steal, when to threaten to steal, how to take extravagant leads, in short, how throughly to distract an opposing pitcher. These many years later, Jackie Robinson remains the most exciting ballplayer I've ever seen. Not the best—that was Willie Mays—but the most exciting.

Tim McCarver, a good catcher turned excellent commentator, once asked me about the difference, which I summarized briefly. Willie had the greatest arm and speed and power, the most remarkable offensive and defensive skills, I've seen in any individual, but the most exciting single play in baseball was this: Jackie Robinson caught in a rundown.

My father tried to conceal his rooting at Ebbets Field, but with the coming of Robinson a new urgency took over Dad's ballpark style. When hard-eyed pitchers threw fastballs into Robinson's body and at his head, I heard my father say more than once, "Oh, Jesus Christ." (He seldom invoked divinities and never cursed.) I picked up his outrage at what white pitchers were trying to do to this "awfully decent fellow." They wanted to maim him, and if that failed, to terrorize him. As a rookie, he was hit by pitches nine times, the second highest total in the league. For someone with Robinson's agility, being hit that often suggests the withering fire of baseballs that pitchers aimed at his person. But the Robinson story transcended terror. It became a triumph.

I particularly remember one 1949 night that matched the Dodgers against the Philadelphia Phillies, a strong club (which a year later would become the last all-white, no-Latino team to win a National League pennant). I'd gotten good tickets through the sports department at the *Trib,* and as my father and I sat close to the field, between third base and home plate, we saw a well-played game that was tied, 2 to 2, going into the last half of the eighth inning. I don't recall the sequence of hits against the Phils' starter, Russ "the Mad Monk" Meyer, but suddenly there was Robinson, the tie-breaking run, caught in no-man's land between third base and home plate. The Phillies' big catcher, Andy Seminick, had the ball and began running Robinson back toward third. Jack was too fast for him. Seminick flipped the ball to third baseman Willie "Puddin' Head" Jones. Robinson stopped dead and started back toward home. Rundowns end quickly for ordinary ballplayers. A throw or two, a little fast footwork, and the victim, often embarrassed, is retired. But with Robinson every rundown became, in Rickey's term, an adventure. Sensing a crisis, the Phillies flocked toward the third-base line. The shortstop, Granny Hamner, came over, and the second baseman, Mike Goliat. Del Ennis moved in from left field. Richie Ashburn raced to the scene from center. The ball moved briskly back and forth, but the lone figure in white, with the muscular black arms, always stayed a few steps away.

The Phils were throwing the baseball to one another without getting any closer to tagging Robinson, and crowd noise rose with the excitement. At length the pitcher, Russ Meyer, stationed himself in front of home plate, as guardian of last resort. After forty breathless seconds and six throws, the gap still had not closed. Then a throw toward third went wild, and Robinson made a final victorious run at home plate. As the ball rolled toward the left-field corner, Meyer dropped to his knees and threw both arms around Robinson's stout legs. Robinson bounced a hip off Meyer's head and came home running backward, saying, "What the hell are you trying to do?"

"Under the stands, Robinson," Meyer said.

"Right now," Robinson cried in his combative tenor.

Police beat them to the proposed ring. "A good thing for Meyer," Pee Wee Reese told me. "If they'd actually started punching, Jack might have killed him."

In that long-ago ballpark, two rites of passage were at play. As I became a baseball writer, I gained entry through the portals of major-league ball. I met Reese and Robinson and Stengel and Ty Cobb and Warren Spahn. I heard their stories. I began to learn advanced nuances of the game the major-leaguers played. A tiring pitcher may first show fatigue by going "wild high," missing with pitches above the strike zone. A prudent baserunner grabs a fistful of dirt as he leads off first and holds on. Making a fist protects a sliding runner's fingers from fielders' spikes. Charlie Dressen, the Dodger manager, taught me how to throw a spitball. Use a fastball motion, and as you release the pitch, squeeze along the wet spot, as you would squeeze a watermelon seed at a raucous backyard picnic. Preacher Roe, whose record across three Brooklyn seasons was 44 and 7, a winning percentage of .863, showed me different grips and wrist movements for curves and sliders. Beyond such newfound knowledge, a modest celebrity went with my job. The ticket takers and the ushers at the ballparks came to know me. A small card indicating that I was a member of the Baseball Writers Association of America opened doors. I never lorded my new ballpark eminence over my father, but it was there. We both knew that it was there. Once he had taken me to games. Now I took my father.

Robinson's rite of passage proceeded on a grander scale. He broke in at first base, an unfamiliar position. He had trouble with the footwork that playing first demands and more trouble with a few batters who tried to plant their spikes in his Achilles' tendon as they crossed first base. One, stumpy Enos Slaughter of the St. Louis Cardinals, drew blood one day in May but missed the tendon. After Stan Musial followed with a single, Robinson said, "I'd like to punch out that fucking Slaughter."

Leading off first, Musial said, "I wouldn't blame you if you did." The Cardinals' first-base coach relayed this conversation to Slaughter. He and Musial never were close after that, and Slaughter began telling sportswriters that Musial was a choke-up ballplayer (who somehow among his chokes managed to lead the league in hitting six times).

As a rookie Robinson batted .297, scored 125 runs, and led the National League with 29 stolen bases. All this amid storms of abuse. At that time, there was only one award for rookie of the year, which covered both major leagues. Thirty-nine newspapermen, from the ten cities and one borough with big-league franchises, made the choice. Almost all beat back the old prejudices. The 1947 Major League Rookie of the Year was Jack Roosevelt Robinson.

He didn't smoke. He didn't drink until the end. But he always loved to eat; rich meals abrim with sugars, starches, cholesterol. His attack on a wedge of apple pie, topped with two stout scoops of vanilla ice cream, was an exercise in passion. For spring training 1948, he showed up in the Dominican Republic at 210, a full twenty-five pounds above his best playing weight. As the black journalist Carl Rowan observed, "Jackie's friends fed him until he was fat and futile."

Rickey was disappointed, a fact he registered by putting Robinson on the waiver list. Any National League team could claim Robinson's contract for $10,000 unless Rickey withdrew Robinson's name from the list within twenty-four hours of the claim. Nobody, not one of the seven other ball clubs in the National League, bothered to claim the great Jackie Robinson. Leo Durocher raged. "That colored son of a bitch got in shape for Shotton, who was nothing. (Burt Shotton, a crony of Rickey's, managed the Dodgers in 1947 after Albert B. "Happy" Chandler, Landis's successor as commissioner of baseball, suspended Durocher for "conduct detrimental to the game.") "I'm the main man," Durocher announced. "I knocked down the petition when those stupid white guys didn't want to play with him. And how does he thank me? He shows up to play for me looking like a tub of lard."

Durocher ordered Robinson into a tan rubber shirt that covered the entire upper body and arms. He stationed Robinson between first and second base and hit ground balls to Robinson's right and left. The temperature on the Caribbean field approached a hundred degrees. Durocher ran Robinson back and forth, barking constantly: "Move, Robinson. Move!"

Whoosh. A grass-cutting hopper to Robinson's left.

Whoosh. A grass-cutter to the right.

Durocher's klaxon voice kept bawling, "Move it, fat boy. Move it." By the time the Dodgers broke camp in Santo Domingo, Robinson had lost fifteen pounds. He remained ten pounds overweight, and he and Durocher were locked into a blood feud that lasted for six years.

A small, quiet sportswriter named Gus Steiger recounted the Durocher-Robinson struggle and took the manager's side. "It's the player's responsibility," Steiger wrote in the New York *Daily Mirror,* "to get in shape and stay in shape." After Robinson heard about the story, he strode up to Steiger near the batting cage and called him "a no-good, fucking bigot." Steiger paled and retreated.

"Jack," Pee Wee Reese said, sharply. "You had no right doing that. Maybe you didn't like what Gus wrote, but you had no business calling him a bigot. I'm the captain of this team. I want you to apologize." Robinson blinked and held his tongue. A day later he apologized to Steiger." It's all right, Jack," Steiger said. "I know you're under pressure. Sometimes a feller has to blow off steam."

Rickey sent the fine second baseman Eddie Stanky to the Boston Braves in March so that Robinson could be moved off first base in his second season to a position where his quickness and remarkable reflexes could be put to better use. Stanky told sportswriters he had given "all my guts" to the Dodgers and that Rickey "has just stabbed me in the back." He then bottled his rage, batted .320 and helped the Braves win the 1948 pennant. Robinson hit .296, and the Dodgers finished third. But '48 was a successful transitional year. On August 24 at Forbes Field in Pittsburgh Robinson showed an increased sense of comfort in his surroundings. An umpire named Walter J. "Butch" Henline called a questionable strike on the Dodger outfielder Gene Hermanski. The Brooklyn bench yapped at Henline and continued jeering after a warning to stop. Suddenly Henline whirled, ripped off his mask, and shouted, "You! Robinson! You're out of this game!" Robinson said afterward, "That made me feel great. Henline didn't throw me out because I was black. He threw me out because I was getting on his nerves. It was wonderful to be treated like any other ballplayer."

In 1949, just two seasons after Robinson's Brooklyn debut, four blacks appeared in the Major-League All-Star Game, which was played at Ebbets Field. These were Robinson, Roy Campanella, and Don Newcombe of the Dodgers, and Larry Doby of the Cleveland Indians. As it happened, Newcombe, after yielding a two-run homer to Stan Musial, became the losing pitcher. (The first non-white, non-Anglo All-Star winner was Juan Marichal of the Dominican Republic, who was credited with the National League victory in 1964.) The black All-Stars of '49 made an emphatic point just by their presence. Some of the best baseball players in the two toughest leagues on earth now, finally, were black Americans.

It was during 1949 that Robinson made his first public foray into politics. Out front, pages ahead of the sports sections, headlines bannered the Great American Red Scare. "The scare had been unsettling the country for some time," my father wrote in the *Information, Please Almanac,* where he was serving on the editorial board. "Back in 1939, Martin Dies, a Texas Democrat, threw suspicion on little Shirley Temple, who was eleven. Her hair was blond; maybe her politics were Red! Now ten years later it became a favorite sport for eager-eyed legislators to hunt for Communists in government, schools, movies, even the clergy.

"Bigger Red Scares were developing abroad. In September of 1949, a fourteen-word White House announcement broke the news that Russia had exploded an atomic bomb.

"The 'secret' was no longer ours."

Some who confuse baseball with Shangri-La assert that the game transcends politics. It did not in the tortured summer of 1949.

Across an epic life, Paul Robeson was a Phi Beta Kappa scholar, an

All-American end, a lawyer, an actor, a singer, and an orator of unforgettable power. During the 1930s he came to admire the socialist ideal and later the Soviet Union. He told an interviewer that Soviet Russia "was entirely free of racial prejudice and Afro-American spiritual music resonates to Russian folk traditions. In the Soviet Union for the first time in my life I walk in full human dignity." He regarded pogroms as part of a dismal czarist past, not the present, and did not see—few did—the anti-Semitism lurking within the murderous mind of Josef Stalin. Robeson is said to have felt that American blacks as descendants of slaves had a common culture with Russian workers as descendants of serfs. Whatever, Big Paul, who spoke no fewer than twenty languages, was a native American radical, strong, sensitive, outspoken, headstrong, and—as described to this day by some Harlem old-timers—"the tallest tree in the forest."

A few weeks before Christmas, 1943, Robeson and several black newspaper publishers presented themselves at the winter meetings of the sixteen men who owned major-league ball clubs. Robeson was starring on Broadway in an acclaimed performance of *Othello,* and his prestige was such that he was permitted to address the owners and Commissioner Landis. "I come here," he said in his matchless basso, "as an American and as a former athlete. I come because I feel deeply." He spoke first to the theme of disturbances—riots in the stands—which some argued would follow baseball integration. He had played football at Rutgers, three varsity seasons of integrated games. There were no disturbances. Now on Broadway he was Othello, a Negro protagonist who eight times a week strangled a white heroine, Desdemona, played by the beautiful, young Uta Hagen. This grim conclusion led to tears, but no disturbances. Robeson's voice rose in passion, "Although Negroes are confronted in far too many American places with random Hitleresque howls of 'white supremacy,' Negro soldiers are giving their blood and sometimes their lives in far-off continents and on distant seas for red, white, and blue supremacy. It would be a fine thing, would it not, to give these selfsame Negro soldiers, and every other Negro who was good enough, a chance to play baseball in the major leagues?"

When Robeson finished, the barons of baseball erupted in applause. But that was all they did. Following the meetings they continued to cling to their racism. Four years later, shortly after Robinson joined the Dodgers, Robeson attended a small reception and promised Robinson whatever support he could provide. Robinson thanked Robeson and moved on. By 1949, with red-baiting poisoning the air, Robeson took certain positions that seemed extreme. How extreme? It is difficult to say at this juncture because both the *Herald Tribune* and the *Times* are suspect as contemporary sources. Even that dogged *Times* defender, Arthur Gelb, concedes in his memoir, *City Room,* that the paper's conduct during "the early period of congressional sleuthing [looking for Reds] was not one of which the *Times* could be proud." Arthur Hays Sulzberger, the publisher, ordered *Times* staffers accused of having had Communist connections to answer whatever questions congressional investigators might pose. Anyone exercising his constitutional right and taking the Fifth Amendment would be fired. During these red-scare days, which Lillian Hellman called "scoundrel time," a dominant emotion at *The New York Times* was fear.

It follows then that what the *Times* printed on the Great Red Scare was slanted, if not by the individual correspondent, then by the various editors who handled his copy as it made its way into print. Across several heated days in June, the *Times* reported that Robeson had said that should war break out between the Soviet Union and the United States, American blacks would refuse to fight. Then the paper used a direct quote, which Robeson later maintained was doctored into inaccuracy: "I love the Negro people from whom I spring in the way that I intensely love the Soviet Union. We do not want to die in vain anymore on foreign battlefields for Wall Street and the greedy supporters of domestic fascism. If we must die, let it be in Mississippi or Georgia. Let it be where we are being lynched." The *Times* topped its story, which ran on June 20, 1949, with a shrill headline: "Loves Soviet Best, Robeson Declares." Subsequently each of the thirty-seven newspapers owned by Citizen William Randolph Hearst published an editorial titled "AN UNDESIRABLE CITIZEN." The Hearst papers declared: "It was an accident unfortunate for America that Paul Robeson was born here."

The furore grabbed the attention of a congressman named John S. Wood, from the then rigidly segregated state of Georgia. Wood, chairman of the House Un-American Activities Committee, announced

that he would hold special hearings on "the loyalty of American Negroes." The committee intended, he said, to provide "a forum for
members of the colored race to express views contrary to the views of
Paul Robeson." Wood then dispatched a telegram inviting Jackie
Robinson to testify.

This was not a subpoena, but the request was weighty. Robinson,
who had not yet achieved political sophistication, felt conflicted. He
talked with Rachel in the modest brick home they had purchased in the
St. Albans section of Queens, a newly black and relatively upscale neighborhood. If he declined to testify, Robinson said, he could stand accused
of agreeing with Robeson's radical positions. On the other hand, the
idea of speaking out against Robeson made him uncomfortable. He
knew at least some of Robeson's accomplishments. "Then I found out
this congressman, Wood, was from the state of Georgia," he later told
me, "and I thought, *Just forget the whole fucking thing.* You remember I was
born in Georgia, and I knew one thing about the place. My mother got
out of there as quick as she could." At length Robinson decided to take
the matter to someone who was increasingly becoming his father figure,
the Mahatma of baseball.

In a highly emotional meeting, Rickey told Robinson that it was an
honor to testify in the Congress of the United States. This was wonderful opportunity to speak out beyond the world of baseball. Some might
oppose Jack's testifying. Such men might well be secret Communists
themselves.

"I'm not sure, Mr. Rickey. I'm not a politician. I'm not a speech-
maker. You know. I'm a ballplayer."

"And an uncommonly fine one," Rickey cried. "Don't worry about
the speech. The congressmen expect a prepared statement, of course.
Don't worry about that. I know you pretty well. I'll write the statement."
Rickey enlisted Harold Parrott and Arthur Mann, two former newspapermen who worked for him, and the three of them, Rickey told me, "got
nowhere. I came to realize that it was a bit presumptuous to believe that I
as a white could speak for a Negro, particularly on so momentous a topic
as national loyalty."

More meetings followed, and Robinson expressed continuing
doubts. Some congressman leaked the news about Wood's plan to have

Robinson appear. Scores of letters came to Robinson at Ebbets Field. Several urged him "not be a tool of witch-hunters." Finally Rickey met Robinson in his office at 215 Montague Street in downtown Brooklyn and summoned up his great oratorical skills. "The overriding issue here," he began, "is how best can an enlightened Negro right the glaring wrongs in America?

"To say, as Mr. Robeson has, that Negroes everywhere are waiting to betray Americans in mortal combat with the godless Reds?

"To suggest, as Mr. Robeson suggests, that the only hope for freedom American Negroes possess is a bloody Red revolution?

"Your triumphs on the ball field give the lie to that.

"Speaking responsibly to the Congress of the United States can be your greatest triumph of all. It will forever establish the Negro's place in baseball and all America."

Rickey paused and puffed his cigar. He blew a thundercloud of smoke. "I'll testify," said Jackie Robinson.

Rickey brought in Lester B. Granger, executive director of the National Urban League, the most conservative of major black organizations, and Granger and Robinson put together this statement, which Robinson delivered in a crowded hearing room on Monday, July 18.

It isn't very pleasant to find myself in the middle of a public argument that has nothing to do with the standing of the Dodgers in the pennant race or even the pay raise I'm going to ask Mr. Branch Rickey for next year. [Laughter.] . . .

I don't pretend to be an expert on communism or any other "ism." . . . But put me down as an expert on being a colored American with thirty years' experience at it.

Like any other colored person with sense enough to look around, I know that life in these United States can be tough for people who are a little different from the majority in their skin color or the way they worship. . . .

I'm not fooled because I've had a chance. . . . I'm proud that I've made good on my assignment to the point where other colored players will find it easier to enter the game. But I'm well aware that even this limited job isn't finished yet. . . .

The white public should start appreciating that every single Negro worth his salt resents slurs and discrimination. That has absolutely nothing to do with what Communists may or may not be trying to do. . . .

If a Communist denounces injustice in American courts, or police brutality, or lynching, that doesn't change the truth. . . . A lot of people try to pretend that the issue [of discrimination] is a creation of Communist imaginations. . . . But Negroes were stirred up long before there was a Communist Party and they'll stay stirred up long after the party has disappeared. . . .

I've been asked to express my views on Mr. Paul Robeson's statement to the effect that American Negroes would refuse to fight in any war against Russia. The statement, if Mr. Robeson actually made it, sounds silly to me. But he has a right to his personal views and if he wants to sound silly when he expresses them in public, that's his business not mine.

There are some colored pacifists and they'd act like pacifists of any color. Most Negroes and Irish and Jews and Swedes and Slavs and other Americans would do their best to keep their country out of war; if unsuccessful, they'd do their best to help their country win, against Russia or any other enemy.

The public is off on the wrong foot when it begins to think of radicalism in terms of any special minority group. Thinking of this sort gets people scared because one Negro threatens an organized boycott by 15 million members of his race.

I can't speak for 15 million, but I've got too much invested for my wife, my child and myself in the future of this country to throw it away because of a siren song sung in bass. . . .

That doesn't mean we're going to stop fighting race discrimination. It means we're going to fight it all the harder. . . .

We can win our fight without Communists and we don't want their help.

Robinson put down his papers. Someone shouted, "Amen!" There followed tumultuous applause.

Robinson flew back to LaGuardia Airport in time to make that night's Dodger game against the Cubs at Ebbets Field. He delivered a bravura performance. With one out in the sixth inning he drew a walk from Bob Rush, a six-foot four-inch right-hander who threw hard. He stole second and went to third when Mickey Owen—the infamous Dodger catcher of 1941 now working out of Chicago—threw the ball into center field. Robinson took a great lead off third and bluffed breaking for the plate. With one out, the percentages demanded that he stay on the base. A fly ball or a grounder would score the run. But Robinson was not only adventure on the ball field, he was surprise. As Rush went into his high-kicking windup, Robinson charged home. Rush saw him go and hurried his pitch. The fastball sailed over Owen's head. Robinson had stolen two bases in the inning; he'd stolen home. Finally, in the eighth inning, he tripled, driving in Brooklyn's third run. The Dodgers defeated the Cubs, 3 to 0, increasing their lead over the second-place Cardinals to three-and-a-half games. Robinson had manufactured two of the runs. That night he was batting .363 and leading the National League in hits, runs, runs batted in, and stolen bases. He felt chipper enough to deal lightly with the press. "I guess public speaking agrees with me," he said.

But in the corridor of time, that day, June 18, 1949, came to weigh heavily on Robinson. When Paul Robeson later spoke before Congress, a politician asked why he hadn't simply moved to Russia and stayed there. "Because my father was a slave," Robeson said, "and my people died to build this country. I am going to stay right here and have a part of it just like you. And no fascist-minded people will drive me from it. Is that clear?" During the late 1940s, under pressure from the increasingly rabid right, concert managers blacklisted—or should the term be "white-listed"?—Robeson. His income shriveled. He was still welcome to sing throughout most of the world, but in 1950 the Department of State revoked his passport, alleging that his traveling abroad was not in the best interests of America. Thus the right to work was taken from him. Although he had committed no crime, essentially he was kept under house arrest in the United States. Enforced silence marked Robeson's elder years. Eventually he grew depressed and suicidal. It was not lost on everyone that Jackie Robinson had been used by right-wing America to launch the assault on Robeson. It was not lost on Robinson, either. Jack burned with a ferocious honesty. In our last conversation, a week or so before his death, Robinson spoke at length about the Robeson episode. As I listened to his voice, I heard agony.

By the time I came to cover the Dodgers in 1952, Robinson had established himself as a premier ballplayer. In 1949 he was close to the top in hits (203), runs batted in (124), runs scored (125, in a 154-game season), triples (12), doubles (38). He led the National League in batting at .342 and stolen bases with 37. Segregation persisted, notably in Cincinnati and St. Louis, leading Dick Young, the mordant baseball writer with the New York *Daily News* to remark, "Robinson leads the league in everything but hotel reservations." After that season, he was chosen Most Valuable Player. The next year he hit .328, second to Stan Musial. Late in 1951 he played what was probably his most sensational single game.

The Dodger lead over the second-place Giants had reached 13½ games during an August doubleheader. That summer I first traveled to the leafy paths of Bread Loaf, where, in Alfred Kazin's phase, writing was everything. Enraptured by the climate of the place and the presence of Robert Frost, and a little weary of daily journalism, I didn't read a newspaper or listen to a radio for two weeks. Driving home in my blue Ford Tudor—it was a *two-door* sedan—I stopped in Millerton, New York, and bought a *Herald Tribune*. It shocked me to see that the Dodgers now led the Giants by only five games. Writing, it seemed, was almost everything. Baseball mattered, too.

In the late days of that season, the Dodgers played inconsistent ball, while the Giants, driving across the stretch, won 37 of their 44 games, a winning percentage of .841. Although the weather was getting cooler, sportswriters described the Giants' play as "torrid."

On September 30, the last day of the regular season, the Giants defeated the Braves in Boston and, with the Dodgers still playing in Philadelphia, took a half-game lead. At Shibe Park Robinson's triple drove in the first Dodger run, but the Phils moved ahead, 6 to 1. Brooklyn battled back and the teams went into extra innings, tied at 8. Robin Roberts, the Phillies' durable ace, came in to relieve. The Dodgers used four pitchers, finally turning to Don Newcombe, who had pitched a shutout the night before. With the bases loaded and two out in the bottom of the twelfth, Eddie Waitkus lashed a line drive just to the right of second base. Waitkus was a left-handed hitter; Robinson had been playing him to pull. Red Smith described what happened next in the *Trib:* "The ball is a blur passing second base, difficult to follow in the half-light, impossible to catch. Jackie Robinson catches it. He flings himself headlong at right angles to the flight of the ball, for an instant his body is suspended in midair, then somehow the outstretched glove intercepts the ball inches off the ground." Smith never forgot Robinson "stretched at full length in the insubstantial twilight, the unconquerable doing the impossible." (For the record, Robin Roberts told me in the summer of 2005 that Robinson did *not* catch the ball. "I was right there," Robert said. "He trapped it [caught the ball on one bounce]." If Roberts is correct and Smith was wrong, Jack deserves an Academy Award for Best Performance by a Leading Man.)

Two innings later, in the fourteenth, Robinson straightened out a Roberts curveball and hit a towering home run to left. That was the margin of the Dodgers' 9-to-8 victory. I wonder if a more exciting baseball game has ever been played. "Just goes to show ya," announced peppery Irving Rudd, "If a game lasts long enough, Jackie Robinson will win it for ya." The regular season was done; the Dodgers and Giants were tied for first place.

On a cool, gray day, October 3, Bobby Thomson's famous home run won the three-game play-off and the 1951 pennant for the Giants. Robinson, Red Smith's unconquerable, distinguished himself even in defeat. As Thomson circled the bases jogging and leaping, Robinson held his defensive position, not joining his teammates' dejected walk to the Polo Grounds clubhouse. He was making sure that Thomson actually touched each base. Then, while Branca, who had thrown the most famous home-run ball in the annals, wept and called for a priest, Robinson dressed quickly. He entered the winning dressing room and mustered a smile, and he congratulated the Giants one after another, Sal Maglie, Bobby Thomson, Willie Mays, and even his brass-lunged adversary, Manager Leo Durocher.

When I walked into the Dodger clubhouse in March 1952—the team had been playing exhibition games in Miami—Robinson was saying loudly, "It wasn't a heart attack. It was just a pulled muscle near the rib cage." He was thirty-three, middle-aged for a ballplayer, and sudden chest pains had given him a scare.

"I'm glad you're all right," I said.

"Thanks."

"I'm, uh, going to be covering the team for the *Trib*."

"That's good," Robinson said. "We can use some better coverage than we've been getting." He said that loudly also; a few older newspapermen stood nearby. He not only refused to bend the knee and flatter the press, he seemed to challenge reporters to like him. I was wondering if he remembered me from our brief encounter in Philadelphia the previous autumn. Apparently he did. "Can we get together for a talk about some things?" I said, a little lamely.

"What things?"

"Integration."

"Have you ever been to a colored hotel?" Robinson said. We settled on a date a few weeks off.

The Dodgers left Vero Beach for exhibition games in Miami and roomed at a comfortable place, the McAllister, on Biscayne Boulevard, overlooking a park with walkways shaded from the Florida sun by stands of palm. The McAllister was open only to whites. The Dodgers booked their black ballplayers—Robinson, Campanella, and Joe Black—into a motel in northen Miami Beach called the Sir John. (Don Newcombe had been drafted into the army and would miss the following two seasons.) The Sir John was situated on the ocean, which didn't matter much to Robinson, who, for all his heroics in so many sports, never learned to swim.

The early-evening scene I found at the Sir John Motel was dreamlike. The building rose a two-story rectangle around a large pool and a wide concrete deck. In dim light thrown out by Chinese lanterns casually dressed people sat about on lounges. The men were mostly musicians who worked in the house bands of Miami Beach resort hotels, white vacationers only, situated a few miles south. The few women looked attractive. There were no children. All around me people were sipping tropical drinks. Nearby a saxophone player ran off jazz riffs. Everyone except me was black.

Robinson, wearing slacks and a dark polo shirt, walked toward me, and we sat at a small table under a folded beach umbrella. "Too quiet for you at the McAllister?" Robinson said.

"I wanted to see you and get your feelings on the state of integration."

"That's what you said. You could get in trouble doing that, you know. Anyway, your paper won't be interested in what I have to say."

By this time, Stanley Woodward was gone, and Bob Cooke, the sports editor from Yale, had risen up foursquare against the integration of baseball. "I don't know just what I can get in to the *Trib,* but I want your thoughts about integration just for myself. If you've got the time."

"Sure I do." (Looking back, I marvel at Robinson's openness and accessability. No agents, lawyers, or publicity men sat with us to direct or censor the conversation. The term "image conscious" was not yet in use. That contrasts sharply with the conduct of most star athletes today.)

To begin with, Robinson said, I ought to understand that barriers were coming down "not just because of me. It isn't even right to say I broke the color line. Mr. Rickey did. I played ball. Mr. Rickey made it possible for me to play." Robinson always spoke of *Mister* Rickey, which in time began to sound subservient, at least to my ears. Sometimes I wished that he would refer to the bushy-browed Mahatma as "Branch" or just plain "Rickey." He never did.

In some ways, Robinson said, the brisk (for the time) pace of baseball integration surprised him. "It's been what, less than six years, since I came to Brooklyn, and certainly half the clubs in our league now will pick up a Negro if he's got the ability."

"I've read that in the beginning, Jack, you had to take a lot of abuse."

"There was a core of 'antis.'" He pronounced the word "ant-ties," rhyming with neckties. That was Robinson's own personal term for bigots. "But then there were guys who were supportive. Lee Handley and Hank Greenberg in Pittsburgh. Stan Musial in St. Louis. And on our club, lots of guys, Gene Hermanski, Branca, Gil Hodges, and, of course, Pee Wee. I've never had a better friend in sports."

He took a breath. "I didn't think the Negro player would be accepted so widely so soon. Neither did Mr. Rickey when he signed me. But, look, as it's worked out, baseball has done more for integration than the FEPC [the federal government's Fair Employment Practices Commission]. The reason baseball has done this is because of . . . well, because of baseball itself. Baseball's that way. You're applauded or booed for what you do on the field. So anyway, whatever you've read, getting accepted by the white players was probably the easiest part of my job."

"I guess it helps that you played like hell."

He nodded. He never seemed to care about compliments on his ball playing, probably because he knew how good he was. "How about the fans?" I said.

"When I first came up," Robinson said, "there was organized opposition coming at me. I could tell when it was organized, because one fan would yell something from one part of the stands, and another would yell the same thing from somewhere else. And the next. It was like a chain; it sounded like it had been planned beforehand. It was that way the first time we played an exhibition at Fort Worth, Texas. Now it's nothing at all in Fort Worth. Only a few yell at you and it's not organized.

"Some people wonder if it hurts me because I have to stay in separate quarters when the team goes to St. Louis or anywhere in the South. No, I'm not hurt. I get treated like a king when I live out like that. People offer me cars, free meals, women. Do they offer you women at the McAllister?"

"I haven't been there long enough to know. But Vin Scully is down in the bar every night, putting on his best radio voice for the cocktail waitresses."

Robinson grinned quickly. "You haven't asked me, but the hardest damn thing has been you guys, the press. Dick Young from the *News* makes things up. Others take shots. There are quite a lot of antis in the press box. Would you believe that you are the first regular Dodger beat writer who has taken the time to talk integration with me one-on-one? In six years. The only one. You're also the only one who has even bothered to come over to see what things are like at this motel."

I was making notes in a small stenography pad, in which I had scrawled some questions. I had a final topic. Rickey had left Brooklyn after the 1950 season. "Do you miss him in the front office?" I said.

Before he spoke, Robinson looked at me very hard. "Just say that I'm not Walter O'Malley's kind of Negro."

"Are you saying O'Malley is prejudiced?"

"No. I guess I'm just saying O'Malley not my kind of white man."

I shaped Robinson's comments into a Sunday feature for the *Herald Tribune* and sent it north by Western Union, night press rate collect. The *Trib* editors were always after me for Sunday features, specifically to fill the columns of the early weekend edition while waiting for later hard-news stories to break. There was no extra stipend for this stuff, which delighted the paper's auditor, Vince Kellett. Columns and columns of free prose was something to his taste. This one—I called it "Jackie Robinson on Integration"—never ran. Sunday space was tight that week, they told me.

"I appreciate your trying," Robinson said, "and look at the bright side."

"There is no bright side, Jack. I just got censored."

"Oh, yes, there is," he said. He started to laugh. "They didn't make you pay the Western Union bill."

The late Allan Roth, the Dodger statistician, a witty Canadian who is the spiritual godfather of today's baseball numbers people, made an interesting point as the 1952 season began. The Dodgers had won the 1949 pennant by one game, clinching it on the last day of the season. Then in 1950 they lost to the Phillies—on the last day of the season—and in 1951 lost to the Giants in the last game of the play-off. "This team has been in a pennant race, an undecided pennant race, every game it's played for the last three years. Every single game, for 465 consecutive games. That has never happened before to any team in the major leagues."

Outbursts of tension, as a hangover from the hard 1951 defeat, came mostly from the manager, feisty Charlie Dressen, who was, among other things, a total stranger to English syntax. Dressen's past tense for the word "throw" was "trun," as in "He trun the fastball by the sumbitch." He told me, "There's tricks to big-league ball that I'll learn ya if you write good. And you better write good. I usta play bridge with yer boss [Bob Cooke]." Dressen's intimate warning about pickpockets was heartfelt. "Stay outa crowds, kid," he said. "One of them pickpockets come after me at the Chicago World's Fair. This was back in 1933. He made his move right into my pants pocket. Now me, I've got small nuts, but even so I felt his hand. You gotta be careful . . ." Wondering how on earth I could stay out of crowds when I was going to a big-league ball game every day, I concluded this conversation by saying thanks.

Dressen said that Robinson was the best ballplayer he had ever managed. This American primitive also had a vivid take on bigotry. "I don't go to church," he said, "but I was raised Catholic in Decatur, Illinois, and one night them Klan fuckers set fire to a cross on the front lawn. I was only a little kid, maybe six or seven, and it scared the living hell outa me. That's what them prejudiced fuckers do, scare little kids."

Robinson had a good, but not a great, year in 1952, batting .308, scoring 104 runs, and stealing 24 bases. (Reese led the majors that season with 30 steals.) Some said Robinson seemed slower in the field, and he made twenty errors at second base. In 153 games the year before he had made only seven. The Dodgers won the '52 pennant with enormous help from their untouted twenty-nine-year-old rookie right-hander, Joe Black. Like Robinson, Black was a college man; he had graduated from Morgan State, a school for blacks located in Baltimore. Joe stood six feet two and weighed 220. He fired high fast balls at ninety-five miles an hour and wicked sliders down and away. He had read quite a bit, taking a minor in psychology, and he had no compunction about knocking down hitters. "We're professionals," he said. "If I send a guy into the dirt, it isn't personal." Most of the time. One day when he was pitching in Cincinnati some of the Reds, still an all-white team, began singing in their dugout "Old Black Joe." Black knocked down two Cincinnati hitters and, as he remarked pleasantly afterward, "The music stopped."

Black grew up in Plainfield, New Jersey, and after college he played with Negro League teams to make a living. "I've seen most of the country," he told me, "through the dirty windows of overage busses." Winters he migrated to the Carribean, pitching in Cuba, Puerto Rico, and Venezuela and in the process he became bilingual. Twelve months of pitching earned him about $5,000 a year. "Could I have made the majors a lot sooner?" he said, "Sure, but I'm a colored guy. All of us, we had to wait for Jack." When I wrote a feature that I called "Joe Black's Odyssey," recounting his circuitous voyage though prejudice from Plainfield, New Jersey, to Brooklyn, New York, the *Tribune* played the story prominently and even ran my picture with it. Black, as a soft-spoken black man who succeeded, drew general admiration. But Robinson, that arrow of dark fire, posed a threat. At the age of twenty-four I began to comprehend that prejudice exists in many forms on many levels at the ball parks, in the newspaper offices, and beyond.

Pitching almost entirely on relief, Black won fifteen games and saved another fifteen. On twenty-one occasions, Dressen brought in Black during the late innings of a game the Dodgers were leading. The team won every one of those twenty-one games. With the Dodgers winning the pennant by fewer than five games, Big Joe was the difference. He started three World Series games and pitched exceedingly well until fatigue overcame him in game seven and the Yankees won a rousing series, four games to three.

During the winter Robinson telephoned and asked me to join him for lunch and a meeting in the Flatiron Building, a venerable steel-framed skyscraper in lower Manhattan. "It will be worth your while," he said. "There's something in it for you." He had been conducting a weekly radio show on WNBC, and I thought he might want help with the scripts. But instead, seated behind a desk, he began to outline the magazine that would be called *Our Sports*. Reading from notes he said that in the days since World War II Negro athletes had reached the top in most major spectator sports. "*Our Sports* aims to corral all the activities of Negroes in sports into one interpretive medium for the vast Negro audience." His manner was alive with excitement. "I'm going to write a column every month. I want you to help me there. I'm a lousy typist. Then I want you to write a story for us under your own name every other month. And meet with some of our editors from time to time. We need as many ideas as we can get." He then mentioned the fee, $150 a month. Since my *Tribune* salary still was only $120 a week, Robinson's offer was a fine supplement. On top of that, his enthusiasm for the new magazine found a match in my enthusiasm at the chance to work closely with a complex, brilliant, and heroic man.

Looking back at the magazine fifty-two years later gives me a sense of paternal, or perhaps grand-paternal, pride. We led the first issue, dated May 1953, of what we billed as "the new monthly magazine featuring

Negro athletes," with a strong piece by Milton Gross, a *New York Post* columnist, called "Will There Ever Be a Big League Negro Manager?" Gross thought Monte Irvin of the New York Giants and Roy Campanella were excellent candidates. Neither became a manager. It was twenty-three more years before the Cleveland Indians broke *that* unwritten color line by putting the estimable Frank Robinson in charge. Although black managers have become fairly common in the twenty-first century, the Dodgers, pioneers under Branch Rickey, have never hired a black to manage. (Nor have the Yankees.)

I led the second issue with a piece Jackie wanted me to write: "What White Big Leaguers *Really* Think of Negro Players." I must have interviewed fifty baseball people. Eddie Stanky, then managing the Cardinals told me, "My relationship with all the Negroes I've played with has been 100 per cent pleasant. Don't mind what I say during a ball game. I want to win and sometimes I get rough. But Robinson does, too, you know. It's part of baseball"

Walter O'Malley, the Dodger president who deposed Branch Rickey, was particularly interesting:

There's the [Dodgertown] dining room. [He pointed to a large room behind screen doors.] Our Negro players and our white players eat in there side by side. This is Florida, but you couldn't tell it.

See the four boys playing cards over there. Two white boys and two Negroes at the same table in Florida. Look at the gang around the piano. Mixed black and white. We aren't boasting about this, we don't ask for credit. We run our organization the right way and you see what we think is right.

In our barracks here Negro boys and white boys sleep under the same roof in Florida. The other days we had some electricians in from Melbourne [Florida] to fix the lights in our new stadium. They worked a long day. When they were through it was late and I asked them if they wanted to sleep over because Melbourne is a forty-five-mile drive. They asked me if they'd have to sleep under the same roof with Negro players and I told them, 'Of course.' They said they couldn't. What did I tell them? It doesn't matter. You couldn't print it anyway.

Jack's story that month, "My Feud with Leo," turned out to be a peace offering. Robinson detailed his Durocher relationship and said it had finally turned for the better after the 1952 All-Star Game, played in the rain in Philadelphia. Robinson homered, but someone drove a hot grounder that went under his glove. The National Leaguers won, 3 to 2; even so, reporters went to Durocher, managing the Nationals, and asked if Robinson should have made the play. Jack said, and I wrote, "If Leo wanted to show me up, this was his chance. But he said on that wet field nobody in the world could have made the play. Then he said. 'Jackie Robinson plays a ton. He doesn't need any excuses.' Anybody can be a needler, but it takes a big man to forget the nastiness and pass up a chance to shoot a sitting duck. It made me feel so good I wrote a letter to Leo thanking him. Leo wrote back that he was really glad that once and for all he could classify me as a friend. People have a lot of opinions about Durocher. Let me tell you something I know. There is not one ounce of bigotry in the man."

Given the intensity of the Dodger-Giant rivalry this was new and exciting stuff, but in the summer of '53, with a great Dodger team on the way to winning the pennant by thirteen games, Jack told me that the future of *Our Sports* was increasingly in doubt. We marched fearlessly into hot-button issues, the sort of stuff *The New York Times* and Bob Cooke's *Herald Tribune* sports section declined to touch. Was the Yankee organization bigoted? (It was. When the Yankees finally signed a black player, in 1955, eight years after Robinson's Brooklyn debut, Casey Stengel referred to the rookie Elston Howard as "my jig.") The Boston Red Sox? (Even worse.) Why were so many reporters hostile to Branch Rickey? (For one thing, his polysyllabic ways made them feel stupid.) We swung freely and encouraged our contributors to do the same. We proposed Satchel Paige for the then all-white Hall of Fame. He made it eighteen years later. We published stories on Sugar Ray Robinson's umpteenth comeback, concerned lest this great boxer suffer brain damage. Before Sugar Ray died in 1989, he had gone prematurely senile. We challenged an unspoken rule that barred blacks from being jockeys and relegated them to the lesser role of "exercise boys."

All this drew spurts of interest from some of the mainstream press (but not from the hidebound *Times* or Cooke's anti-Robinson *Tribune,* which both doggedly ignored *Our Sports*). The Negro reading public, and many whites, swamped us with mail. But the economics of American journalism ran against us; we were not attracting sufficient advertising revenue to stay afloat. Could Robinson personally have solicited major advertisers? Perhaps. His celebrity would open almost any door, right up to Dwight Eisenhower's oval office. Had we thought of hustling that way, would it have helped? Probably not. When that Lord of the Press, Henry Luce launched *Sports Illustrated* a year later, the magazine began by losing $60,000 a week. Luce maintained a large and tough advertising sales force, but the early issues are littered with advertisements for cheap shoes. It was a decade before *SI* broke even. Sports, went the conventional thinking, were for kids. And Negro sports? Well, what colored child could afford to buy a nineteen-inch Admiral television, a set of Firestone tires, or a Packard convertible? Why advertise, went the conventional thinking, to the young and the impoverished? Had Jack and I trekked to the offices of corporate presidents, some certainly would have asked for his autograph. But the business of America being business, as Silent Calvin Coolidge put it in a burst of verbiage, I doubt that any would have sent serious advertising dollars our way.

Robinson then set out to compose an illuminating valedictory called "Have I Achieved My Goals?" I had better explain right now how we worked. Jackie would talk and I would take longhand notes. If I didn't agree with a point, I'd say so and we'd argue it out. Then I'd type a draft and we'd go over it and I'd mail the finished copy to the magazine's offices in the Flatiron Building. We worked out "goals" in a couple of cramped rooms in the Hotel Schenley, a dreary setting that Duke Snider described as "the Pittsburgh old ladies' home."

Teams put two ballplayers in each room in those days, even outstanding ballplayers, and Robinson was booked with the rookie second baseman, Junior Gilliam, a one-time star with the Baltimore Elite Giants of the Negro National League. Gilliam lay on a bed as Robinson and I talked, showing no interest. "First," Jack said, "I better define my goal, don't you think?"

"What do you think, Junior?" I said.

"Ain't none of my business, man."

"Don't worry about him," Robinson said. "He's going to be learning."

Robinson said his goal was this: "That all ballplayers, regardless of race, creed, or color, be accepted in baseball as ballplayers only and that they be judged simply on the basis of ability."

"Don't you think we should go beyond baseball and extend this equal opportunity theme to society in general?" I said.

"You're right, but I think that's another story. Right now could you set down that my personal goal is to be accepted as just another ballplayer?"

He first talked about on-field needling. "When one or two of the St. Louis Cardinals shouted 'porter' and 'shoeshine boy' at me, I was steamed but not insulted. If a great many Negroes have to earn their living as porters and shoeshine boys, we know where the fault lies. For the most part, it is not with the Negroes themselves." Moving to the press, he said he had met many honest reporters but "careless and prejudiced newspapermen have done a great deal of damage—more than the honest men can undo." He singled out several teammates for praise: Carl Erskine, Ralph Branca, and Pee Wee Reese. "It's hard to put into words the decency, the honesty, the real Americanism of this gentleman from Kentucky." He spoke fondly of Ford Frick, who after blocking the 1947 players' strike as National League president, had gone on to become commissioner of baseball.

"But my own goal has not been achieved," he said. "If more Negroes before me had achieved their goals, my goal would not be what it is. Negroes would have been playing in organized baseball before I was born and I would have been just another ballplayer.

"I am not just another ballplayer. I don't suppose I ever will be. But some day—I hope in my lifetime—one Negro will be. Until that day comes, all of us must work and fight to bring it closer. If we do, it is only a matter of time."

It was tragic that this brave, purposeful magazine died aborning, tragic and absurd as well. In the very first issue, an advertisement appeared on page 67 featuring four hairless people and a sheep. The headline read "Did You Ever See a Baldheaded Sheep?" The copy explained that wool contained lanolin, an oily substance that when applied to human heads would keep hair "growing thick, luxurious, soft, shiny and handsome. All you have to do is order NIL-O-NAL [lanolin spelled backwards] $3.00 a jar."

To survive we needed ads from Campbell's Soup and General Motors. Rich, ripe, red tomato soup. Big, shiny Cadillacs with fins. What we got was lanolin spelled backward. The magazine folded in the autumn of 1953, and when the backers failed to pay me my final $150, Robinson walked me into the magazine headquarters, stood over the publisher, and glared. I settled for $120. Robinson then took me into a clothing store in which he had an interest and commandeered $30 worth of shirts, which he presented to me. I never had a better collection agent than Jackie Robinson.

In 1954 I made a Dodger trip that ended with a stormy flight back from the Midwest. We were flying in a chartered Constellation, a four-engine prop aircraft that could not fly high enough to rise above wretched weather. My late first wife, Joan, was pregnant at the time, and as the plane shuddered through a thunderhead, Robinson, seated four rows behind me shouted, "Hey, Kahn. It's too bad you're not gonna live to see that little baby." The weather continued to worsen, and one of the stewardesses suddenly announced, in frightened tones, "Hold on. It's going to get really rough."

Lightning flashed outside the windows. Hail beat on the wings. The pilot turned on the headlights but visibility ended at the wingtips. We were caught in the middle of large and angry storm clouds. After one long shuddering drop I unclasped the buckle of my seat belt, half-stood, turned, and called, "I don't hear you now, Robinson."

He said in a small voice, "It's not funny now."

When finally we landed, a few Dodgers came up to me and said things like, "Good going. You really put that Robinson down." Whatever, I thought his needling had crossed the line. Late that October, I telephoned him about a story. "How's the baby?" he said.

"The baby died, Jack. A little girl named Elizabeth. The baby died the day after she was born."

"What's you wife's number?" As soon as I told him, Robinson hung up. Later Joan remarked that his consolation call had been a marvel of sensitivity. "I hope my bringing this up doesn't upset you," Jack said, "but I just wanted you to know I'm sorry."

After my marriage to Joan broke down, amiably, as such things go, I married an ardent Quaker girl from Pennsylvania named Alice Lippincott Russell. Alice had the fair-haired good looks of a college-football cheerleader, which she had been while studying ceramics at Alfred University. She proved a loving stepmother to my son Gordon, who was born in 1957, and then had two children of her own, Roger Laurence, who arrived at about the time the Republican Party nominated Barry Goldwater in 1964, and Alissa Avril, who was born three years later. Coming, or perhaps escaping, from rural Bucks Country, Alice embraced New York, with its great theater, where we saw Alec Guiness portray the doomed Dylan Thomas; concerts at Carnegie Hall, where we heard Heifetz play Bach; ball games at Yankee Stadium, where we saw Koufax overwhelm the Yankees; and everywhere exciting people and beguiling parties. Some of her old farm-country friends told her she truly had become Alice in Wonderland, and for a time she was content and seemed to sparkle. She found us a gorgeous apartment on Riverside Drive overlooking the Hudson and began working toward a master's degree in fine arts education at Columbia Teachers' College. Certainly a lot was going on.

Although Alice's pottery had won prizes at Pennsylvania craft fairs, the chairman of ceramics at Teachers' College did not offer her a fellowship. She painted bright, colorful, free-form canvases that I proudly hung about the apartment. People looked and made courteous remarks, but no one offered to buy. "Don't be down, Allie," I said. "Same thing happened to Van Gogh."

At length she turned against New York, saying with jaw outthrust, "I have no intention of raising my children in this city." The sparkle was gone. We abandoned Riverside Drive and the apartment, which now is a co-op worth about $6.5 million, and moved into a rambling colonial, in exurban Ridgefield, Connecticut, with an old slate roof that leaked. We knew few people there, but the Robinsons, in North Stamford, were located within an easy drive. One evening Rachel served us martinis in the living room of the big, stone house. Jackie, feeling tired, did not appear for quite some time. Then he entered, wearing dark slacks and a gray, short-sleeved T-shirt, looking handsome under his white hair and remarkably muscular. After a brief greeting, he stretched on a couch, doing isometric exercises that emphasized the sinews in his arms. Rachel was saying that no one had ever asked if Jack, following a tough day at the ballpark, took out his frustrations on the family. "He never did," she said. "But I could tell when he'd had a bad time with racism, or whatever. He'd take a bucket of golf balls and his driver and bang them one after another from the back lawn into the lake."

Robinson fixed Alice with an intense look. "The golf balls," he said, "were white." He then resumed his isometrics and I noticed Alice was sitting up very straight. A few days later my mother told me that Alice had really enjoyed the evening at the Robinsons and had told her that Jackie was "the sexiest man" she had ever seen.

"How did I fare in the sexy-man sweepstakes, Mom?"

"Alice didn't mention your name," my mother said with amusement, laced with a dash of maternal malice.

With his legs gone and his bat slowed, Robinson quit baseball after the 1956 season and signed for about $50,000 annually plus stock benefits with a chain of Manhattan lunch counters, Chock full o'Nuts. His title was personnel director, and virtually everyone working underneath him was black. "You see," Jack said, when were lunching at an upscale restaurant, "these people all have a good deal. The president of the company is a fine man. And now some of them want to start a union. That doesn't make sense with things being as good as they are."

I said unions gave working people a sense of independence. "A good boss is fine, of course, but good or not, without a union people are at the mercy of a boss's favors."

Robinson listened carefully, without agreeing. In a year or so more sophisticated blacks were calling Chock full o' Nuts "Jackie's Plantation." But Robinson was working to catch up with the world beyond baseball, and he found a good mentor in Franklin H. Williams, a lawyer with the NAACP, who was later Lyndon B. Johnson's ambassador to Ghana. Williams, who died in 1990, reported that "Jack takes coaching on new topics very well."

In 1960 Robinson went calling on John Kennedy who said (Robinson reported to me), "I haven't known too many Negroes, Mr. Robinson, being from New England." Robinson next sought out Richard Nixon, who was much more the earthy baseball fan. Nixon spoke of "my own and the Republican party's historic concern for Negroes and the wrongs done to them."

"So I'm for Nixon," Robinson said. "Any senator like Kennedy should make it his business to know Negroes, no matter where he's from."

"But can you accept Nixon's sincerity?"

"On this one issue, yes."

"But there are lots of issues." That may have sounded patronizing.

Robinson took no offense. "Sure there are, and there are pressure groups working on all of them. I'm a pressure group for civil rights."

He moved on from Chock full o' Nuts and took jobs with a variety of start-up enterprises: an insurance company that would provide coverage to blacks, often denied by the white insurance giants; a Harlem bank called Freedom National; a company named Sea Host that was projected to become a seafood McDonald's. None of these ventures were notably successful, and Dick Young wrote kindlessly in his tabloid column, "Robinson's tragedy is that nothing he has done outside of baseball equals what he accomplished within the game."

"How could it?" Robinson said, more hurt than angry. "How possibly could it? And I'm not tragic. What a stupid fucking thing to write." Young's good reporting skills increasingly were corroded by his malice.

When Robinson and I discussed school integration, he made a stimulating point that presaged the final and most successful phase of his life after baseball. "Most people think that integration is the biggest single issue in civil rights. I don't agree. Housing is the biggest issue. If you integrate the schools, when you integrate the schools, what happens if the black kids have to live in lousy housing? They won't want to go home. So they'll leave their integrated classes and hang out on the streets and get into trouble. I'm all for integrated schools, of course, but the most important single thing for Negroes is the right and the economic means to live in decent homes."

★ ★ ★

Early in the 1960s I accepted a position at *The Saturday Evening Post* called editor-at-large. The work consisted mostly of undertaking major writing assignments for what was developing into the finest magazine around. Working closely with two extraordinary editors, William A. Emerson Jr. and Otto Friedrich, I had some input on the magazine's overall content. Robinson never spoke to me about the Republican organization as "the party of Lincoln." He championed it, he said, because he wanted more blacks voting Republican. "It would be a terrible thing," he said, "if every Negro voted Democratic. Then we'd be on the way to having a white party and a black party in America. That would be a disaster for me—my whole career has been about integration—and, more important, it would be a disaster for the country." With the help of a black journalist named Alfred Duckett, he expanded that theme into an article which I placed in the *Post,* in which he warned that the nomination of Barry Goldwater in 1964 "would ensure that the GOP became completely the white man's party." The piece was called, "The GOP—For White Men Only?"

Robinson supported Nelson Rockefeller, and he said the Goldwater supporters during the Republican convention in San Francisco were "full of such hatred toward us Rockefeller people that surrounded by them I thought I felt a little of what it must have been like to be a Jew in Hitler's Germany." Jack was a man of action, and it dismayed him that Rockefeller did not mount a forceful response. Politics was losing its allure.

He seemed to be aging unusually quickly and I brought my children to meet him one cool May day in 1971. Rachel was away, and Robinson said first that his son, Jack Junior, "got himself in a scrape last night. You know he came back from Vietnam a heroin addict, but he's doing better now, trying to help others. He goes into bad neighborhoods and it caught up with him. Someone hit him with a board and split his forehead. I've got to pick him up later at New Haven Hospital, but we've got plenty of time for a visit."

Young Roger, almost seven years old, was captivated by a football in Robinson's trophy case that had been signed by the entire 1940 UCLA varsity. "Dad," he said, "can we take the football so you can throw me some passes?"

"That's not a football to throw. You admire it."

"Like hell," Robinson said. "Balls are for children to play with. Go out on the lawn and toss some passes to your son."

The signatures were in ink. The grass was wet. "Don't drop any, Rog," I said. I must have thrown him twenty passes and he caught every one. The trophy football remained dry.

The morning of June 17 brought terrible tidings. Jackie Robinson Jr., twenty-four, had been found dead in a wreck of a yellow MG. He had driven off the Merritt Parkway at such high speed that the car demolished four oak guard posts and one door came to rest 117 feet distant from the chassis. I telephoned and Robinson answered the phone himself. I stumbled, then said, "Jack, I'm trying to say you have our love."

His voice was high and strong. "You don't have to say that. By making the phone call you already did."


Near the end, with his sight all but gone, Robinson spoke with great excitement about a housing concept. "You know in lots of these ghettoes, there are plenty of what used to be fine private homes."

I knew that well. My great grandmother, Lilly Lasar Weill, inherited a splendid brownstone at 702 Greene Avenue, in what became known as the Bedford-Stuyvesant section of Brooklyn. I had often sat on one of her ebony rocking chairs in a high-ceilinged, damask-curtained drawing room and listened to her warn me against misbehavior. "You dasn't do bad things," Nana Lilly said, "or God"—she pronounced the word *Gawd*—"will punish you." Years later perhaps fifty people, all black, were living in what had once been Nana Lilly's single-family house.

"Here's the idea," Robinson said. "The insides of a lot of these places are falling apart. You have rats running around, and worse. Now I'm putting together a company that is going to buy up some of those homes. We hire people from the neighborhood, carpenters, plumbers, and the rest, and we put them to work restoring the old brownstones. In the remodeling we'll create a lot of nice apartments. We make work for people having a hard time in the ghettoes, and we make fine, affordable housing for ghetto people at the same time. What do you think?"

He was sitting at his kitchen table in the house on Cascade Road. His eyes were red from diabetic bleeding. I knew, because I opened his mail, that he was two months behind on his mortgage payments. But here, infirm and blind, beset by money problems, he exuded the old concern for others, the old fiery optimism that spoke banners.

"Jack," I said, "that's a brilliant idea."

"For a second baseman," Robinson said.

He had been musing lately about Paul Robeson. He didn't agree with Robeson, but he would not now, with the knowledge he had acquired over time, testify against him before an all-white committee in the Congress chaired by a Southerner. "Here's something bigger than our disagreements," Jack said. "The salient fact of Robeson's life and my life is pretty much the same. We are black men in a bigoted white society."

I was part of white American society. I wanted to burst forth with an eloquent, sweeping apology, but none came to mind. I reverted to baseball talk. "Jack," I said, touching his arm, "I'm fucking sorry."

"Don't you be sorry," he said. "You did what you could. We both did."

I felt proud that he regarded me as a warrior by his side.

Robinson's intellect was catching up with his accomplishments and then, before the two could join, on the mild morning of October 24, 1972, death interceded. Specifically, a heart attack felled Jackie Robinson as he was preparing to fly to Washington, D.C., to lobby for his housing plan. At 7:10 A.M., he died in an ambulance en route to Stamford Hospital. He was buried at Cypress Hills Cemetery near the border of Brooklyn and Queens, under a modest stone and an epitaph he had written for himself. "A life is not important, except in the impact it has on other lives."

His own life was too short, of course.

But what a legacy.

# CHAPTER 5

# "The Time Is Out of Joint"

Roving far beyond sports, I wrote politics and current affairs for *The Saturday Evening Post* in its fascinating last years, when the late Otto Friedrich was making it a great magazine. I found political and intellectual extremes in two leaders who did not become president of the United States: Barry Goldwater and Eugene McCarthy. Twenty-first-century America is rooted deeply in the 1960s and in the failed campaigns of these two men.

## I

### *A Midsummer Night's Madness*

The 1960s came hurtling in to a different drumbeat. Often journalists, and even some historians, point to the election of John F. Kennedy as both hallmark and overture for a period of astounding change. Having lived the 1960s and covered many of its most significant persons and places and episodes as editor-at-large at *The Saturday Evening Post,* I have a different and admittedly personal view. (Tip O'Neill famously said that all politics is local. At the core, all writing, or anyway all serious writing, is personal.)

To me the tumultuous '60s began metaphorically on July 13 in the Memorial Coliseum at Los Angeles when a little-known Democratic senator from Minnesota, Eugene Joseph McCarthy, spoke out against Kennedy and in favor of yet another presidential nomination for Adlai E. Stevenson of Illinois. Quoting from *Hamlet,* McCarthy began, "These times, men say, are out of joint." The full quotation serves as a superscription to Gene McCarthy's own political career, one illumined by intelligence and nobility.

> *The time is out of joint; O cursed spite,*
> *That ever I was born to set it right!*

Presidential politics soured during the 1960s, with Lyndon Johnson and Richard Nixon scheming in the White House. More than anyone else, Gene McCarthy sustained my faith in the political system. His bid for high office ultimately failed, but the bid itself, and the great concepts that energized it, showed something significant and comforting. Even in a time rife with cynicism and murder, American idealism still survived.

Before Neil Armstrong walked on the moon in 1969, the 1960s presented a stunning, troubling cavalcade. With the founding in New York City of the Students for a Democratic Society during June 1960, a new and militant campus left appeared. Eight years later the SDS shut down Columbia University. In that same 1960, Nikita Khrushchev, the Soviet premier, spoke to the United Nations in New York and promised Communist support for "wars of national liberation" anywhere on earth. At one point during the debate that followed, Khrushchev took off one of his shoes and banged it on a desk.

Khrushchev told western journalists more than once, "Our grandchildren will bury you." Still later, on a momentous and confrontational New York visit, Khrushchev met with Fidel Castro, conjuring up visions of Cuban marines landing in Fort Lauderdale while Soviet paratroopers were dropping into the Bronx and the two columns proceeding to mount a monstrous pincer movement on the White House.

Actually the next invasion went the other way. On April 15, 1961, some 1,400 insurgents, armed by the Central Intelligence Agency, landed at Playa Girón on the Bay of Pigs, which lies on the southern shore of Cuba, about forty miles from Havana. Within three days all these benighted warriors were captured or killed. Kennedy had ordered the strike. Now he and his people variously blamed Dwight Eisenhower (bad planning), Adlai Stevenson (opposed air support for the invaders), and the Cuban populace (failed to mount an island-wide anti-Castro uprising). It was an embarrassing American adventure and terribly dangerous. By September President Kennedy was advising Americans to build fallout shelters. The Soviet response was to test a thermonuclear weapon that exploded with the force of 57 million—not thousand, but million—tons of TNT. For shelter from that, I thought, one would do best to move to the planet Saturn.

Freedom Rides, a new and militant form of black protest, began in the segregated South. Since there was nothing funny or even light-hearted in the front-page news, one had to turn to the sports pages for comic relief. With the Dodgers and Giants fled to California, the first wholly synthetic modern major-league baseball team was cooked up. The result, the New York Mets, lost 120 games in 1962. With stinging sarcasm Casey Stengel, the seventy-three-year-old manager who had previously won five consecutive World Series with the Yankees, called this team "the youth of America."

That October the appearance of Russian missiles in Cuba brought the world close to nuclear war. Neither Khrushchev nor Kennedy seemed able to control events, but across thirteen days a desperately bro-kered truce emerged. Having looked into the abyss, all mankind shud-dered. Many wept thirteen months later when the dashing, young president was assassinated on a political trip to Dallas.

Harlem broke out in race riots during July 1964. "I don't approve of that sort of violence," Jackie Robinson told me. "First of all, violence is wrong. Second, the whites have more guns." In an angry and not en-tirely honest speech that August, President Johnson charged that North Vietnamese patrol boats had attacked U.S. destroyers cruising the Gulf of Tonkin. A clarion call to nationalism, the speech stirred memories of the devastating Japanese attack on Pearl Harbor. The Vietnam War was under way. Soon thousands of young people would be marching to the chant: "Hey! Hey! LBJ! How many kids did you kill today?"

With student leftists becoming more numerous and more vocal, with American blacks becoming more combative, and with the Soviet Union apparently becoming a sort of thermonuclear loose cannon, hard-line conservatives, the "Radical Right," seized the Republican Party. These were people who spoke out strongly against what they called "godless, atheistic Common-ism." The right-wingers then nominated Barry Goldwater for president at the Republican convention in San Francisco. Goldwater was the son of a Jewish dry goods merchant in Arizona who had changed religions. "I always knew," someone said, "that the first Jewish president would be a Presbyterian." Running as a peace candidate, Lyndon Johnson defeated Goldwater by 16 million votes and an Electoral College margin of 486 to 52. That being done, Johnson proceeded to escalate military action in Vietnam until half a million Americans were fighting there, and the nation was more angrily divided than it had been at any time since the Civil War. Battles raged in such obscure places as the Mekong Delta. On native American grounds, racism persisted. Hate seemed to be lurking on every balcony, in every corner. Martin Luther King Jr. was murdered in April 1968. Robert F. Kennedy was shot to death two months later. Some wondered, Was the great American experiment drowning in the wash of blood? But most people most of the time went about their daily business, carried out garbage, puffed Marlboro Reds, drove wide-track Pontiacs, and bought Preparation H Ointment to shrink their hemorrhoids. That was the 1960s, or a part of the '60s, as I remember the time. It was also the decade in which two historic beacons of journalism, the New York *Herald Tribune* (1966) and *The Saturday Evening Post* (1969) ceased to be.

I did not come charging into the '60s in the imperial style of Jack Kennedy or, for that matter, in the blustery manner of Nikita Sergeyevich Khrushchev. I sidled up, circuitously, leaving second base and taking a detour through the badlands of Hollywood. Following the success of my Robert Frost article, Irving Goodman, then New York editor of *The Saturday Evening Post,* which continued to base its main offices in Philadelphia, asked what I wanted to write next. I suggested that I fly to London to visit Sean O'Casey, the great Irish playwright, who, like so many other Irish writers (Oscar Wilde, George Bernard Shaw), had elected to live among the Sassenachs in England. I remembered my O'Casey assignment from Bill Zinsser years before at the *Herald Tribune* and I had since read O'Casey's lyrical six-volume autobiography, an attempt, a commentator observed "to wrest some order and significance from the anarchic events of the first half of the twentieth century." A few days later Goodman reported that Bob Fuoss, the executive editor, had told him, "We don't think too many people in Kansas City care about an expatriate Irish writer, particularly one whose politics are pinko." But the *Post* wanted "everything I wrote," Goodman said, and asked me to collaborate with the former child movie star, Jackie Cooper, in an article Cooper wanted to call "Unfortunately I Was Rich." At the time, he was performing in a pleasant CBS television series called *Hennessey,* playing a kindly navy doctor.

When I reached Hollywood, I found Cooper had an interesting story to tell. Big money appeared early when Cooper played a poignant urchin in *The Champ* (1931) and young Jim Hawkins in the hit film made from Robert Louis Stevenson's *Treasure Island* (1934). But along with success came battering incidents. When young Cooper was supposed to cry in one scene but could not summon tears, an assistant director told little him that his pet dog had been run over and killed. The child actor burst into tears. When the scene was done, the director cheerfully said that he had made a mistake; the little dog actually was fine. The article wheeled around Cooper's difficult relationship with his father, John Cooperman, who had abandoned his family early. I wrote the piece, far from my best, collaboration not being my forte as I've noted, and Cooper turned it over to his lawyer, who at the last minute decided that it was "unwise" to tell the honest story of Cooperman and Cooper, father and son. He deleted the core of the piece, which he was empowered to do, since the article bore a double byline, Cooper's and mine. That left me on deadline having to fill in gaps with fluff. Later, when Clay Blair was editing the *Post* and a pretty brunette editorial assistant gushed about me and my prose, Blair found the Cooper piece, presented it to her, and said, "See. He can also write lousy."

But lousy is in the eye of the beholder. Soon after the Cooper article ran, a publisher asked if I would consider writing a book with a yet more famous former child star, Mickey Rooney. The initial offer, which Rooney and I would split, was $75,000, something like $500,000 in today's dollars. My half would more than cover the costs of my divorce, and years of alimony and child support after that.

"But it's not the sort of thing I want to do," I told my agent, a bright, driving Brooklyn native, Herb Jaffe.

"Take the money," Jaffe said. "You can knock off this job in three months. Then you'll have all the cash you'll need to write serious books."

"I was hoping to write a serious book that generated cash."

"That sort of thing is rare," Herb Jaffe said.

When I met Rooney in a small office near Sunset Boulevard in Hollywood, he was primed. "This book is the story of a loud little guy who doesn't want to be loud," he said in a tempo that made me think of a Gatling gun. "It's the story of somebody who thinks well—twice a month. It's about a man who loves women so much he's married five of them and every time for love." Rooney continued this rapid-fire performance for twenty minutes.

"I understand you first appeared on stage when you were seventeen months old."

"Right," Rooney said. "Before that I just lay around the house."

"So you must really know show business and Hollywood."

"The trouble with Hollywood," Rooney said, "is that it has too many girls with open legs who ought to have open hearts."

"Would you say you've learned from all the hit movies and your romances?"

"I'm still learning," Rooney said. "Even Einstein died with something more to learn." We went to contract quickly, and he introduced me to the fifth Mrs. Rooney, a willful blonde named Barbara Ann Thomason, once chosen by a jury of weight lifters as "Miss Muscle Beach," and to his "money guy," an amiable lawyer named Dermot Long. "I have some advice for you," Long said over a drink in the vanished restaurant the Brown Derby. (The building that housed the place was shaped like a hat.) Long then remarked, matter-of-factly, "Don't fuck Barbara Ann."

If my father were alive and with us, I thought, he would not believe this conversation. I said, "I wasn't thinking of it." (That may or may not have been true.)

"Perhaps," Long said, "but I know Barbara Ann, and *she's* thinking of it. That girl is all hormones, so I've got detectives on her. If they catch someone in bed with her, they might get rough." Rooney had fared badly in three of his four previous divorces, Long explained, and as a lawyer he was protecting his client from yet another expensive split.

I rented an apartment in the Chateau Marmont where my friend the blacklisted screenwriter Ring Lardner Jr., was working on a script (and living) under the front name of Robert Leonard. "That way the initials on my briefcase still match my working name," Ring said. "The studio people think that's a good idea. But my cover isn't perfect. A call came for Mr. Leonard the other day and the Chateau telephone operator said, 'That's you, isn't it, Mr. Lardner?'" I thought briefly that a society in which a man named Ring Lardner could not write under his own name was lurching toward madness, but Ring's wry humor brightened my mood. Presently Rooney and I divided the first check, $50,000, and toasted one another with martinis. Then the little actor disappeared.

He was not a bad fellow, really, and a terrific performer, but Rooney did not want to confront, much less tell the reading public, the dismaying story of his life. I imagined the book as an up-close study in self-destruction, a genre that had recently succeeded in Errol Flynn's best-selling posthumous memoir, *My Wicked, Wicked Ways* (1959). But if Rooney thought of the book as anything more than a payday, he disguised his thinking.

He was born Joe Yule Jr. in Brooklyn; his father was a vaudeville comic, and his mother, Nell, was an "end pony" in burlesque. The taller women in the second row of strip-house dancers were called chorus girls. The shorter ones, up front, were "ponies." Nell Carter Yule worked at one end in the front line of the mostly naked dancers.

At the age of fourteen Rooney played Puck in Max Reinhardt's gorgeous black-and-white production of *A Midsummer Night's Dream*. Here he got to utter the memorable Shakespearean line: "Lord, what fools these mortals be!" His exuberant performance drew him a long-term contract at Metro-Goldwyn-Mayer, the huge studio that advertised "more stars than there are in the heavens." In *A Family Affair* Rooney was cast as Andy Hardy, a clean-cut Midwestern adolescent virgin whose father was a judge and whose love interests were played by, among others, Judy Garland and Lana Turner. MGM shot no fewer than sixteen Andy Hardy movies starring Rooney, and many film historians still cite the set as the most successful family series of all time. For three years, from 1939 through 1941, Rooney was the number-one box office draw in America, more popular than Clark Gable, Gary Cooper, or Cary

Grant. He is a durable character, who was eighty-five years old and still working in 2005, but after Hardy his career declined.

He earned about $13 million before his twenty-first birthday and lived in a sprawling ranch house in then semirural Encino. He, or his mother, had workmen install "sterling silver faucets in every bathroom." He married repeatedly, the first time to the great beauty Ava Gardner. She was a quick-witted, edgy woman who wanted to be loved for something more than her willowy body. Rooney remembered one night when he took her to the Hollywood Palladium, a theater on Sunset Boulevard. He moved on to the stage, did some dance steps, played drums for a while, and began doing imitations of such stars as Lionel Barrymore and Spencer Tracy. At length Ava called a taxi and went back alone to their new home in Stone Canyon. When Rooney arrived there in the small hours, he rolled her over and had sex. After that, Gardner started for the bathroom, then turned around. "She was a beautiful nude," Rooney told me. "Looking at her I started to come on again."

Naked Ava Gardner stared down at him. "If you ever knock me up, you little son of a bitch," she said, "I'll kill you."

By the time I came around with the book contract, four marriages and all the of Rooney's star money was gone. Following one particularly disastrous night at a dice table in Las Vegas—he lost $55,000 in a few hours—he stopped paying his income taxes. Two or three years later agents of the Internal Revenue Service appeared and said, in effect, "We don't want to destroy you, Mr. Rooney. We want to be your partner."

Subsequently, all checks to Rooney, for personal appearances, television shows, movies, went directly to Dermot Long. The lawyer then contacted IRS, and he and IRS agents would allocate the funds. So much for back taxes, so much for current taxes, so much for groceries, so much for clothing, so much for the pediatrician, and so on. Past the age of forty, with his sterling silver bathroom fixtures long gone, Rooney was put on an allowance of $100 a week. That would not go far if you liked to play the horses at Santa Anita, and Rooney loved to play the horses. Living in the lap of the IRS, he was desperately broke—in time he declared bankruptcy—and desperately borrowing. But he was never charged with income tax evasion.

As I said, not a nasty sort at heart, but he didn't want to talk about most of the things—divorce, bankruptcy, decline, and fall—that made his life story especially commercial. A retinue of Hollywood bit players still hung out with him, and each day as I prepared to leave the Chateau Marmont and go to work at Rooney's home, the phone would ring. "Mickey can't make it today," one of the bit players would say. "He's got to go rehearse." Or "Mickey can't make it today. He's had to visit his in-laws in Arizona." Or "Mickey can't make it today. He misses God. He needs to spend the day in church." This continued for three months, and I filled in my time by writing magazine articles, on Stanley Kramer, the director-producer, and Joan Baez, the singer. In a casual way, I looked for work on screenplays, but I was joined at the hip with Rooney, now a Hollywood outcast. That was not an impost I could overcome.

I told my agent, Herb Jaffe, that I was prepared to give back most of my advance. The editor, Howard Cady, had left the publishing company, which meant, in the parlance of book publishing, that I had "lost my rabbi." The head of the house summarily took the position that I was Mickey Rooney's business partner. I personally would have to return Rooney's share of the advance as well as mine, if I wanted to escape the book contract from hell. To argue I would have to bring a lawsuit against a rich, powerful corporation.

"Bankruptcy seems to be contagious," I told Jaffe.

"Don't give up," he said. "After this I can get you really good bucks to write a book with the Three Stooges." The thought of them made him giggle.

"Senses of humor differ, Herb."

In the end, after litigating with Rooney, not the publisher, I got some time with my supposed partner. By this point, predictably, we were getting on each other's nerves, but I put together a first chapter that caught his Gatling-gun style. It began:

"Had I been brighter, had the dice been hotter, had the gods been kinder, had the ladies been gentler, had the scotch been weaker, this might have been a one-sentence story.

"Once upon a time Mickey Rooney lived happily ever after."

Those lines survive on an least one Internet site today. By now Rooney probably believes he wrote them. I did the best I could with the rest of the work, but finally, litigations be damned, I walked away. Dermot Long, among others, filled in data to Rooney's dictates, and Rooney titled the finished product, *I.E.* Dismayed, I had my name removed from what I regarded as a hopeless hodgepodge. *Look* magazine quickly bought American serial rights for $25,000 and a British Sunday paper paid $50,000 for rights in the United Kingdom.

I enjoyed the fiscal comfort, but the creative (or noncreative) experience had beaten hell out of my psyche. I sold some free-verse poetry to *Esquire,* found an ideal bachelor pad diagonally across Fifty-seventh Street from Carnegie Hall and wondered what on earth I would do next.

"You are just going to have to write seriously," Candida Donadio, Herb Jaffe's partner, told me. She was warmhearted, plump, and intellectual and would become truly a *literary* agent. "You've been given a gift to write serious things," Candida said. "When you let yourself be tempted into silliness, like the Mickey Rooney book, you get into trouble and you always will get into trouble. That's because God means for you to write seriously. Your gift has a price. When you don't write seriously, God leans down from heaven and gives you a rap on the head."

As for Rooney, he presently found tragedy. Rooney first wanted to dedicate the book to "Barbara Ann, who taught me the meaning of the word 'woman.' " But they argued and the dedication would read, "For you, Mother." Just after *I.E.* appeared, Barbara Ann was murdered by her latest lover, Milos Milosovic, a Yugoslavian actor, who then turned his pistol on himself and committed suicide. My business with Rooney was done. I had been walling myself off from his chaos. He and almost everyone close to him was out of control. If you venture too far from the norms of society, I thought, as these people were doing, if you live simply on whim and impulse, you place yourself in nothing less than mortal peril.

I don't know the names of the sixth Mrs. Mickey Rooney. Or the seventh. Or the eighth.

## II

### *White Against Black*

"The Curtis Publishing Company is committed to the goal of becoming the voice and conscience of the competitive free-enterprise system, which is the foundation of a progressive economy and a democratic way of life." With this extravagant statement in 1962, Matthew Joseph Culligan, a swaggering Madison Avenue star, famous for his salesmanship and his trademark black eyepatch, assumed the presidency of the company that published *The Saturday Evening Post*. The year before, Curtis had lost money—$4,193,000—for the first time since its incorporation in 1891. The magazine was selling 7 million copies a week, every week, and still managing to lose money. Put simply, the underlying problems at Curtis were an antiquated corporate structure and the hidebound belief that if you sold copies of *The Saturday Evening Post* very cheaply, losing money on most sales, advertising revenue would more than make up the difference. That had once been so, but with the rise of television, advertisers could get their sales pitches to more people more cheaply on, say, *CBS Evening News with Walter Cronkite* than in any of the big general magazines, *Life, Look,* or *The Saturday Evening Post*. The admen talked about "cost per thousand"; they really were concerned with cost per million. When it came to advertising to the American millions, for General Electric Roll-Out Freezers, "You'll never have to fill another ice tray," or Anahist, "continuous-action cold-relief medication," or Sylvania, "color TV with a flair for elegance," let alone Campbell's Soup or Ford Motor cars, magazines and newspapers could no longer compete with television. As surely as the pioneering Negro magazine *Our Sports* was killed by advertising perceptions of its audience, the huge national magazines also were doomed.

Why not simply start charging more for each issue? At the *Post* 80 percent of the 7 million weekly copies had been sold by subscription, many running on for several years. Those prices were locked in, and that was a dismal, immutable fact of corporate economics. But putting journalism ahead of economics, as far as possible, a new generation of *Post* editors began talking about creating "the greatest magazine in the entire history of magazines." Without altering the rules of Joe Culligan's "competitive free-enterprise system," that effort made for some of the most exciting times I've known.

I signed on as editor-at-large beginning in 1964. I would do some consulting, mostly on sports, but Clay Blair, the editor in chief, said he wanted me to spend 95 percent of my time writing "important articles."

He added, "We are bringing magazine journalism into the twentieth century."

"Clay, *The New Yorker* has already done that."

"Into the second half of the twentieth century, I mean."

The eventual editor of *The Saturday Evening Post,* William A. Emerson Jr., described Blair as "an earth force lightly filtered through a personality." Bulky, black-haired Clay Blair was a zealot, fired by the idea of making the *Post* great and contemporary. He was fearless and sometimes even profound. "I'll fire any writer who tries to bullshit our readers," he said. "It's wrong and, believe me, sooner or later the bullshitter gets found out. Never forget that." But as zeal fired him, it also would be his undoing. Blair was often right, *always* convinced that he was right, and inclined to trample on the checks and balances that are an essential part of rational magazine editing. Without seeming to realize it, or care, Clay Blair, a political conservative and a devout Roman Catholic, was passion's slave.

In 1963, after too many martinis on a Sunday night, he and the *Post*'s Philadelphia lawyer, Philip Strubing, decided to run "the story of a college football fix," implicating Wally Butts of Georgia and Bear Bryant of Alabama in a conspiracy to rig a game. Blair and Strubing had ignored my own initial counsel: You hear "fix" stories all the time in sports, but without confessions, proving them is just about impossible. Both the accused men sued, and the *Post* had to pay about $760,000 in damages. More important, as Otto Friedrich pointed out, "The *Post* had lost a dangerously large part of its reputation for accuracy and responsibility, the reputation on which all its other stories had to rest." A year later Blair launched a carefully plotted attack on Joe Culligan, grasping to capture the presidency of the Curtis Publishing Company for himself. The insurrection failed, and before Blair was dismissed, some hard-edged and nasty reporting by *The New York Times* made Curtis appear to be a Byzantine madhouse. (In 1901 Adolph Ochs bought a sagging newspaper called the *Philadelphia Times.* When he was forced to sell it in 1913, the purchaser was Cyrus H. K. Curtis, who insisted that the sales contract be signed on his private yacht. Ochs and his strong-willed daughter, Iphigene, felt that Curtis was humiliating the family. Iphigene, who lived until 1990, had an enduring taste for vengeance, and I believe that colored the *Times*'s coverage of the Curtis Publishing Company's last days.)

After I signed on as editor-at-large, Blair said, "You seem to have a good rapport with Negroes. How about giving us a profile of Paul Robeson? I mean, was he a Commie, yes or no, and what the hell has happened to the guy?" Robeson, it turned out, had grown depressed and was in no shape to be interviewed.

"Then write that," Blair said, when I reported back to him. "I mean, imagine what you think he's going through, and set it down."

"I won't, Clay. Robeson is ailing. I'm not going to make matters worse."

We were sitting with Otto Friedrich on a banquette at Toots Shor's restaurant. Suddenly plaintive, Blair said, "We just got to get some colored stuff in the magazine. There's a Negro revolution going on."

The solution, suggested Friedrich, was for me to go to Harlem "for as long as it takes" and write "the definitive story" on life in the ghetto. This roused Blair, who said, "We'll pay you whatever you need."

That began an unusual routine. Each morning after breakfast I put on shabby clothing and left my comfortable bachelor pad, which I was now sharing with Alice Russell, the Quaker girl from Bucks County. She seemed to understand my project and encouraged me. She had once dated Julian Bond, she claimed, and "I even let him kiss me good night." She thought racial problems would end eventually after worldwide mixed dating created a human race that was uniformly the color of light coffee. Alice's overviews tended to be simplistic, charming, intuitive, and sexual.

I wore the shabby clothing as a shield. Many streets in Harlem were infested by drug addicts, and a white man who walked into them when well dressed was asking for a mugging, or worse. I wandered Harlem, its many neighborhoods, for days and nights, weeks and months, and finally wrote a 15,000-word article, "White Man, Walk Easy," which the *Post* published in its issue of June 13, 1964. I shared the cover with Former President Harry S. Truman, who had composed a lively article, "My First Eighty Years." The president's story was full of sunlight and optimism. Mine was not. I wrote:

While much of New York, and much of the country prospers, the people of Harlem are still living in the great depression that began almost thirty-five years ago. Except for a brief period during World War II, Harlem never emerged from that depression. Today clusters of men loiter on Harlem street corners. They have no place to go. One out of every four able-bodied Harlem males is unemployed.

Approximately 60,000 citizens of Harlem are addicted to heroin or to the "white lady," cocaine. A fix costs about five dollars, but many addicts require as many as a dozen a day. Addicts, desperate for cash, commit between 60 and 70 percent of Harlem crimes.

Police in Harlem do not enforce all of the laws. Goods advertised as stolen—phonograph records, furs, television sets—are offered to anyone wearing a white shirt and a tie. . . . Say the police: "We only have time to worry about crimes of violence." Say Harlemites: "The police are corrupt."

Conditions are getting worse not better. Talk of violence is common. Extremist groups are gaining numbers. No organized rehabilitation program is in effect. . . .

The story concluded with an episode, in which Tony, a lean black buck, had tried to break my arm before a bigger, stronger black man, a friend of mine, slammed him into a wall.

Tony screams, "Oooh!" Then having made his protest, he grows defiant.

"He's an Uncle Tom," Tony cries. "Ain't he? Ain't he?"

Tony's big black eyes bug out. They look around and look at you. I hold my arm. It hurts where Tony twisted it.

And I see Tony, against a wall like Harlem itself, needing my help and hating me to my grave.

The only black I saw on the floor of the epochal 1964 Republican National Convention in San Francisco—where many believe today's neoconservatism began—was Jackie Robinson. It was July 13, and Nelson Rockefeller was trying to introduce a resolution denouncing extremism. He could not be heard. Supporters of Barry Goldwater stood and booed Rockefeller for more than three minutes; Republicans hooted and jeered a fellow Republican. Robinson, an honorary delegate from Connecticut, was standing up and shouting through cupped hands, "Come on, Rocky." As it happened, Jack was positioned close to the all-white delegation from Alabama. Robinson's cheering enraged one beefy Alabaman. He moved toward the aisle as if to charge. The delegate's wife threw her arms around the man and cried, "No, no."

"Turn him loose, lady," Robinson yelled. "Turn him loose."

The woman continued to restrain her husband. "Luckily for him," Robinson said later, "he got smart enough to listen his wife."

Like most of the country's major publications, *The Saturday Evening Post* had long published editorials that followed the Republican party line. The magazine that Clay Blair had commandeered was widely considered, in Otto Friedrich's words, "old and stodgy, edited by the old and stodgy to be read by the old and stodgy." In reality it was better than that; the *Post* had published F. Scott Fitzgerald, Ring Lardner, and William Faulkner, but shied away from their most adventurous works. Quiet, firm pro-Republican editorials fit the back pages of the old *Post* just as Norman Rockwell's deft, upbeat illustrations fit its covers. For all Blair's talk about creating an entirely new magazine, he himself followed a moderate Republican line. But, as I hope is abundantly clear by now, Blair was not a moderate man.

Most candidates for the Republican presidential nomination in 1964 fell out of contention during the primaries. The final primary, California, would decide the race. Two ambitious rivals remained: Senator Barry Goldwater of Arizona and Governor Nelson Rockefeller of New York.

During the California primary, Rockefeller attacked Goldwater as Mr. Doom. In a pamphlet mailed to 2 million voters, he asked, "Do you want this man in a room with the H-bomb button?" Goldwater's response was personal and pelvic. After years of marriage, Rockefeller had left his first wife for a younger woman, Margaretta Murphy, nicknamed "Happy." She had been divorced by *her* first husband, a prosperous physician with whom she had conceived four children, and in 1963 married Nelson. As she did, Happy agreed to surrender custody of her offspring. This opened the field of virtue for Goldwater. Rockefeller had no respect for family life, Goldwater's aides charged, and what sort of woman could his new wife be, giving up her kids just to satisfy her lust? Three days before the primary, Happy Rockefeller gave birth to a boy, Nelson Jr. That event gave new vigor to the Goldwater family-values offensive. Trumpeting his own resolute marriage and unshakable morality, the senator won the California primary on June 2 by three percentage points.

Now, in San Francisco, I remembered covering the New York Giants of 1954 when they trained in Phoenix. There the largest department store was Goldwater's. The lingerie department was peddling a curious item: brief white women's panties with a design in front and back of crawling black ants. The designer? Barry Morris Goldwater. Up close, I remarked, the Battle of San Francisco, 1964, pitted unconventional morality against bad taste.

"Great," Clay Blair said. "That's what I want from you. Keep your eyes open. Write what you see. Put your guts into every story you write for me."

The entire Republican hierarchy had gathered in San Francisco during the second week of July 1964, and I was determined to talked head-to-head with all of them. Dwight Eisenhower had taken a floor—not a suite, an entire floor—at the St. Francis Hotel. Sorry, but no interviews at this time; the general was working on his speech and on another book as well. He had no free time. The tough-minded general had come to prefer royalties to dialogue. I collared Robert Finch, the most appealing member of the group around Richard Nixon, and was told, "I'll see what I can do." I did hear from Dick Nixon later—much later. In 1991 he wrote me a longhand letter praising *The Boys of Summer*. He did not, however, get back to me in 1964. The political establishment and its secretive ways were fixed of old and founded strong. But my effort to change things was not entirely unsuccessful.

I wandered the floor of the San Francisco Cow Palace seeking other subjects. Everyone had to display a credentials badge, which the men wore on their lapels. To this the Goldwater supporters added their own special Western symbol, a gold-colored miniature bucking bronco.

In the midst of the California delegation, Ronald Reagan stood up, and when I made a small wave, Reagan waved back. He said pleasantly that he didn't want to be interviewed just then. "I'm not a candidate for anything. I'm just an out-of-work actor." Reagan wore a Goldwater Bronco. He waved again, but not to me. He seemed to know everybody on the floor. For a noncandidate, his energy was impressive.

John V. Lindsay, the tall, handsome congressman representing the Upper East Side of Manhattan, said, "Sure we can talk, if you'll buy me a sandwich for lunch." We moved to a concession stand, and over a ham and cheese on rye Lindsay said, "You know I'm on the outside here."

"If Goldwater wins the nomination . . . " I began.

"That's not an if. He has it."

". . . will he get your vote?"

"Yes, but I won't be voting for Goldwater. I'll be voting for the Republican Party." John Lindsay's presence called to mind Edward Arlington Robinson's phrase, "He glittered when he walked."

"Can you tell me how the Goldwater people took over this convention?"

"Kind of dry," Lindsay said, looking down at his sandwich. "Would you get me a container of coffee?"

"*The Saturday Evening Post* gives me an expense account for just such contingencies."

Lindsay smiled broadly. "Look, what did you say your name was? Right. Look, Roger. I think those of us they call liberal Republicans were too diffuse. We had Lodge, Scranton, and Rockefeller. We scattered our firepower. The conservatives, and there are some reactionaries in there, focused all their energies in backing Goldwater."

"If Eisenhower had come out for Rockefeller, would that have made a difference?"

"If my aunt had balls, she'd be my uncle."

Feeling suddenly close, I said, "Can I use all this stuff, John?"

"Sure. Just remember I'm helping you, so don't embarrass me. And if you want the nuts and bolts of how Goldwater nailed down the nomination, I'm the wrong man. Talk to Bill Miller, the congressman from upstate New York. He's got the vice-presidential nomination locked up. But he's tougher than I am. You won't get him for just a ham sandwich."

"What will he want?"

"An endorsement from *The Saturday Evening Post.*"

William E. Miller, short, black-haired, and dapper, received me in his duplex suite on the top floor of the San Francisco Hilton. A press release reported that Miller had grown up in Lockport, New York, graduated from Notre Dame Law School, served as "an assistant prosecutor of Nazi war criminals" during the Nuremberg Trials, and been national chairman of the Republican Party for the three years leading up to the Goldwater convention. He said in a businesslike way that he could give me half an hour, no more than that, because *Newsweek* was coming in next and after that *Time*. "They're settling for fifteen minutes each. The *Post* is a bigger magazine. That's why you're getting more."

While Miller was willing to be interviewed, he was not willing to engage in conversation. That is, whatever I asked produced a preformed answer, usually identical to the printed text in the position papers someone had placed on his desk. Goldwater's upcoming nomination was not "politics as usual. It was the will of the American people who were sick and tired of big government and big spending.

"Let me quote the greatest Republican, Abraham Lincoln. He said that to arrest the progress of slavery, we formed a party composed of 'strained, discordant, and even hostile elements.' That's what you're seeing here. But just like Lincoln we're going to save the country." There was no questioning dapper Bill Miller's zeal.

Could he be specific about how the Goldwater camp lined up its delegates?

Hard, dark eyes fixed me. "You're a reporter. Find out for yourself."

He told me that Lockport, his hometown near Buffalo, was the site of a factory that manufactured radiators for General Motors cars. His personal background? He didn't want to talk about that, but his grandparents were immigrants from Ireland and Germany and his parents didn't have any money.

"How could you afford Notre Dame?"

"A widowed aunt stashed away funds. I was her favorite nephew."

"Can you tell me about her?"

"*Newsweek* is here," said an assistant.

Miller gave me a dismissive nod. I never got the name of the widowed aunt.

Rockefeller made his last stand the night before voting began. "I've warned of the extremist threat to the party and danger to the nation,"

Rockefeller said. He was speaking slowly. The crowd at the San Francisco Cow Palace chanted, "We want Barry."

"These extremists feed on hate and terror," Rockefeller said. "They operate from dark shadows of secrecy. It is essential that this convention repudiate any militant minority, whether Communist, Ku Klux Klan, or Birchers." Now the booing rose. More than one Republican delegate that summer was a member of the Ku Klux Klan. Untold numbers belonged to the John Birch Society, an organization on the radical right. The Birch Society published pamphlets alleging that Soviet Communism had already established control over the American government. According to the John Birch line, "dedicated, conscious agents of the Communist conspiracy" included Eisenhower, Allen Dulles, director of the CIA, and Earl Warren, chief justice of the United States.

A day later Goldwater won the nomination and made an uncompromising speech. "The Democratic administration," he said, "has failed and failed and failed in the works of freedom. Failure cements the wall of shame in Berlin. Failures blot the sands of shame at the Bay of Pigs; failures marked the slow death of freedom in Laos; failures infest the jungles of Vietnam."

Then he responded directly to charges of extremism. "I would remind you," said Barry Goldwater, "that extremism in defense of liberty is no vice!"

The big hall rocked with cheers.

By the time I left the Cow Palace it was close to midnight. A chilly San Francisco fog was swirling outside the lobby. Pickets trudged about, silent and orderly. Many were black; black men and women were picketing the Republicans who had become, as Jackie Robinson warned, a party of, by, and for white people. The blacks bore sandwich-board signs with a militant message. "Bury Goldwater."

"Come on," Clay Blair said, "I'm taking you somewhere great."

"I want to run down a few more politicians."

"Some other time." Blair directed me into his limousine and we set forth toward the North Beach district. "There's a club there with a babe," Blair said, "who comes down from the ceiling in a gilded bird cage. Bare-butt naked. She's got a forty-four-inch bust."

I was trying to come to terms with a great deal, and I didn't want to go slouching into a strip joint. But Blair was the boss and he was insistent. Soon we were sitting in a nightclub, tables ringing the stage, where female dancers were bouncing about and shedding clothes.

A pause. A fanfare. A drum roll. A blur of lights. And then the star—her name has long since escaped me—descended. The bird cage was a kind of swing. The woman sat with her legs crossed, looking vulnerable. Her body swayed. Loudspeakers blared the throbbing song "Night Train." The woman's bust was so large as to approach the grotesque. The San Francisco strip joint rang to cowboy whoops. I got up and walked around.

Most of the men cheering the woman with the huge breasts wore bucking broncos on their lapels. Having trashed Nelson Rockefeller for immorality, the Goldwater delegates were having fun, country-western whorehouse style.

"Hey," a stranger shouted at me. "How'd ya like to sink your face in them two milk jugs?" I wondered where the Republican wives were, but I suppose that didn't matter.

When I call *The Saturday Post* a great magazine during the years from 1964 through 1969, I don't imply perfection. Before Clay Blair was forced out of the Curtis Publishing Company late in 1964, he contributed great energy and, as we will soon see, demonstrated for one final time, great excess. The magazine's layout was not consistently pleasing, and the covers sometimes looked too busy. But the writing, the depth, variety, and splendor of the prose, has, I suggest, not been matched by any other periodical. In its late years the *Post* published nonfiction by Ben Bagdikian, Russell Baker, Jimmy Breslin, Truman Capote, Joan Didion, John Gregory Dunne, John Kobler, Edward Linn, Alex Haley, Pete Hamill, W. C. Heinz, John Hersey, Sanche de Gramont (a.k.a. Ted Morgan), Lewis Lapham, Peter Maas, Robert K. Massie, Willie Morris, Budd Schulberg, Wilfred Sheed, Gay Talese, Evelyn Waugh, Yevgeny Yevtushenko—pretty much everybody who was anybody in the craft. Then there was the fiction, composed of, among others, Thomas Berger, Shirley Jackson, Arthur Miller, Frank O'Connor, John O'Hara, James Michener, William Saroyan, Isaac Bashevis Singer. To play off Hemingway's title, the *Post* was a portable feast. At least it was for people who loved to read. Bill Veeck, the baseball entrepreneur then living on the Eastern Shore of Maryland, telephoned and told me jubilantly, "Great news. They've started stealing the magazine out of my mailbox again."

My assignment was to cover Goldwater, and his followers, across the summer and on up to October 15, a span of more than three months. Then I'd have a week to write a final draft. This was Blair at his editing best. "Research and report the story for as long and as hard as you can. Don't worry about costs. That's my problem."

I started with background. Barry's grandfather, "Big Mike" Goldwater, escaped from the ghetto in Konin, Poland, in 1848 and made his way to the American West. He learned English, of course, and started a peddling business. Big Mike went from town to town in the rugged, sparsely settled land, selling pots and pans and socks and shirts from a horse-drawn wagon. He was tough. He could handle a gun. He had a good head for business. In 1876, Mike opened the first Goldwater store in Prescott about ninety miles north of Phoenix. He was nineteenth-century American individualism personified, albeit with a Polish-Yiddish accent.

One of Mike's sons, Baron, moved to Phoenix and started the Goldwater Department store there that swelled the family fortune. Baron, reserved and quiet, was Barry's father. Mike's other son, Morris, stayed in Prescott. He wore a handlebar mustache and a gold nugget stickpin and carried a cane. During political arguments, he waved the cane like a baton. Uncle Morris, a conservative, states' rights Democrat, was Prescott's mayor for twenty-six years. He had been, Barry told intimates, "my boyhood idol."

I talked with the men around Goldwater, most of whom have been forgotten—who today remembers Denison Kitchel, Stephen Shadegg, or Harry Rosenzweig?—and I came to learn their grand design for victory. The candidate would win large blocs of the old Confederacy because he stood with Southerners on the issue of states' rights. "But," Goldwater's brother Bob told me, "don't think for a minute that Barry is racist. When we were kids we played baseball and football with Negroes. Barry has always been for the colored people."

You could not win an election just with Southern states. Elsewhere,

Goldwater and his people believed, they could scramble the old voting patterns. In Illinois and Indiana, in Michigan and Pennsylvania, and maybe in California and just possibly even New York, Goldwater would draw voters because he stood foursquare against big government, big labor, big business, big-city bosses, and (in the White House) Big Brother. He was the anti-Establishment candidate, who was running, his spokesmen said, on behalf of the unorganized, overtaxed, overregulated, unlobbied middle class. To be sure, this strategy was unorthodox and a long shot, but moving from a Polish ghetto to the United States Senate in three generations had made unorthodoxy and long odds part of the Goldwater tradition. Whatever one's politics, and I was trying to make myself completely apolitical, his was a remarkable American story. I looked forward to sitting down with Barry Goldwater, one-on-one, as I had with Pee Wee Reese and Robert Frost. I approached Paul Wagner, a crew-cut, thin-lipped man whom Goldwater employed as press secretary, and said I'd like some time with the senator.

"I'll let you know," Wagner said.

"I'll be writing a cover story for *The Saturday Evening Post*."

"I'll let you know."

"We're selling seven million copies a week. They tell me that works out to twenty-one million readers. Most of them vote."

"I'll let you know."

Thus began a journey in which I followed Goldwater about the country, from Prescott to Boston, from Oregon to Memphis, from border unto border, listening to what he said and watching how audiences reacted. One day, memorable for mileage, began in Wichita Falls, Texas, moved on to Dallas, Mason City, Iowa, and Madison, Wisconsin, before we arrived in Boston for an evening speech. The next day we flew from Boston to Albany, to Louisville and then New Orleans. The campaign had chartered a Boeing 727. Goldwater and his wife, Peggy, stayed in an up-front suite, equipped with beds and a bar. The rest of us rode in cramped airline seats that made sleep difficult.

During the first week of the campaign, he attacked the draft (end it), income tax (reduce it), and federal power (curtail it). As the weeks wore on and the incessant air travel wearied everyone, he spouted apparently sincere opinions in reckless ways. He said that violence in the

streets, wanton crime, and race riots, sprang from federal amorality. The
living symbol of that was President Lyndon Johnson, "the most dishon-
est man I've ever met." Hubert Humphrey, the Democratic candidate
for vice president, was "a socialistic radical." In Winston-Salem, a tobacco town, he said, "Now they're trying to tell you what you have to
print on cigarette packs." I asked Wagner to find out if Goldwater was
advocating "a fair deal for lung cancer."

Often Goldwater took positions that were downright contrarian. In
Orlando, speaking mostly to retirees, he condemned the idea of provid-
ing medical care for the aged under Social Security. (Johnson signed
Medicare into law a year later.) In Knoxville, Tennessee, the heart of
TVA country, he talked about dismantling the TVA. In Charleston, West
Virginia, deep in depressed Appalachia, he said that Johnson's war on
poverty was "phony." About this time *The Washington Post* published a
telling Herblock cartoon. With a briefcase in one hand and a winter
coat on one arm, Goldwater is telling a homeless woman, dressed in
rags, who is clutching her two children, "If you had any initiative, you'd
go out and inherit a department store."

Before the campaign, Goldwater assumed a comfortable position on
integrated education. Personally, he believed that black and white children should go to school together. Personally, he believed that segregation was wrong. But this was not a federal matter. It was a matter of the
individual heart. The Supreme Court was mistaken in ordering school
integration, and Congress had been mistaken in enacting the Civil
Rights Act. But now, as a candidate, he stood shoulder to shoulder with
Strom Thurmond, whose strident speeches against civil rights approached fanaticism. Moderates became resentful and blacks were furious. Outside one Midwestern county courthouse, black men refused to
shake Goldwater's hand. In Michigan a black chef refused to give Goldwater his recipe for barbecue sauce. "I don't like to give it to nobody,"
the chef said. "But especially not to him."

The campaign was going badly. Some called Goldwater "the fastest
lip in the West." Someone else corrected that. Goldwater was "the fascist lip in the West." He kept saying more than made political sense.
"The United States should act like a world power and quit groveling on
its knees to inferior people who like to come to New York.

"Some day I am convinced there will either be a war or we'll be subjugated without a war. I think a general war is probable."

The conservative columnist Stewart Alsop, wrote, "Lyndon Johnson is lucky in his opponent. A Republican candidate who did not scare the pants and the petticoats off the voters would have given this President a real run for his money. That might have been a very good thing for the country." Other commentators and all the polls suggested a Johnson landslide. Convinced by September that he could not win, Goldwater fell back on delivering three set speeches in flat tones. In time I could repeat them by rote.

Social Security bankrupted France; it will bankrupt America. We have to make Social Security a voluntary program.

Because of the Earl Warren Supreme Court, your wives and daughters are no longer safe on the streets. We have to appoint justices who care more for law-abiding citizens than they do for criminals.

The best way to bring peace to Southeast Asia is to defoliate Vietnam. We have chemicals to do that which are harmless to people. (Back in May he had told a *Newsweek* reporter that "I'd drop a low-yield atomic bomb on Chinese supply lines in North Vietnam.") Now he was advocating widespread use of Agent Orange, which has turned out to be just as harmless as arsenic.

"If you expect me to make sense out of this campaign," I said to Paul Wagner, the grim press secretary, "you have to get me with the candidate, one-on-one."

"I'm working on it," Wagner said, and turned away.

In its issue of September 19, *The Saturday Evening Post* published an astonishing editorial. It had been written by William Miller, 1964 being a busy year for William Millers. This one was a moonlighting *Life* magazine writer who wrote the editorial (for a fee of $250). Clay Blair made the assignment and rushed the piece into print, without showing it to Bill Emerson or Otto Friedrich. Warming up, William Miller asserted that Goldwater had "a mind of quicksand and a tongue of quicksilver." The editorial went on, "Goldwater is a grotesque burlesque of the conservative he pretends to be. He is a wild man, a stray, an unprincipled and ruthless political jujitsu artist. . . . For the good of the Republican Party, which his candidacy disgraces, we hope that Goldwater is crushingly defeated." This ran anonymously, as editorials do, in solitary splendor on the back page of 7 million copies of the *Post*.

As Friedrich commented, "Obviously, we should have come out for Lyndon Johnson against Goldwater, but we should have done so in a thoughtful, well-reasoned editorial. Miller's harangue was as extreme as anything Goldwater himself had ever said." After the issue appeared and I reported to Dulles Airport for my next swing with the candidate, Paul Wagner came striding toward me and said in a belligerent tone, "Change in plans. We can't accommodate you on the jet. You'll have to follow on the DC-6 [a prop plane that was about 150 miles an hour slower]. You'll miss some stops, but I'll get you tapes of what the senator said."

That the *Post* had paid for my jet travel in advance was swept aside. I didn't trust Wagner to supply tapes, so I contracted with Andrew Glass, of the *Baltimore Sun,* to cover the Goldwater appearances I would miss. After checking with Emerson, I said the *Post* would pay him $1,500. Glass was delighted to do some extra reporting for me.

To protest the wild and wooly editorial, about ten thousand readers canceled subscriptions to the *Post*. Given the magazine's circulation, that was relatively unimportant. But several large companies responded to the editorial by pulling their advertising. One was Timken Roller Bearings whose slogan—"Wherever Wheels and Shafts Turn"—described the widespread use of its product. Another, the Admiral Corporation, manufactured large appliances and television sets. A third was Kraft Foods. The best estimate I got from *Post* executives was that the Goldwater editorial led directly to the cancellation of $3 million in advertising. For a struggling magazine that was catastrophic.

The harangue did however get me my first direct contact with the Goldwater family. To attend the late cocktail parties that invariably concluded the senator's day, I had to wear credential badges identifying me and the publication I represented. In a large suite at a Kansas City hotel, Peggy Goldwater, stared at my lapel. She'd had more than one drink. At length Mrs. Goldwater said a bit thickly, "*Sharturday Evening Posht!* What are *you* doing here?"

"I'd like to talk to you about that," I said.

Security men briskly steered her out of range.

My story in the October 24 issue began, "Barry Morris Goldwater does not seem to be a man of hatred but hatred surrounds him this strident autumn. Wherever and however fast he travels, the hatred of both his supporters and his opponents travels with him." I then chronicled the wanderings of someone who seemed sincere and personally likable, but kept committing dreadful gaffs.

> Goldwater is a country-club man. His famous outrageous remarks, many of which he has recently disavowed, are the kind of strong talk that sounds grand back in the locker room at the Coyote Gulch Country Club after a rousing 18 holes of golf. . . .
>
> A determining factor in Goldwater's campaign has been his inability to remember he's not back at the club. Country-club talk is not always out of place in the Senate, itself a kind of club. But as a candidate for President, Goldwater moved into a different and vastly more public world.
>
> Some people close to him have remarked that he seems frightened. They say at times he seems to be wondering how he ever happened to become a Presidential candidate. Whether he is motivated by fear or resentment, Goldwater has barricaded himself from the press. (He has not held a single on-the-record press conference all campaign.) Refusing to answer questions has helped Barry Goldwater stay out of further trouble, but it has also left everyone wondering what on earth he means.

On Election Day the American public put Goldwater to rout. Lyndon Johnson polled 43,126,506 votes to Goldwater's 27,176,799. Johnson's margin, just under 16 million, was larger even than Franklin D. Roosevelt's edge in his 1936 landslide over Alf Landon. Goldwater won only five Southern states and Arizona. Johnson's margin in the electoral college was 486 to 52.

Trying to sum up Goldwater's effort, Theodore H. White, the gifted presidential campaign scribe, used one word: dismal. I suggested in my story that Goldwater had neither the intelligence nor the adaptability to become a successful president. I didn't think Goldwater was dismal. I thought he was dumb.

As my visit with Robert Frost had drawn four hundred letters, so did my Goldwater story. But these were unpleasant. Almost all were signed "100 percent American." Most offered me the same inelegant sentence, "I'm glad I read your article near the bathroom, because it made me have to go and throw up."

Looking back, I think, like Teddy White, I really missed the point, which was not whether Goldwater was dismal or dumb or both. Actually, I wrote the point close to the end of the article, but in the press and stress of journalism I failed to think it through and expand it as I wish I had. The shadowy, ominous John Birch Society claimed as members John Wayne, Hedda Hopper, and a lapsed New Deal Democrat named Ronald Reagan. (Reagan in time denied membership.) Unlike Goldwater, leading Birchers were willing, even anxious to talk one-on-one, but always with the proviso that I agree not to print their names. As they were messianic, they wanted to be anonymous. It was not widely acceptable to stand publicly in a group that called Ike Eisenhower a dangerous Red. I no longer remember the name of the Bircher who handed me a key to what happened within the Republican Party in 1964. I do know that he was Midwestern, a hand surgeon, a short, balding fellow who wore eyeglasses and bought me a few drinks.

"You've really accomplished something," he said, "becoming a big writer for an important magazine. I'll bet you've gotten where you are on your own."

"Mostly, Doc," I said, "but not entirely."

"Same with me," the surgeon said. "I didn't need a handout from the government. I've worked my tail off and now I make a lot of money. The colored, they want a lot of money but they're too lazy to work for it, like you and me. Here's the thing. We have to stand up to the Commies, or they'll destroy us. And we've got to kill welfare and make the colored go to work just like the rest of us, or the whole country will go under."

I said nothing. I waited to see where he was going. "We're not happy with Goldwater," the surgeon said. "He's just the best that we could do—this time.

"Well, the hell with this election. We know we're going to lose. But at least we've gotten control of a party. Whatever happens, we aren't letting go."

Across all these intervening decades, from the 1960s into the twenty-first century, that is what hard-right conservatives have accomplished, capturing the Republican Party, driving from power the liberals and the moderates and the Easterners, even as Barry Goldwater, the dumb or dismal candidate who marshaled all that thunder on the right, eased back into conventional respectability, irrelevance, and old age, before he died in 1998 at the age of eighty-nine, in an Arizona town called Paradise Valley.

## III

### *The Benedictine*

To use a phrase originated by Fred Allen, the 1960s put America on a treadmill to oblivion. Lyndon Johnson talked about creating a Great Society, but blacks rioted, first in Harlem, then in the Watts district of Los Angeles. The enlightened leadership of Jackie Robinson and Martin Luther King Jr. was being challenged by such nihilists as H. Rap Brown. Running as a Republican, the glittering John Lindsay became mayor of New York in 1966, defeating Democrat Abraham Beame and that elegant, UnGoldwater conservative, William F. Buckley, and all at once the city stopped working. On Lindsay's first day as mayor, brisk and wintry, the Transit Workers Union called a strike. All the wheels on all of New York's busses and subway trains halted. How was one to go to work or get around the chilly town? Rent a bicycle? They all were snapped up within hours. Horseback? There were no longer hitching posts in Manhattan; even if you knew how to ride, where would you park the animal? The so-called subway strike went on for twelve foot-blistering days. Two years later, on February 2, 1968 the Sanitation Workers quit their trucks and stayed idle for nine days. Nine days of piling garbage bags, one on the other until the noxious mounds reached ten feet high and higher. New Yorkers saw rats scurrying on sidewalks, amid the stacks of garbage, even on Fifth Avenue and Central Park West. More than one serious citizen worried about a recurrence of bubonic plague. Was New York, the capital of the world, doomed to chronic chaos? I found myself considering Lewis Mumford's lines from *The City in*

*History*: "Necropolis is near, though not a stone has yet crumbled. For the barbarian has already captured the city from within. Come, hangman! Come, vulture!"

And beyond New York, like a drumbeat for the dead, war in Asia pounded on.

In October 1964 the directors of the Curtis Publishing Company fired Clay Blair. William A. Emerson Jr. replaced him as editor of *The Saturday Evening Post* and Otto Friedrich became managing editor. Emerson was a spirited son of the South who, the story went, lost his Southern accent during his days as a Harvard undergraduate, then reacquired it as his New York career burgeoned, while he was living in Westchester County. Emerson was enlightened, passionate, and very funny. "Just the other day," he wrote in one brief column "From the Editor," "on my commuter train from Larchmont, I rode over a bump that wrinkled every thread in my suit." He possessed a treasury of stories, which he fervently related to corporate executives, prospective advertisers, nervous staffers, and friends. I liked the one about the last whore in Waxahatchie County, Texas, and the one about his uncle from Bottom Dollar, Tennessee. My favorite was "The Curse of the Plotnik Diamond." In the end the curse turned out to be Mr. Plotnik. Bill Emerson was a brilliant editorial mind and splendid company.

Friedrich and I shared many enthusiasms: Tuscan food, rose gardens, women of restraint and passion, Beethoven's *Hammerklavier* Sonata, *The Mayor of Casterbridge,* nicely played major-league baseball games, the clarinet works of Brahms, and—most of all—writing as well as we possibly could. When Friedrich lived in Paris during the early 1950s, Alice B. Toklas, Gertrude Stein's colleague and lover, pronounced him "the finest young American writer since Thomas Wolfe."

As the country snarled and rattled under Lyndon Johnson, I prospered under Emerson and Friedrich. I wrote the story of a bizarre murder in Manhattan, a long account of the mighty institution *The New York Times,* and an extended consideration of American Jewish life, which would become in 1968, when I was forty-one years old, that long-awaited (at least by me) first "serious" book. The publisher insisted on calling it *The Passionate People.* (I had titled the work *Jews in*

*America: A Passionate Portrayal,* which has, of course, an entirely different emphasis.)

I wrote a shorter piece about the musicians Jacqueline Du Pré, the haunting, doomed English cellist, and her husband, the Israeli pianist and conductor, Daniel Barenboim, and another about Frank Ryan, a quarterback for the Cleveland Browns, who had acquired a Ph.D. in topology, the abstract mathematical study of surfaces. Du Pré looked dewy and sexy. She wore a short plaid skirt, and as we talked, facing one another she frequently crossed and uncrossed her long legs, flashing firm thighs. Barenboim was assertive and kept calling his wife "Smiley," as in "Smiley, get our guest another tray of canapes." Frank Ryan's gifts and humor proved to be remarkable. In the Browns' training camp on the day when media photographers were permitted to run free, Frank, who was right-handed, threw every forward pass with his left hand. Afterward, as a swarm of picture editors cursed, Ryan grinned and said, "Wouldn't you think one of the photographers would have noticed?"

Late in 1967, Friedrich asked me to look into a growing movement within the Democratic Party. "These people want to drop LBJ from the 1968 ticket," he said over lunch at a restaurant called the Italian Pavilion, where the veal and the Barolo wine were delicious. "The man won by sixteen million votes. Three years later half his party wants to dump him." He sipped some more Barolo. "I don't know if you agree with me," Otto said, "and of course you don't have to, but it seems to me that we are turning Vietnam into an Asian Auschwitz."

Throughout the twentieth century, we both knew, the Democrats had given the country multiterm presidents: Woodrow Wilson, FDR, and Harry Truman, although Truman stepped aside in 1952 rather than run against Eisenhower, the conquering hero. The power of incumbency had been mighty. Now the Vietnam War was changing everything.

Back when Vietnam was part of French Indochina, France established a military base called Dien Bien Phu in northern Vietnam near the border of Laos. The native forces of Ho Chi Minh engaged the French and, under massive air bombardment, encircled Dien Bien Phu, trapping 13,000 elite troops. Despite a plea from Georges Bidault, the French foreign minister, President Eisenhower declined to let U.S. forces intervene. The general told associates, "I never want to see this country bogged down in a land war in Asia." On May 7, 1954, the French garrison at Dien Bien Phu surrendered. Vietnam subsequently was partitioned.

Eisenhower did send hundreds of military "advisors" to South Vietnam, men charged with training the new nation's army. In 1959, when North Vietnamese guerrilas attacked a base at Bienhoa, Major Dale R. Buis and Master Sergeant Chester M. Ovand became the first Americans to die in the Vietnam War. Russia and China shipped supplies and technicians into North Vietnam, adding that developing country to the Communist bloc. President Kennedy expanded Eisenhower's commitment and dispatched American paramilitaries in order, some said, to defend his coreligionists, the Roman Catholics of South Vietnam, from the aggressive atheists of the north. In this version, which now can be neither confirmed nor disproved, Francis Cardinal Spellman of New York was dictating some of America's foreign policy.

As president, Lyndon Baines Johnson wildly expanded the American role, sending more and more troops, promising to bomb the Viet Cong into history, until in 1967, more than 500,000 American servicemen were on the ground in a small corner of Southeast Asia. The Viet Cong fought defiantly and well, and there we were, stuck with Ike's dreaded land war in Asia. Casualty lists appeared daily in major newspapers. The draft forced hundreds of thousands of young men into service, mostly, the Congress of Racial Equality charged "from minority groups and the poor." The Defense Department turned to universities for research, and by 1967 war contracts had become a greater source of academic income than tuition. MIT signed $92 million dollars worth of military contracts that year. Johns Hopkins came in at $71 million, Stanford at $45 million, and Columbia at $16 million. Many professors chose the increasingly profitable business of war research over the less lucrative activity of teaching undergraduates. The American student class felt alarmed by the draft and spurned by the colleges they were attending. One popular and inflammatory campus pamphlet appeared under the heading "The Student as Nigger."

"Let's just quit and say we won," someone suggested. But that was not Lyndon Johnson's way. The war was stretching on, war without end, and to what purpose? "If we don't stop the Communists in Vietnam," argued the warriors of the right, "we'll be fighting them on the streets of San Francisco." But Johnson had run in *opposition* to the warriors of the right. In what remains a memorable one-liner, the author Norman Mailer spoke for many when he said, "The shits are killing us."

I began with an exploratory tour, east to west. New York Democrats seemed stoutly against the war and dismayed by Johnson. A young lawyer there named Allard Lowenstein was organizing "Democrats in Dissent." I checked in with Democratic Party people in Des Moines. Same thing. An Iowa legislator named Harry Beardsley said, he was leading a group that "actively seeks an alternative to Johnson." I flew on to San Francisco. No one I talked to there was worried about fighting Communists on Lombard Street. Or on the slopes of Candlestick Point, for that matter. I heard expressions of anger and one very telling joke. A Democrat named Gerry Hill said he had been approached by a Republican who asked, "Remember what you told me in 1964? You told me that if I voted for Goldwater bad things would happen. You said the Negroes would riot in the streets and we'd have half a million men in Vietnam."

"Yeah," the Democrat said.

"Well, I have to confess," the Republican said, "I did vote for Goldwater, and you were right." Betrayal was on the minds of many Democrats. More than one told me, in effect, "That gunslinging son of a bitch from Texas has betrayed us."

An early morning telephone call awakened me in the St. Francis Hotel. "You'd better get to Washington tomorrow," said Don McKinney, Friedrich's deputy. "Some guy named McCarthy is going to announce he's running for president."

I remembered the "guy"—Eugene Joseph McCarthy of Minnesota, and his great speech for Adlai Stevenson eight years before. (Stevenson had fallen dead on a London sidewalk in 1965.) Back in 1968 only fourteen states offered voters presidential primaries. The convention delegates were handpicked in back rooms by party bosses, playing power games with one another. In essence the public was barred. There was more suspense to conventions then, but an outsider with no ties to bosses simply could not win.

In the 1960s as today, the sitting president dominated the news media, supervised the disbursement of hundreds of billions of dollars, and hired major national officials. His autocracy within his own party was limited only by his guile, his energy, his ambition, and, to a lesser degree, his popularity. I asked a fair question: Could guileful, energetic, ambitious Lyndon Johnson actually be deposed?

"No," insisted Friedrich when I reached him, "but this is a major story just the same. A strong challenge just might force Johnson to modify his policies." Friedrich and I both had sons growing toward draft age. The possibility of losing one of our children in what seemed a pointless war was so horrifying that we never spoke of it.

Snow fell on Washington in the morning of November 30, 1967. It fooled the weather forecasters and snarled a city that liked to think of itself as Southern. Around the Capitol lay unplowed snow, and a mean, wet wind sprang up. Inside, Eugene McCarthy, pale-skinned but robust, wearing a gray suit, stood before marble pillars in the Senate's vaulted caucus room. "I intend to enter the Democratic presidential primaries in New Hampshire, Wisconsin, Oregon, California, and Nebraska," he said, speaking softly, almost diffidently. "My decision to challenge has been strengthened by recent announcements of the administration, the evident intention to escalate that war and the absence of any indication of a compromise." He had declaimed the Adlai Stevenson speech with ringing tones. Speaking about himself, he was restrained. Still talking quietly, he began to itemize the cost of the Vietnam War:

"The physical destruction of a small nation. . . . The fracturing of the society of South Vietnam. . . . For the United States, over 15,000 combat dead and nearly 95,000 wounded. . . . A monthly expenditure of between two and three billion dollars. . . . The failure to provide adequate funds for the poverty program here. . . . The drastic reduction of foreign aide elsewhere. . . . A dangerous inflation. . . . A deepening moral crisis: discontent, frustration. . . . Alienation from politics, particularly on campuses. . . . A tendency to withdraw in frustration or cynicism.

"I would hope not to be misunderstood. I am not for peace at any price, but rather for an honorable, rational, and political settlement to this wicked war." Were there any questions? He wanted to know.

"Sir," a woman began belligerently, "hasn't the administration sought the rational solution you suggest and offered to meet with Hanoi?"

"To suggest a meeting anytime, anywhere," McCarthy said, "is not an offer. An offer would be 'Let's meet next Tuesday morning in Warsaw.' "

"Don't you believe," another woman reporter said, also belligerently, "that we should stop Communism?"

"Yes, I do," Gene McCarthy said. "And South Vietnam is the worst possible place to try."

"Sir, aren't you committing political suicide?"

He gave a small smile. "It won't be a case of suicide, but it might be an execution."

The assembled Washington press corps burst into giggles.

Where most campaigns open with martial trumpets, Eugene McCarthy began with civility. He felt, he would tell me later, that the Kennedy style and what went with it, the troops of publicists, the hired cheering claques, the wheeling, the big-money dealing, demeaned the democratic process. He believed in the intelligence of the voters—Robert Frost's "wisdom of the mob"—and he cherished Adlai Stevenson's phrase, "Let's talk sense to the American people." The telephones in his office rang all afternoon, and telegrams of support began to arrive. But, and this is very significant, no senator, not one, not even such so-called doves as Albert Gore Sr., William Fullbright, and Wayne Morse, moved to his side. There were 248 Democratic members of the House. Only one, Don Edwards of California, spoke up in favor of McCarthy. In opposing Johnson and his hawkish cadre, McGeorge Bundy, Arthur Goldberg, Hubert Humphrey, Robert McNamara, Dean Rusk, Walt Rostow, and General William Westmoreland, McCarthy stood alone. That is not a comfortable situation when you are bidding for popular votes; McCarthy sharply felt his isolation. In all of the Congress, the House and the Senate, where he had served for eighteen years, only one supporter came forward. But, and this is even more significant, McCarthy did not waver.

A few days later a Gallup poll reported that 58 percent of those sampled had never so much as heard of him. The senator refused to be discouraged. "Had they asked," he said, "they would have found that fewer still have heard of Saint Benedict of Nursia, but that detracts not one whit from his importance." (Benedict, who lived from 480 to 544, is the patriarch of Western monks and founded the Roman Catholic order that bears his name.)

On the first weekend in December, McCarthy flew to Chicago for a gathering called the National Conference of Concerned (that is, anti-Johnson and anti-Vietnam War) Democrats. More than five hundred of them, well groomed, middle-class, polite, paid their own way to Chicago and took rooms at the Sheraton Blackstone Hotel where nineteen years earlier Harry Truman began the give-'em-hell campaign that defeated Thomas E. Dewey. This weekend the Blackstone was installing new elevators. The Concerned Democrats waited for cars with patience and minimal profanity. These people were dignified and intelligent, like their candidate.

McCarthy took questions at the Hotel Hilton across the street. Was he going to drop out if Bobby Kennedy ran? "If Kennedy moves, we'll have to see. I don't know what he'll do. There is no conspiracy between us, no collusion, no common plan."

What about the militants? The reference was to extremist antiwar groups, gathering, mostly on campuses. McCarthy said, "This group is militant enough for me."

How about black militants?

"I'm indifferent to color."

It was going well. When McCarthy walked into the delegates' cocktail party at 5:45, portable spotlights fixed on him and men bearing television cameras closed in. McCarthy was a big man who played a lot of hockey. He moved strongly among the people, his pale face looking bloodless under the cruel lights—moving and clasping hands and saying, several times, "No, thank you. I don't need another drink just now." He was gentle and attentive. As people spoke to McCarthy, adoration brightened their eyes.

Later two thousand Democrats crowded into the grand ballroom of the Hilton to hear him. Perhaps four thousand more milled outside in the cold, angry at being denied admittance by the fire department. Chicago's mayor, Richard J. Daley, was no friend to political dissent. Allard Lowenstein of New York delivered a fiery introduction.

"We are not trying to beat somebody with nobody," he shouted. "We are trying to beat somebody with somebody." Cheers.

"Get this straight about Lyndon Johnson. If a man cheats you once, shame on him. But if he cheats you twice, shame on *you!*" Cheers.

"They say we're trying to lick Goliath with David. Well, who the hell do they think won that one?" More cheers.

The style was rough, reasonably effective, and totally uncongenial to the mood of Gene McCarthy, who was standing with his head bowed and his strong hands held before him, as if in prayer. When Lowenstein finished, fifteen minutes later, McCarthy walked to the podium and read through his prepared speech. He told the delegates that the Dreyfus case in France indicated that a society cannot accept a single injustice without spreading corruption. The war in Vietnam was an amalgam of injustices. He told them what the Punic Wars had done to Rome. Even though the legions were victorious, even though Roman troops under Scipio Africanus obliterated Carthage in 142 B.C., Roman society was so disrupted by the wars that it never recovered. The Republic fell, and then came the Caesars. Vietnam could be our Punic War. Unlike Lowenstein, McCarthy did not attack Johnson, nor did he raise his voice. The applause was subdued.

Someone asked afterward why he had not been more galvanic. "At this stage of the campaign," McCarthy said, "what would you have me galvanize them to do? At this point I am raising questions, hoping to get everybody to think."

This approach was not popular with rank-and-file political reporters. Many felt McCarthy was talking down to them. Others found him belligerently obscure. *I mean exactly who was this French-Jewish fellow Dreyfus, and who the hell ever won a presidential campaign by invoking Scipio Africanus? Could you spell out that Roman name for us, Senator? Does it take a c or a k?*

"You could look it up in Toynbee," McCarthy said, and then a reporter asked him how to spell *that*. McCarthy was rousing the anti-intellectuals in the American press. *The New York Times,* where the hawkish and anti-intellectual editor, A. M. "Abe" Rosenthal, was becoming powerful, buried his Scipio Africanus speech amid bouffant Christmas advertisements on page 42.

* * *

A few days later, at Temple Emanuel in Great Neck, a Long Island sub-
urb with a prosperous and generally liberal population, McCarthy outlined a remarkable domestic program. No position papers. No prepared
texts. He was running his own campaign in his own way and if you
wanted to cover the story accurately you had to pay attention.

Standing before bronze emblems representing the twelve tribes of
Israel, he began by saying that underlying all American freedoms was
"the right of every person to be free from unwarranted public disgrace." The Bill of Rights, with its famous dicta, freedom of speech,
freedom of and freedom from religion, freedom of the press, and freedom peaceably to assemble, was without doubt a remarkable document,
but it was a document created in the eighteenth century. Now in the
twentieth century the American government was able to guarantee further rights. He enumerated four:

> "The right to a job, employment or decent income. This right has been
> established by our mastery over our economic system.
>
> "The right to an education, not just for the most talented, but for those that
> are least talented, the mentally retarded and the handicapped, so that they
> can become more fully human. The need for an education during the early
> years of the nation was limited,
>
> "The right to health. We have moved too slowly in this respect but we
> are coming to understand that even the mentally ill have a civil right to
> the best treatment possible.
>
> "The right to decent housing. The housing should be in a community
> where a citizen can live free from threats on his person, and also free from
> poisons in the air and in his food and water.

"Jobs, education, health, housing," McCarthy continued, "have always been *human* rights, but now we see them as civil rights, something
that civil authority must provide and guarantee."

It was apparent that he was not a one-issue candidate, but before the
clear, cold night in Great Neck grew very much older, McCarthy was

again addressing himself to the pervasive issue of Vietnam. Specifically, he responded to those who asked, "Suppose we withdraw and the Communists charge down and burn and pillage, rape and sack and murder?"

"Vietnam," he said, "presents us with a situation in which everyone must be somewhat uncertain and no one can be quite sure that his judgment is right. Under these circumstances you say to a people, as I say to the American people, be prepared to make a mistake, if you are going to make one, on the side of an excess of trust. Be prepared to make a mistake on the side of an excess of generosity with man and with history. Be willing to make a mistake on the side of trust in the future, rather than on the side of despair. That, as I see it, is the ultimate test, the basic test to which, for the first time in the history of this country, we are each and all being placed."

The audience in the synagogue, 1,200 strong, warmed slowly but deeply. McCarthy had stirred his listeners into thought. They responded with a confusion of questions and submitted them on cards to the temple's rabbi, Dr. Avraham Soltis, who was also the Jewish chaplain at West Point. "Wasn't erring on the side of generosity what America did during Hitler's rise?" the white-haired rabbi read from a card.

"No," McCarthy said. "We should have responded earlier than we did, but what with the depression and endemic isolationism in the wake of World War I, by the time we got around to noticing Hitler, we weren't *able* to do anything about it."

"I understand," Soltis read, "that you once studied to become a monk. How has this training influenced your political philosophy?"

McCarthy smiled his small smile. "One of the lines in the Benedictine Monastery is to keep death daily before your eyes, which never hurts in politics." Then McCarthy switched back into a serious mode. "I don't think spending a year in retirement and meditation ever does anyone harm. I suppose I'm the only member of the Senate who knows what the eighth degree of humility is. They say the last degree of humility is very close to the ultimate in pride, in the same way that the pale horse of death and the white horse of victory are almost indistinguishable."

This eloquence made no visible impact on the political reporters who gathered afterward for a brief press conference. Their questions were flat, and suddenly a man from the *New York Post* exploded. "I notice,

Senator," he said, almost shouting, "that you are answering question for the TV guys and you're ignoring us in the print media. What the hell is going on?"

McCarthy sighed. "To tell you the truth," he said coldly, "I can't tell you apart. But I do wish you'd get your jurisdictional disputes settled among yourselves."

We met two days later in a room—not a suite but a room—at the Plaza Hotel on Central Park South, and we spent an entire morning together. This was no Bill Miller, parroting position papers and hustling me out before I could probe or, even better, turn an interview into a conversation. And this was certainly no Barry Goldwater secluding himself from the dangers of dialogue in apparent terror of his own tongue.

McCarthy greeted me pleasantly and said he was familiar with some of my sportswriting. Why in the world was I leaving the sunlit world of baseball for the murk of politics?

"I believe," I said, "it was Scott Fitzgerald who wrote that the world is larger than a diamond."

"Yes," McCarthy said. "Something like that. But if you have no objection, I'll mark you down as a sportswriter who's gone straight, a reformed sportswriter."

"You can put that on my stone, sir," I said. "Anyway, all of this is accidental. I meant to write like Keats."

"You are not alone," said Gene McCarthy. He got up from the desk and suggested I sit there, where it would be easier to take notes. He moved to a deep hotel chair. He was wearing shirt sleeves and looking more rested than he was, a big, sensitive man with a fine-featured face who displayed the splendid political knack of talking to me as though I were the most important person on earth. (Twenty years later, at a small, White House party, Ronald Reagan did the same. There may well have been something magical in the Irish waters that the ancestors of these two men imbibed.)

McCarthy began to talk about his family and his youth. His father was in the livestock business in Watkins, a Minnesota community of five or six hundred. His grandfather had been a teacher. "I went to a Benedictine College, St. John's. Minnesota was a fine state, without class distinctions because everyone arrived at about the same time. The Methodists went to Hamline. The Presbyterians went to Macalester. The Norwegian Lutherans went to St. Olaf's, and the Swedish Lutherans went to Gustavus Adolphus. We were ecumenical way ahead of our time. The state was influenced by co-ops and a genuine communal feeling. Certain reforms were made in the Catholic Church in the 1930s and interfaith conferences frequently went on. I majored in English at St. John's and centered the line in hockey. It was a good place to go if you were alert and open."

He played jazz clarinet and first base for a team in the Great Soo League, a semipro circuit in the northern prairies, then tried the monastic life. He retired from the monastery and married the late Abigail Quigley, by whom he fathered four children. (He and his wife eventually separated. Until a few years before her death in 2001, Abigail Quigley wrote a column for the intellectual Roman Catholic magazine *Commonweal*.)

Back in Minnesota, McCarthy took a master's degree and taught in schools and colleges. He became a member of a liberal group that purged the Democratic-Farmer-Labor party of Stalinist influences. He was chairman of sociology at the College of St. Thomas in St. Paul when he was elected to Congress in 1949.

"When did you decide to run for president?" I asked.

"When I heard [Secretary of State] Dean Rusk warn the people that one billion Chinese soldiers were poised to march into Vietnam, each one armed with a nuclear bomb."

"Seriously."

He sat up. "When a hundred thousand American soldiers could not bring peace to Vietnam. That should have been the limit of our commitment. That should have made the administration aware of the limits of power."

"Won't Lyndon Johnson start a vendetta against you?"

"That's not Johnson's way," McCarthy said. "His way of eliminating people is to let 'em die on the vine. He doesn't waste time in the name of vengeance."

Once they were close, and I cited a Johnson quote. "Gene McCarthy," the president had written, "is one of those uncommon men who puts his courage in the service of his country. He's the kind of man—as we say in the ranch country of Texas—who will go to the well with you. That's a homely way of saying you can count on him in dark days or bright ones."

"I'm still a good man to go to the well with," he said, "but not to a wasteful war in Vietnam"

He talked about certain poems then, and certain poets. "It's good to read poetry, and not impractical. I suggest it is as important to read Sandburg as well as the *Tribune,* if you presume to understand the city of Chicago. It is important to read Allen Tate's "Ode to the Confederate Dead," as well as the speeches of George Wallace, if you presume to understand the South."

Our common love for poetry quickly brought us close, and I heard myself asking with real concern why he was putting his political life on the line right then. He mentioned Dylan Thomas, the glorious Welsh bard who tried to drink all Scotland dry and failed and died. "Near the end of his life Dylan Thomas said immortality now mattered less to him than did the deaths of his friends." McCarthy looked straight at me. "My own political survival matters less than the deaths of other men."

I must have misted at the nobility of his words, his person. He rose, walked to the desk, and now his eyes possessed a twinkle. "If you want to get heavy," said Senator Eugene J. McCarthy (D. Minn.)

What happened next will be familiar (and ultimately dismaying) to many. In the weeks after my story was published in *The Saturday Evening Post* of February 10, 1968, thousands of college students rallied round McCarthy. At his urging they got their hair cut and shaved their beards. They said they were becoming "clean for Gene." Many of these students traveled to New Hampshire and stumped door-to-door through bitter New England winter days and evenings. When the primary results were announced on March 12, McCarthy had won twenty of the state's twenty-four delegates. In the popular vote of party regulars, he polled 42 percent to Lyndon Johnson's 49 percent. The American system had spoken. Johnson was beatable. Four days later Robert F. Kennedy announced as yet another candidate for president. He would now also oppose the war in Vietnam, although he had been one of its strongest early proponents. On March 31, Lyndon Johnson announced that he would not seek reelection. The dragon, some wildly claimed, was slain.

McCarthy won Wisconsin. Kennedy took Indiana. McCarthy won Oregon. Kennedy won California on June 4. Then came his murder. After that the antiwar movement was never quite the same. Hubert Humphrey, the choice of party bosses and big unions, the hidebound Democratic Party establishment, was nominated for president on the first ballot in Chicago with 1,760 votes. Gene McCarthy drew 601. On Chicago streets students ran wild in dismay. Mayor Richard Daley's police assaulted the young protesters and beat many into unconsciousness.

That autumn, on the fifth of November, 31,710,470 Americans voted Richard Nixon into the White House. Humphrey fell about a million votes short and lost in the electoral college, 301 to 191. George Wallace, running with what *The Saturday Evening Post* called "the anti-Negro vote," won five Southern states.

The last U.S. troops quit Vietnam in 1973. A year later the impeachment proceedings began that drove Nixon from the White House. In 1976, North and South Vietnam were united as a single Communist nation. The effect on the world balance of power was negligible. In the twenty-first century large American clothing chains sell polo shirts and shorts manufactured by Communist workers in Vietnam.

After 1968 Gene McCarthy never made it back to the center stage of American politics. He ran for president four more times, without coming close, and in 1980 startled some old party-mates by supporting Ronald Reagan over Jimmy Carter in the presidential campaign. Aside from everything else, McCarthy told me, "Carter's heavy pomposity ill becomes a lightweight."

He wrote countless essays and twenty books, including four collections of poetry, and his witty commentaries often drew blood. "The rejection of presidential responsibility reached institutional status in the George [H. W.] Bush administration. Bush did not even take responsibility for his choice of running mate. He treated Dan Quayle as a kind of accident or an act of nature—something found on the doorstep one morning." During the late 1990s a movement began to gain McCarthy a Presidential Medal of Freedom. Previous winners included a comedian

(Bob Hope), and a chef (Julia Child), and a first-lady (Nancy Reagan). I know from personal experience, that the second President Bush is a man of great personal affability and unbending partisanship. The effort to honor McCarthy in life perished on the desk of George II.

McCarthy died at 89 in December 2005, an insufficiently honored American.

What, some ask, would the young McCarthy of '68, have to say about the raging issues of today: abortion, social security, Iraq. A key, it seems to me, is his comment that underlying all American freedoms is "the right of every person to be free from unwarranted public disgrace." A single woman in a small town, pregnant and unable to obtain an abortion, will suffer public disgrace. If Social Security benefits, already less than generous, are cut, millions of older people will be forced into the public disgrace called poverty.

What of Iraq and Muslim terrorism? I would begin here by repeating McCarthy's thoughtful words on Southeast Asia. "Vietnam," he said, "presents us with a situation in which everyone must be somewhat uncertain and no one can be quite sure that his judgment is right. Under these circumstances you say to a people, as I say to the American people, be prepared to make a mistake, if you are going to make one, on the side of an excess of trust. Be prepared to make a mistake on the side of an excess of generosity with man and with history."

That is not a very satisfactory answer, plucked as it is from a talk of almost forty years ago, but surely it can make us consider and debate and think. That, finally, is what Gene McCarthy was about, making his countrymen think.

I dismiss ambient attacks leveled against his career. I remember a good man in his prime standing against a wicked war, when he was, in words originally written by Anatole France, "a moment in the conscience of mankind."

CHAPTER 6

# Rescuing Roger

The chaos that followed the 1968 political campaigns was all
about during the life of my second son, Roger Laurence
Kahn, who had been born four years earlier. That chaos, I
believe, contributed to his death.

*If I could dwell*
*Where Israfel*
*Hath dwelt and he where I,*
*He might not sing so wildly well*
*A mortal melody,*
*While a bolder note than this might swell*
*From my lyre in the sky . . .*

—EDGAR ALLAN POE

On a hot, dry California night in the summer of 1987, as my son Roger
Laurence Kahn lay dying amid tubes and wires and flickering digital
readouts, a nurse at Los Robles Hospital hurried up to me and said, "Sir,
we have a note." She handed me an envelope marked in thin, severe
lines of black ink, "To my father!"

Roger lay motionless and silent under a coverlet on a bed in the
unit called intensive care. A middle-aged internist told me, "There isn't
any care that will help now. The poison [carbon monoxide] and its

effects have pretty much destroyed his brain. Nothing will occur from here on, except further deterioration." The doctor paused. "He's a good-looking boy, isn't he?"

"He always was."

"The nurses keep talking about that. They even trimmed his mustache. See how neat it is." The doctor loosed a shuddering sigh. "I thought I had a chance to bring him back. I went into the hyperbaric chamber myself, which is risky for a man of my years. But it was too late. If only we had gotten him sooner. Even ten minutes might have made a difference. Are you religious?"

"Not particularly."

"I'm a Methodist. There's nothing more I can do here. I'm going home to say a prayer for your son."

I walked by myself down a corridor into an empty waiting room, where I opened the envelope Roger had left. Again I saw the thin, severe, black lines.

*Dear Dad:*

*After twenty-two years in the amusement park, this roller coaster isn't fun any more, so I'm getting off the ride.*

*Roger*

*PS—As my mother is worth neither my time nor a postage stamp, send her a copy of my death certificate, as you would my grades.*

My immediate response mixed surprise and sadness with cold, defensive impersonality. I liked the imagery of the first sentence, the one about the roller coaster. Poor kid, I thought, to do this to yourself at twenty-three and leave a note that tells me you could have been a writer. I would have liked that for you. I would have liked that very much.

What of the postscript and the ferocious words Roger fired at his mother? Absolute honesty is imperative here; I am reporting on the impact of words from beyond the grave. In shock and confusion and rage, I thought: *That proves it. I knew it all along. I was the better parent. This tragedy is her fault, more than mine.*

According to the American Association of Suicidology, a Washington, D.C., group dedicated to the understanding and prevention of suicide, anger is common as grass among "suicide survivors"—that is, the family members of the one who has died by his own hand. I know whereof the association speaks. "Our estimate," writes Edwin Shneidman, Ph.D., the president of the organization, "is that in the last twenty-five years five million Americans have become survivors of suicide."

Under such terrible circumstance, you recognize as you never have before that death is an unspeakable enemy. Yet you must speak. For another and more subtle enemy is silence. Many families deny or disguise the fact of suicide. They feel stigmatized by the truth. For months Mary Welch Hemingway said that her husband died while cleaning a shotgun. Ernest Hemingway committed suicide. So did Bruno Bettleheim, Spalding Gray, Abbie Hoffman, William Inge, Arthur Koestler, Jerzy Kosinski, Jack London, Sylvia Plath, Hunter Thompson, Jean Seberg, Anne Sexton, Virginia Woolf and, for that matter, Mark Anthony, Cleopatra, and, in a sense, Socrates. In the most famous meditation offered by our greatest literary figure, Hamlet considers making his "quietus with a bare bodkin"—stabbing himself to death.

A disheartening telephone call had come close to the end. "It's me," Roger began and plunged ahead. "The best thing you've ever written is the passage in *The Boys of Summer* where your father dies. When I die, promise me you'll write something like that about me."

"You're not going to die."

"That's not up to you. Promise me."

"You're going to make it, son."

"No. Promise me, Dad. Please."

He did not let up.

Whenever I remember that conversation, I also hear lines by Robert W. Service:

*Now a promise made is a debt unpaid, and the trail has its own
  stern code.*
*In the days to come, though my lips were dumb, in my heart
  how I cursed the load.*

I promised.

We were a small group from the east, summoned 2,500 miles west to
a community called Thousand Oaks, by Roger's desperate deed.
Thousand Oaks! What a California name, I thought, like Twentynine
Palms or San Luis Obispo or Eureka. Nutley goes with New Jersey
and Worcester goes with Massachusetts. Thousand Oaks goes with
California.

The message I heard on an answering machine was that Roger lay
in critical condition. "It's really worse than critical," Gordon said on the
airplane flying toward Los Angeles. "Someone at the hospital told me
that Roger will never again be the person we knew." I thought about
Roger as a hockey star and as a prep-school quarterback. For the moment it became impossible to believe that he was immobile. Even as a
baby he was seldom sick. I thought some more. I began to hope our
plane would never land.

The mother, Alice, flew out of Boston with Roger's sister, Alissa, and
his uncle Jim, a Massachusetts surgeon named James E. Brackbill, whose
brother David, also a physician, had extinguished his own life with a pistol several years before. Inside the hospital, I shared Roger's note with
Gordon, but not the others. "Dad," Gordon said, "we can't let Allie see
this. It would hurt her too much."

"We have no right to censor Roger."

"Dad, I'll handle this." Gordon corralled some nurses and they pho-
tocopied Roger's death note, using a blank white sheet to blot out the
postscript. Alice studied the doctored version. She nodded, looking
grave but with no tears. She had always before cried, at even trivial disturbances. "My therapist asked me the other day," she said, "how much
longer I intended to allow myself to be held captive by a terrorist."

"I don't care about your therapist," I said. "My boy is dying. My
boy is not a terrorist. Fuck your therapist."

A supervising nurse appeared and asked me if I would consider letting Roger's vital organs be used for transplants.

Before I could answer, Alice said, "Yes. That's very important."

"Nothing is very important," I said. "My boy is dying."

Sometime in the spring of 1963, when the Los Angeles Dodgers were coming east to play, and overwhelm, the nascent New York Mets, Allan Roth, the Dodger statistician, telephoned. For many the baseball life is a ceaseless pursuit of companionship or just raw sex on the road, and Roth, witty and gregarious and a brilliant baseball analyst, had a predicable question. Could I get him a date in the big city? I was struggling through a long divorce, and as an almost single man of thirty-five, I'd made some friends. I called a brunette secretary at *The Saturday Evening Post* and she said, yes, she had a chum from her prep-school swimming team who would be in town for a few days, a lively potter who lived with her family in a place called Newtown, Pennsylvania. That turned out to be Roger's mother, Alice Lippincott Russell, a fresh-faced twenty-two-year-old with a pleasing wit, eyes full of mischief, and light brown hair, cut in a short (and rather boyish) style, who was eager to experience the world beyond a place called Newtown, Pennsylvania. By midnight on that distant spring evening I was ignoring the bouncy brunette secretary and found myself in a close embrace. Alice's splendid bottom gyrated. She stepped back flushed. "We'd better remember whose date is whose."

I saw her again just before Labor Day. She had been summering with her mother on the Jersey Shore, and the sun had lightened her hair and graced her with an inviting tan. (Is there anyone among the heterosexual male population who has not longed to see where a pretty woman's tan ends?) "Anything ever happen with Allan Roth?" I asked.

"He called from Philadelphia and said he had a ticket for me to the Dodger-Phillies game and I could pick it up at the Warwick Hotel. When I got there, we had a misunderstanding about why I was in his hotel room. I haven't seen him since."

"He's married, you know."

"And you?"

"I'm getting divorced. Don't you have a boyfriend?"

"I'm trying to break it up. His mother doesn't approve of me. I think that's because I'm not Jewish."

We went to a small East Side club to hear a forgotten duo billed as "the first integrated comic team." The jokes were broad, as when the black comic told the white one, "I don't care if my kids go to school with yours or not, just so long as I get to sleep with your wife." Then we repaired to an apartment, where Alice was a house guest, and sat on a living-room couch and talked till dawn. I had been editing Robert Frost's letters. Frost, Alice said, was the favorite poet of her father, a lovely man, who liked to farm and died of "chemical poisoning" on Alice's seventeenth birthday, March 8, 1958. The father's name was Laurence but everyone called him "Mush." Mush Russell. He looked a bit like Gary Cooper, she said, and he was a pacifist.

"Aren't all Quakers pacifists?"

"There are three kinds of Quakers," Alice said. "Pacifist Quakers. Warlike Quakers. And then there's the third kind, with names like Biddle. They own Pennsylvania. Biddles are the other side of my family."

I loved her looks and I liked her wit and I admired her artistic nature. Two days later she moved into my Fifty-seventh Street apartment, in a building called the Osborne, after its designer, Thomas Osborne, who went bankrupt before the structure opened to tenants in 1883. He created a landmark. Eighty years later, most of the huge original Osborne apartments had been partitioned. Mine, number 4FF, probably servants quarters long before, consisted of a large living room with a bay window, a modest bedroom, also with a bay window, and a sizable bathroom with a large tub that sat on clawed feet, and on which someone had painted bordello-red fingernails in a way that suggested a woman beneath the rim was bathing. The ceilings were fourteen feet high. On solitary nights, I tossed up thirteen-foot pop flies and practiced catching them behind my back. (I'd once seen a Cincinnati shortstop named Eddie Miller snare eighty-foot pop files that way in infield practice. Miller caught hardballs. In deference to my Osborne chandelier, I caught rolled-up socks.)

Mostly during 1963, I had been editing and much of what I edited was sports stuff. Despite the *Post*'s generous rates, I found few people who could meet a deadline and deliver an interesting, well-written story. Such writers as Bob August of Cleveland, Myron Cope of Pittsburgh, and New York freelancers Frank Graham Jr. and Ed Linn, were pleasant exceptions. But mostly I found myself editing mediocre articles, and here my native facility served me well. I was not trying to make of these pieces eternal lines to time, but simply good adult reading. Doing that came with relative ease. The *Post*'s offices at 666 Fifth Avenue were an easy walk from my apartment building, and so were such haunts as Toots Shor's and the 21 Club on Fifty-second Street. As I mentioned, Carnegie Hall was diagonally across the street, along with the vodka and blini of-ferings of the Russian Tea Room. When Alice realized that the Radio City Music Hall was only eight blocks distant, she began referring to that mighty cavern as "our neighborhood movie house." My rent for high-ceilinged apartment 4FF, in one of the most desirable buildings in one of the most desirable locations in Manhattan, was $250 a month. In an up-scale neighborhood today that does not cover garage space.

I'd taken the editing job because it seemed a stable place to perch until the squall of my divorce passed, assuming that it would pass, which was not certain. The understanding was that I would edit for one year, not a day more, and then return to writing. So in late summer and au-tumn, 1963, I was wrapping up the misadventures of Mickey Rooney, quite casually now, since he had destroyed my interest in the project, and editing *Post* sports articles, seriously, but pretty much with my left hand. Mostly, as my thirty-sixth birthday approached, I was trying to think of a book, a real book, that would challenge me. But I had not found that book. To an extent I was idling, playing a lot of tennis and weekend softball, happy that the days were mild and that I had found a bright and pretty companion to share my apartment. It was, in short, a fine time (and the Osborne was a fine setting) for carefree romance.

I can't recall the date when Alice told me that she was pregnant, but when she did, the carefree romance changed. It became a relationship of suffocating intensity.

"How can you be pregnant?" I said. "The pill." (Enovid, the first of the birth-control pills, appeared in 1960. By 1963, its use was wide-spread.)

"I don't take the pill."

Silence invaded my apartment. Then, after a while, "How far along does the doctor think you are?"

"I haven't been to a doctor."

"So how do you know?"

"I just know."

"Don't you have a doctor back in Newtown?"

"The doctor back in Newtown is senile."

From the second time we met I had thought about marrying Alice. I wasn't much good at being a bachelor, but almost all the women I encountered in New York were freighted with complexities and neuroses that I was not inclined to share. (I had enough complexities of my own.) With her humor, her bucolic freshness, and her trim young body, which featured one of the better bottoms of the century, Alice seemed enchanting. Besides, I was *ready* to remarry when and if, and even as, my divorce came through. In the closing soliloquy of *Ulysses,* Molly Bloom thinks, before she draws her first lover down to her breasts, "well as well him as another." At first I thought that of Alice and marriage. "Well, as well her as another." But in time I found myself deeply in love.

I introduced Alice to my six-year-old son Gordon. Her eyes misted as she watched him sleep. She said, "He's beautiful." She bought brightly colored construction paper and created a hutch in front of the bedroom bay window, marked "Gordon's Corner." I drove to Brooklyn and introduced her to my mother, who prepared a specialty from her then current Anglophile Period, roast beef and Yorkshire pudding. "If you stay with my son," Olga said, "what do you intend to do?"

"First, I want to look after Roger and love him."

While Alice rose and studied one of my mother's paintings, an abstract of Wallace Stevens's poem, "The Man with the Blue Guitar," my mother whispered to me hoarsely and harshly, "No Jewish girl would admit to such limited ambitions."

"If that's The Man with the Blue Guitar,' " I said, "why is the guitar in your painting green?"

"Obviously because that's the way I see it," my mother said, as though I had raised a foolish question.

Alice and I would get no support from Brooklyn Heights. Later, at the Osborne, I asked Alice if she had mentioned me to her mother, back in Newtown.

"Of course."

"Well, is this Jewish thing a problem? Is she going to object to your marrying somebody who's Jewish?"

"Not at all," Alice said. "But she would object to my marrying somebody who is married."

We looked ahead. I would write. Alice, who had majored in ceramics at Alfred and had won prizes for her work, would throw pots at one of the craft guilds in New York. She had just finished a striking blue and ivory tea set and told me she would like to present it to my mother. Touched, I quoted from *The Merchant of Venice*:

> *Sweet lady, you have given me life and living:*
> *For here I read for certain that my ships*
> *Are safely come to road.*

We embraced and slipped into tranquil sleep. But the next day Alice was still pregnant, and I was still married to someone else.

The late Charles "Cy" Rembar was my softball buddy and lawyer. He had gained a national reputation with his defense of *Lady Chatterley's Lover* against charges that the D. H. Lawrence novel was obscene, a victory he celebrated in his own book *The End of Obscenity*. It had been a crime to buy or sell *Lady Chatterley* in the United States until Rembar built his case, arguing powerfully and with some humor that eroticism was neither criminal nor obscene. He was also a rakish character, enjoying many romances, without ever considering a divorce from his first and only wife. "No marriage," he liked to say, "is perfect. And every divorce is expensive in time and emotional energy and most of all in money."

Rembar had been negotiating my divorce slowly, not trying to run up a bill—we had agreed on a fixed fee of $2,500—but because time, a lack of any urgency, was important in the negotiation. After invoking client-lawyer confidentiality, I told him that Alice seemed to be pregnant, and could he hurry matters along so that I could marry her? In a manner that was both businesslike and friendly, he suggested other choices. We could go off somewhere so Alice could give birth in a private setting and subsequently offer the child for adoption. Or Alice could undergo an abortion. The famous Supreme Court decision making abortion legal,

*Roe v. Wade,* lay ten years in the future, but abortion, with anesthesia, was easily available through a Manhattan underground for $500 up front, cash only. "There is some possibility," Rembar said, "that your divorce won't ever come through, unless you agree to give away half of what you earn for the rest of your life. I'd hate to see you do a thing like that."

As calmly as I could, I summarized this conversation for Alice. Her response came as an outburst. She had no intention of giving up any child of hers for adoption. Her Quaker tenets prohibited taking human life. Abortion was out of the question.

"But suppose," I said, "my divorce simply does not come through."

"Then I'll have the baby," Alice said, "and commit suicide." She articulated the last word as a shrill, alarming war whoop. SIOUX-is-cide!

Alice was confronting the possibility of one form of what Eugene McCarthy would describe five years later as "unwarranted public disgrace." Sex between consenting adults, was, of course, private. Walking about Newtown, Pennsylvania, pregnant and single, was not. That possibility must have terrified Alice. On the surface she was something of a free spirit, but within lay a conventional morality and a profound concern for appearances. She favored bikinis in the Caribbean but at her mother's summer home in the Pocono Mountains, she always wore conservative bathing suits that revealed less of her form, if perhaps more of her underlying psychic needs.

I told Rembar to settle the divorce case promptly. "A life may be at stake."

Rembar shook his head.

"I don't want to argue, Cy. Just get the divorce."

I subsequently agreed to give up about half my income, and on the morning of November 22, 1963, the day John Kennedy was assassinated, Alice and I obtained a marriage license at City Hall. Ours was the last license issued before the municipal offices shut down. Much to Alice's dismay, her Quaker group declined to marry us at their meetinghouse. A New York Justice, Will Midonick, performed a civil service before a dozen of our friends, and a few days later we flew off to a Bahamian resort called the Ocean Club, on Paradise (formerly Hogg) Island. Clay Blair had invited "my key *Saturday Evening Post* people" on an all-expenses-paid junket to "rethink" the future of the magazine.

Diffident servants surrounded us. The house wine was Lafite Roth-
schild. Alice water-skied gracefully wearing stylish bikinis, newly purchased at Bergdorf Goodman. I began to learn scuba diving from Blair,
who was an expert. Rethinking the future of the *Post* eluded me, but I
did discover that when a boost in newsstand sales became urgent, a
cover photograph featuring Elizabeth's Taylor's cleavage worked best.
"That's out front," Blair said. "The think pieces and the short stories
go inside."

"Suppose we need a circulation boost Christmas week?" I asked.

"Then we run a cover that features Girl Scout cleavage," Blair said.
"Julie Andrews."

"You look a lot like Julie Andrews," I said to Alice.

"Don't mistake me for a Girl Scout," she said. "I've had some adven-
tures." Late one night, I began setting up one of those folding beach
chairs that always seems to come with awning-stripe fabric. "I'm terrible
at this," I said, but after a while I prevailed without crushing any fingers.

Alice settled into the chair. I sat on the sand, my back against her
legs, listening to the sea, and considering the perfectly clear tropical night
sky. After a bit I heard sobs.

"What's the matter?"

"Being with you here is so beautiful, it makes me afraid to die."

Back in New York the following week, a doctor I had met when
undergoing an insurance physical solemnly confirmed that Alice was
pregnant and would give birth in late June or early July. Then he wished
us luck. That meant the baby would be born about seven months after
our wedding. Happy and relieved to be married, Alice said, "I told you I
was never any good at math."

The pregnancy that would produce Roger appeared to proceed nor-
mally. As Alice and I settled into married life, she concentrated on finding a two-bedroom apartment, setting my days and wardrobe in order,
and bolstering Gordon. She removed the tension from midweek visitations by turning them into ice-skating outings, usually at a rink at
Prospect Park in Brooklyn. Gordon never cared for games of ball, but he
became a fine skater and swimmer and later a good skier, all with loving
guidance from his stepmother. I commuted from Fifty-seventh Street to

Harlem for my involving *Saturday Evening Post* assignment, perhaps most dramatically when I toured a half block of dreadful tenement buildings, guided by a local housing activist named Jesse Gray, who was organizing a rent strike. The inhabitants, almost all women and children, lived from one welfare check to the next.

A Black Nationalist had recited a bit of doggerel that he said summed up everyday Harlem life:

> *If yo' black,*
> > *Git back.*
> *If yo' red,*
> > *Yo' dead.*
> *If yo' white,*
> > *Yo' perfectly all right.*

"The black man in America," he said, "has been abused, misused, confused, and refused." He wanted the federal government to buy enough territory in Africa so that every American black could emigrate and find land for a new home. "The United States government done that for the Jews. That's how Israel got started. We need a Israel for the black man. Trouble is, the black man, he ain't real slick, like them Jews."

Jesse Gray was local, not global, and so a more effective short-term leader than the nationalist. He showed me a warren of one-room apartments on 123rd Street that violated all manner of building codes and sanitary rules. A small, placid brown-skinned single woman named Luanna, mother of nine, lived in the worst, a reeking, unheated room. One of the children, a girl of three, was asthmatic. Luanna said "street air" was bad for asthma, so she had to keep the windows closed. I listened to her story: Up from the Carolinas, doing the best she could, deserted by boyfriends. "The colored man," she said, "is no-kinda builder. Tha's the big trouble with colored men. They don' build nothin'" I gave her fifty dollars. Luanna started to take off her blouse.

"No," I said. "Thanks, but no. The money is for the children. Get some asthma medicine from the drugstore for your little girl."

Back at the Osborne, I walked directly to the shower, turned on the water, and started tearing off my clothing. I was sure I'd contracted something in Luanna's apartment, or anyway that my clothes had picked up dangerous microbes, and I didn't want to infect Alice or the baby she was carrying. But the next day everyone was fine, except that musing about what would become of Luanna and her nine children left me feeling low. Did these little wide-eyed Harlem kids have anything? Did they even have so much as a dream? Our child to be, Alice's and mine, would be entering a world of privilege.

Before Alice gave birth to Roger in the small hours of July 1, 1964, at Doctors' Hospital on East End Avenue, she underwent seventeen hours of battering labor. When it was done, part of her lower torso was severely bruised. We named the baby Roger Laurence Kahn, the middle name coming from Alice's late father. Young RLK looked robust and normal until I noticed that one side of his skull rose up in a cone, a witch's cap. "Nothing to worry about," said the obstetrician, a plump, outgoing Italian-American woman. "Just a bruise picked up in transit. He's fine."

I said the bruise looked sizable and was located uncomfortably close to the brain.

"Nothing to worry about," the obstetrician repeated. "He's fine. With a few days' rest, Alice will be fine. And you'll be fine after you pour yourself a drink."

But when Jim Brackbill, Roger's physician uncle, saw the traumatized head, he took the baby to Boston Children's Hospital. Neurological tests showed no abnormality but those tests, almost a half century ago, were not definitive. In Roger's later years, I asked myself whether some undetectable but terrible damage had been visited on his brain during his turbulent journey from womb to light.

In 1966, when Roger was two, Otto Friedrich proposed another of his compelling assignments. "The longer Vietnam goes on," he said, "the more I miss reporting of the kind Hemingway did during the Spanish Civil War. The sense of battle. The noise of shells. The pity and the horror of it all. How would you feel about going to Vietnam?"

"I took risks in the drug neighborhoods of Harlem."

"This could be worse. I'm not interested in press releases from the Pentagon or interviews with generals. I'd like you to give us the sense of what it is to patrol the Mekong Delta. If you're willing, I'll have our

Washington people start making arrangements. You'll probably need some inoculations. One other thing. Before we go further, I want you to run this by Alice."

As with the pregnancy, her response took the form of an outburst. "If you go to Vietnam," she said, "don't look for me and the baby when you come back. If you go to Vietnam, you'll never see either of us again."

"It's an assignment," I said. "Vietnam is the most important story in the world. Pilots have to fly through thunderstorms. Doctors have to breathe close to people with TB. Journalists have to cover wars."

"I'm not listening to you. I've married you and I've had your baby. I don't want to be alone. I don't want to be a widow. If you go to Vietnam, then that's good-bye."

Alice, someone later observed, tended to deal with frightening issues by issuing ultimatums, and that precluded dialogue at important times. I can't say that I was eager to trudge through swamp and jungle, under fire, halfway around the world. My late friend, John Lardner, who landed on Iwo Jima with a Marine division on February 19, 1945, spent three days under mortar bombardment, which he summed up succinctly. "The shrapnel makes for disfigured dead." But I was willing to take the risk, and the more I thought about it, the more important the assignment became. Grantland Rice trudged through trenches in France. Hemingway covered wars with reckless bravery. Stanley Woodward landed behind Nazi lines. They all had children.

"I don't want to hear about them," Alice said. "I don't care about them. But if you go, it's good-bye, and if you really loved me and little Roger, you would even consider abandoning us to go to war."

I reported this conversation to only two people, my mother and Otto Friedrich. "I certainly don't want to see you killed," Olga said, "but I have no right interfering with you career. Neither does Alice." Friedrich thought for a few moments, then said, "I'll send someone else."

"I want to go."

"I know. I'll send someone else."

Friedrich spoke to another journalist, and when he asked what that man's wife would say, the journalist said, "I won't tell her." The man went, and it was harrowing, but he survived.

My next assignment turned out to be a profile of the brash baseball man Leo Durocher, who had started managing the Chicago Cubs. While I watched ball games in the sunshine in San Francisco, Los Angeles, and Chicago, I repeatedly thought, *I'm cheating doing this. I ought to be in Vietnam with the troops.* For a season after I could not shake such soundings. My home life became less harmonious than it had been.

Alice found a splendid apartment at 131 Riverside Drive with nine rooms and eight windows overlooking the Hudson River. I bought a piano, where I hoped Roger would begin music lessons, and began practicing some of the chords and arpeggios that resonate through *Götterdämmerung,* the twilight of the Gods. Playing the famous Georg Solti recording of Wagner's enormous work, I'd seat Roger on my lap and tell him the plot as the music progressed. He particularly liked a passage where two giants, Fafner and Fasolt, who built Valhalla, march toward Wotan to collect the gold they have been promised. Heavy bass tones mark the giants' footsteps, and Roger would listen in delight and then cry, "Protect me, Daddy. Protect me from the giants." I'd hug him close. Then at the piano I'd sound out the lyrical theme that goes with Wagner's words, "My father promised me a sword . . ." I would do that, I thought: I would find Roger a sword, to arm him against all the giants, all the dragons.

Trouble came after we enrolled Roger in kindergarten at the Calhoun School on West End Avenue, a few blocks from home. Toward March a school official said that Roger was causing disruptions in class. "Striking other children. Refusing to follow instructions. His disruptive behavior is such that we have no choice but to direct you to withdraw him." The college phrase for expulsion was "the boot." Twelve years before college Roger had gotten the boot—in kindergarten.

The Calhoun people suggested that Roger was hyperactive and recommended neurological tests. These showed a certain irregularity in a brain wave, but nobody knew just what that meant. The neurologist at New York Hospital prescribed the drug Ritalin. The next autumn we placed Roger in the first grade of the Cathedral School, which was affiliated with the Church of St. John the Divine. Education was formal and conservative. Roger, a dark-eyed, handsome, sturdy six-year-old, started wearing blue blazers to class. The Ritalin quieted him, and in the Christmas pageant he performed well as a Palestinian shepherd. True melting pot stuff, I thought merrily. A half Jewish kid with a Quaker mother playing an Arab at an Episcopalian prep. Some time after that the explosive success of *The Boys of Summer* reshaped our lives.

The Curtis Publishing Company continued to lose money—$18 million in 1968—and on January 10, 1969, a small, taut Wall Street hustler named Martin S. Ackerman, the latest president of Curtis, announced that he was folding *The Saturday Evening Post*. "It's a sad day for me and the American people," Ackerman said, "but no other decision was possible."

At the Post's last offices on Lexington Avenue, an eighteen-year-old secretary named Linda Leto told a reporter from *The New York Times*, "I just said my prayers this morning and hoped that all this wouldn't be true." One of the cleaning ladies, an old woman called Louise, wept noisily and cried, "Oh, where was St. Anthony?"

I sat with Otto Friedrich behind closed doors. He had five children. My daughter Alissa arrived in 1967; I now had three. "I guess we should have stayed with *Newsweek*," I said with more lightness than I felt.

"Compared to what we've been able to do here at the *Post*," Otto said, "everything we did at *Newsweek* seems so . . . well . . . *small*." He handed me an envelope; in it was a check for $5,000.

"What's this?"

"A thank-you. After today I won't be authorized to issue Curtis checks."

Lavere Lund, a short, stocky man who was Ackerman's chief assistant, burst in without knocking. Otto looked up and scowled. "We were talking," I said to Lund.

"Well, now you'll have to *stop* talking, cowboy."

It was a measure of my distress that I began circling Lund, looking to throw a right-hand punch. Friedrich, not athletic but quite tall, hurried between us and extended his long arms, like a fight referee breaking up a clinch. Lund withdrew. Puffing, Otto said. "Why don't you go home? We'll get together at my place tomorrow night."

The idea for *The Boys of Summer* traces first to the evening in the early 1950s when I heard Dylan Thomas recite his stirring poem. Across decades the idea developed, as I watched athletes who had been heroes trying to contend with life after their athletic skills had fled. I began specific work on the book on December 15, 1968, a few weeks before the *Post* closed. (I had hoped the magazine would help bankroll a project that would require many months of travel from New England to San Diego.)

Alice still was unconnected to a craft guild and she had recently enrolled at Teachers College and started studying for a master's degree in fine arts education. I thought that she would become a star there and presently begin teaching art, ideally at Columbia, and also return to the ceramic work at which she excelled. She did well as a graduate student, even writing an essay on the failure of New York City schools meaningfully to integrate minority children. She maintained that integration by itself was insufficient. Schools would have to offer fresh curriculums to get the children of the black ghettos involved. Did it make sense to teach a period-piece English countryside novel, say *Silas Marner*, to a fatherless black child who lived in Harlem and had never so much as seen a meadow? She made her points with great humanism and passion. "Would you like me to polish this?" I said. "I can tighten it a bit."

"I know," she said. "My English teacher at prep said I was 'wordy.' Anyway, I've already turned it in."

I edited for a few hours, and she decided also to submit the version with my revisions. The professor marked that with a B. He rewarded Alice's original with an A plus. "The other draft is smoother," he wrote, "but this one burns with a real fire. Congratulations."

Like most serious books, *The Boys of Summer* was a consuming enterprise. I heard out the old Brooklyn Dodger ballplayers. Common to all their stories was an underlying sadness. They could not play major league baseball anymore. I heard them out and wrote about their lives and talked about what I was writing. That led Alice to remark one night, "I've become the world's leading expert on Pee Wee Reese under the age of thirty-five." But she liked Reese, and the death of Jackie Robinson moved her to tears.

At length Alice said that she did not intend to teach. As far as I know she wanted to be a sort of über-housewife, giving small dinner parties for intriguing people, watching her family thrive, and dabbling enthusiastically in sports and the arts. But for me, with three children and a nonworking wife, the loss of the Curtis retainer became troublesome. Just maintaining three children in Manhattan private schools was daunting.

In the autumn of 1971 we moved into an eighteenth-century colonial house, eleven rooms on four acres, in the manicured village of Ridgefield, Connecticut. Our fortunes and our lives were changing dramatically. The Book-of-the-Month Club chose *The Boys of Summer* as its special spring selection in 1972, and hired Red Smith, to write a profile of me for the *Book-of-the-Month Club News*. Celebrity came in a clamorous rush. My share of the book club advance was $50,000. Paperback rights sold for another $100,000 and a fully paid two-week vacation for all of us at a villa on Barbados. Back in Connecticut Alice became friendly with a carpenter and began remodeling our rambling old home. By June, *The Boys of Summer* reached the top of the bestseller lists. (The book currently is in its eighty-fifth printing.) That autumn I collected a significant royalty check. The following spring Alice sued for divorce.

Why? We seemed to get along better in lean times than we did amid prosperity. Alice needed large measures of bolstering, attention, and love; the nature of the work I was doing often moved my focus away from her. I've heard from homicide detectives, physicians, and trial lawyers that their job seriously detracted from family life. Work and family time appear to be natural enemies, and I know that creating complex stories can commandeer most of my energies and a sizeable chunk of my soul. Ernest Hemingway maintained that a writer's life simply was uncongenial to the institution of marriage. "A woman," he said with characteristic certitude, "can stand a writer for from five to seven years. After that she moves on to someone else."

During one dispute Alice said, "All of your goodness goes into your books. You have none left over me." On another occasion she said, "Even if I stood naked painted green in the living room, you wouldn't notice me." I said, "If you stood naked in the living room, painted or unpainted, I would notice, and so would the carpenter working outside the windows." The comment was too flippant for the occasion. As best I can remember, Alice came to feel deprived of affection, and that created a sense of hurt. In time her love, her raw passion for me, ebbed, simmered, and became transformed into a hot anger that blocked other emotions, as anger does.

Outside a courthouse in Bridgeport where lawyers were preparing to do battle, I said. "Alice, whatever happens, part of me will always love part of you."

Alice stared. The mischievous look her eyes once had was history. Her jaw jutted. She said, "I'm not your friend."

I stood no chance of gaining custody of Roger. One of the Connecticut lawyers told me, "In this state the mother always gets custody, unless it can be proven that she is a prostitute working the streets. And even then the father may not win." Beyond taking the house, the car, the furniture, the carpets, the bedding, the china, the silver, the glassware, the television, the stereo, and my collection of phonograph recordings and books, Alice and her attorneys grasped for a mammoth share of *The Boys of Summer* royalties. I resisted. Divorce lawyers battled for years. I wrote letters, once citing the Shakespearean sonnet that begins "When in the chronicle of wasted time . . ." We were, I suggested, creating our own wasting chronicle. Alice declined to respond and presently moved on, or attempted to, by marrying an airline pilot. In the midst of all this, civil strife, changing locales, and shifting characters, young Roger was trying to grow up.

As we have noted, the 1960s were a time of war, tumult, and assassinations, but in many ways, Roger was awash in love. His older brother, Gordon, became a steadfast companion. His mother, while not affectionate, said she admired his sturdiness. On our visitations I skated with him, pitched to him, took him to ball games and movies. Roger enrolled at a fine day academy, the Harvey School in Katonah, N.Y., and soon showed promise in a variety of areas, along with a strain of rascality. He studied Latin and posted nice grades. Accompanied by a teacher, he and some classmates went on "a history tour of Russia." They ran afoul of the police in Kiev for dropping water bombs out of a hotel window. The Soviet Union was no country for boyish pranks.

Roger played quarterback on a good Harvey football team and starred as a wingman on the excellent hockey squad. He had good skating speed, bodychecked lustily, and developed a hard, accurate shot. It was from Roger that I learned the five "holes" toward which a hockey player shoots the puck: over the goalie's right shoulder or left shoulder, outside the goalie's right skate or left skate and—the so-called five hole—between the goalie's feet. Why wouldn't a goalie keep his feet to-gether? To skate laterally, you have to open up, and to cover the width of the goal mouth you have to skate laterally. (Like so much else in sports, this is simple enough, once explained.)

In 1975, when Roger was almost eleven, David Lowrey, the hockey coach at Harvey, said he might improve further if I found him a good summer hockey school. That turned out to be Holiday Hockey Camp, located in Banff, Alberta, amid the fierce beauty of the Canadian Rocky Mountains. It was owned and supervised by Glen "Slats" Sather, at this writing president of the New York Rangers and before that architect of the Edmonton Oilers, five-time winners of the Stanley Cup. Sather and his wife, Ann, organized the school with thought and care. The boys lived in a ski resort called Sunshine Village, 7,500 feet above sea level on Brewster Mountain. The peak was 1,500 feet higher, and each morning the boys tramped under an idle ski lift, moving in quick time to the top. "Look down as you go," Sather counseled. "Rich skiers use the lift in the winter, and lots of coins fall out of their pocket. Finders keepers." After that, busloads of young hockey players reported to the Banff rink, about 4,800 above sea level. I mention altitude because everybody worked and played and lived in thin air. Hockey is the most exhausting of team sports. Conditioning is critical.

Before organizing power skating drills, Sather and his staff—all prominent players in the National Hockey League—showed the boys how to measure their own heart rates from a carotid artery running down the side of the neck. Every camper had to pass a physical exami-nation before enrolling, and for healthy boys of eleven or so, the idea was to get the heart rate up to 180 beats a minute. (For a thirty-year-old the maximum safe rate is said to be 155.)

After hockey, the boys could try a variety of other sports at Sun-shine Village, from Ping-Pong, to boot skiing, which meant skidding down a glacier and keeping your balance wearing no skis, just boots. Sather posted boot-skiing prizes for speed and hotdogging. Like most of the others hockey campers, Roger seemed fearless. His New York accent must have been more pronounced than I realized, for in western Canada he picked up a nickname. I'd hear teammates say to him after games, "Nice shooting, Bronx."

Glen Sather did not ignore young minds. He hired Red Fisher, then sports editor of the *Montreal Star*, to lecture on hockey tradition and history and to quiz the boys. Some days into the camp session, Roger came to me looking surprised. "You know what, Dad? You won't believe this, but Mr. Fisher says July 4 is not a holiday in Canada!"

Doug Risebrough, a center for the Montreal Canadiens, later Calgary, refereed Roger's first game. The teams were tied at two with time running out as Roger skated hard toward a loose puck. Someone cross-checked him and knocked him down, smashing a stick held laterally into his face. The buzzer sounded. Roger got up and skated off with a small shrug that seemed to say, "That's hockey." Risebrough blew his whistle and called for a penalty shot. The two teams lined up against the sideboards, watching. Roger took the puck at center ice and sped down on a large Native American youngster in goal. He faked once, twice, and ran out of room without ever getting off a shot. Then he smashed into the goalie and said something.

Risebrough and I were drinking coffee when Roger hurried up to us, fresh from a shower, wearing only a white towel. "Dad," he said. "I missed a penalty shot."

"I saw. What did you say to the goalie?"

"I smashed him pretty hard. I asked him if he was all right."

"Roger," Risebrough said, "when you miss a penalty shot, don't *ever* ask the goalie if he's all right. Don't give him the satisfaction."

Risebrough became a favorite of Roger's and showed him a series of small, significant things that markedly improved his game. Even in 1975, there was considerable talk about the mercenary bent of professional athletes. I was touched that an NHL star took time out of his summer vacation to work for a token salary with young people, including my son.

On the farewell night at Sunshine Village high on Brewster Mountain, the young athletes had to perform skits. Roger wrote one in which he starred as a hockey coach whose team was having a terrible game. At the end of the first period, the coach said, "You fellers are disgracing your uniforms." The second period was worse. The coach repeated himself. In the end, the game became an utter rout. The uniforms were permanently disgraced. At a final meeting the coach said, "All right. I'm buying you all new hockey shirts."

Nerves gave Roger laryngitis that diminished his robust voice, but he still was honored for writing and playing a squeaky lead in the best skit of the night. Ann Sather presented the award. It was a roll of hockey tape. That cleared the larynx. "Thanks, Mrs. Sather," Roger said in loud clear tones, through a broad grin. There was also an award for most improved player, a statuette of a hockey player on a walnut base. Roger won that as well. As we flew home from Alberta, Roger guarded this trophy as if it were a Medal of Honor. Would he play in the National Hockey League? I wondered. No one knew, but surely he would excel on the ice at prep school and at college. "I'm very pleased with you, son," I said.

Roger took that in and responded with the careful nonchalance I had observed in other athletes, say, Mickey Mantle.

"Yup," Roger said.

Alice moved to a northern Massachusetts river town called Merrimac, which jerked Roger away from his firm base at the Harvey School and complicated my visitations. To see Roger now, meant a shuttle ride and a car rental. That stressed us both, but in a year or so, when Roger reached high school age, he was accepted as a boarding student at Milton Academy, a renowned prep that had been chartered in 1798 and was located eight miles south of Boston. This would be Roger's sixth school in his thirteen years, but remembering his early success in formal settings, I thought Milton would be just fine. "We do good works here," one of the deans told me. "We even educated Teddy Kennedy."

"You accepted my son quickly."

"We knew he could skate."

Roger never played a game of hockey for Milton Academy. He made the football varsity as a running back, but the schoolwork swamped him. That was puzzling. He had always been a quick study. His faculty advisor was a soft, plump Southerner, an overgrown Truman Capote, who had a difficult time relating to a vigorous jock. I visited the campus three times and one Saturday saw Roger run for successive first downs, bowling over older, larger tacklers. But something was going wrong. The advisor said Roger was unable consistently to focus on his studies. The football coach said he was forgetting his role on various plays. Roger's memory had been one of his strengths. It was stronger even than his hockey shot. What was to be done? Nobody at Milton told me anything helpful, but Alice took Roger to an elderly psychiatrist whom the school recommended, a classic Freudian.

"Lie down on the couch," the psychiatrist said.

"No," Roger said.

"Then I won't treat you," the doctor said.

Alice burst into tears. Then she said furiously to Roger, "Can't you do anything right?"

A few days later Jerome A. Pieh, the Milton headmaster, telephoned me in New York. Pieh was in his midthirties and had a doctorate from Harvard, but he was a relatively inexperienced headmaster. He spoke impersonally. "I want your son off the campus by five P.M."

"What has he done?"

"I'm not going into that. He has to be off the campus by five P.M."

"I'm not the custodial parent."

"We can't locate the mother. You'll have to pick him up."

"I'm in New York."

"I know where you are. Pick up your son by five P.M."

If Pieh felt compassion for Roger or for Roger's family, he disguised it exceedingly well. In pain and concern, I simply did what Pieh demanded, and for a few tense days Roger and I lived together in a motel. Roger may have brought marijuana onto the Milton campus. Smoking pot could explain his lack of focus. Another possible cause was the collapse of his first big teenage romance, with a girl who was a football cheerleader as his mother had been. Distraught, Roger may have skipped campus for several nights to search for her and, spurned New England Romeo, plead his case. Whatever actually happened, his family was not informed, and Roger would say nothing. But it was clear that despite its success with Teddy Kennedy, Milton Academy under Jerry Pieh was no place for my middle son.

An educational counseling service in Cambridge suggested that we send Roger to "a therapeutic boarding school that combines a college preparatory program with individual and group psychotherapy." That turned out to be a demimonde called the DeSisto School, set in the Berkshire Hills on three hundred acres near Stockbridge, Massachusetts, not far from the Tanglewood Music Center. Alice and I had been stirred one summer night at Tanglewood following the anti-Soviet uprising of 1968, the so-called Prague Spring, when a Czech expatriate, Karel Ancerl, conducted an impassioned performance of Dvorak's Eighth Symphony. But now in another decade, as I drove into the Berkshires on a murky autumn day, I heard not even an echo of great music.

It was a measure of my desperation that I accepted the prodigious costs that went with sending Roger to DeSisto without seriously investigating the institution or its founder. Here was Roger, bright and talented, strong and ambitious, dark-eyed and handsome, getting the boot at Milton as he had gotten the boot at Calhoun. He didn't fit in at school. His mother would not relinquish custody, but neither would she let him live at home with her second husband. Where, then, did Roger fit in? Where was Roger's place on earth, if anywhere?

A. Michael DeSisto, scraggly bearded and fat, the founder of the school that bore his name, said, "He'll fit in here. No matter what. Did you bring the down payment on his tuition and therapy? Before we do anything else, we have to have your payment. Ten thousand dollars."

He looked at my check and nodded. We were standing on a campus path outside the main building, a rambling nineteenth-century mansion. DeSisto wore a lumber jacket, a white shirt, unbuttoned at the collar, wide, unpressed slacks, and muddy shoes. I stared, and remembered the immaculate Carlton Saunders of Froebel. I thought, "What manner of headmaster is this?"

Inside his office DeSisto discoursed. "At Milton Academy, or at Andover, they try to hide the craziness. That's why Roger was expelled. They've hidden him and as far as they're concerned, he doesn't exist anymore. Because they try to hide it, at Milton and Andover, the craziness goes on from one generation to the next. Family misery persists. If I were you, I'd start a lawsuit against Milton.

"Here we confront craziness head-on. All the kids are in therapy. All the faculty and the dormitory parents are in therapy. I'm in therapy myself."

"Why?"

"Mostly because I'm fat. Where did you get your blazer and slacks? Brooks Brothers? I wish I knew how to dress like you. I hate being fat.

I hate being a fat slob. I hate it." Through the beard, his lower lip quivered, and A. Michael DeSisto abruptly began to cry.

When he recovered, he said, "Do you get along with your ex-wife?"

"I've tried, but no luck."

"Do she and the new husband get along?" DeSisto said.

"That's none of my business."

"Wrong. It *is* your business. You and Alice had a child together. You're connected. You always will be. You can't get out of it. How do you think she feels about you now?"

"I don't mean to overstate, but I'd say she's come to hate me."

"That means she loves you," DeSisto said. "She may not want to love you anymore, but she does. Probably she always will. And the deeper the hate she displays, the stronger the love that she is driving herself crazy trying to deny. The opposite of love, you see, isn't hate. The opposite of love is apathy."

After a while he said, "You've heard of schools that use animals as symbols. The Princeton Tigers. The Michigan Wolverines. Our symbol is the butterfly." He handed me a paragraph he had written:

"The butterfly is the most 'human' of all insects, for the pain of its metamorphosis most clearly resembles the pain experienced in human growth. If we know that the beautiful butterfly inside the cocoon is fighting to get out and we love it and help it by minimizing its struggle, we kill it. The struggle that it undergoes is what gives it the strength to live. Children also, if we really love them, must be allowed to struggle, for only through the struggle of adolescence can they acquire the security of adulthood. At the DeSisto School, loving is not 'doing for' but 'sharing with.'"

"Robert Frost has written a lovely work called 'My Butterfly,' " I said. DeSisto looked impatient. He didn't seem to care about other people's butterflies, only his own.

Mike DeSisto was an intuitive man. He attended well-regarded Catholic schools in the Boston area, St. John's Seminary and Stonehill College, where he earned a baccalaureate. But he never acquired the graduate degrees that are coin of the realm among educators. He started DeSisto in the 1970s—he would not disclose the sources of his funding—and he embraced gestalt therapy. When I asked him to describe gestalt therapy, he read from a pamphlet. "'Gestalt therapy takes as its centerpiece two ideas. The first is that the proper focus of psychology is the here and now. The second is that we are inextricably caught in a web of relationships with all things. It is only possible to know ourselves truly as we exist in relation to other things.' Roger is all about here and now. Most kids are. You and Alice exist in relation to each other."

"Where do Freud and Jung fit into this gestalt approach?"

"They don't, except maybe peripherally. These kids don't care about an old, bearded Jew from Vienna. I don't myself. Here and now is what we deal with, and we do it in the here and now."

"Could you give me a rough percentage of your failure rate?"

"Not rough. Exact. Zero. We can't fail because we never give up on a kid."

"But these children are severely troubled. Have you had many suicides? What's the suicide rate?"

"Another zero," DeSisto said. He was not weeping any longer. My suicide question angered him. He looked defiant, even pugnacious. As well as being intuitive, Mike DeSisto was one angry character.

Trying to conclude the conversation I said, "Thanks. You've given me a bit to think about."

"Don't think," DeSisto said. "*Feel*! This place will be a change for you. You may feel confused. Change is always frightening . . . *but stay with your confusion!*

"One more thing. All the kids are here because they need to be here. So do the parents. Both parents. Whatever happened, the kids didn't do it to themselves. So every parent, including you, becomes a part of the process here, just like the kids."

I was witnessing a performance. In time, considering DeSisto as a school director and unlicenced therapist, I saw him in many guises: actor, manipulator, cultist, publicity hound, necromancer, mercenary, entrepreneur, and, when it suited what he thought was a larger purpose, liar. There had indeed been suicides among DeSisto students. There would continue to be suicides among DeSisto children until Massachusetts authorities closed the school in 2004, a year after DeSisto died of a cerebral hemorrhage at the age of sixty-four. An official statement charged that the school "failed to provide the students with a safe environment." Had DeSisto been alive, his response would have taken the form of a tantrum rumbling from the Berkshires clear to Portland, Maine.

Discipline at DeSisto was enforced by faculty, dormitory parents, and the students themselves, gathered in ad-hoc groups that decided what to do by consensus. (Reaching a consensus could take hours, even days.) Breaches of conduct drew punishment. The offender sometimes was forcibly held down by others until he or she admitted the offense and promised to do better. Several students, boys and girls, said they were stripped naked in front of a group. "I had to stand in my birthday suit with thirty people staring," one attractive redhead told me, "Mike De-Sisto calls that 'tough love.'" DeSisto denied that anyone was forcibly stripped. "But we do use humiliation as discipline," he said. "We have truants here and petty thieves. We have to shock these kids back to rationality."

Consistently unacceptable behavior was punished by a sentence to work on the campus farm. There young people were put to hard labor and looked after chickens, pigs, and cattle. "After they start relating to the animals," DeSisto said, "we work on getting them to relate to other humans. Overall, we say to all of them, 'Here are the rules. We love you. Break them and you'll be punished, but we'll still love you.' Naturally they test us in every way they can."

The most severe punishment was called expulsion. That did not mean the student was expelled in the accepted sense, as at Calhoun or at Milton. It meant that the student was put off campus until he or she pleaded to come back. Then a consensus had to agree that the "expelled" student was sincere. School "expulsions" led to runaways, and DeSisto informed parents: "If your kid comes to your door and says, 'Take me in, please,' you have to be strong. Slam that door shut!" The expulsions led to at least one fatality when a boy, put off campus in mid-winter, froze to death on an icy Berkshire Hill.

Where were the cops? Somehow DeSisto the necromancer reached a quid pro quo with the surrounding police. He would take responsibility for the DeSisto kids, if the cops agreed to look the other way. As far as I know, that is what went on until, after almost thirty years, the

Massachusetts Office of Child Care Services finally intervened, which is what led to the closing of the school.

In mid-December 1979, a dormitory parent telephoned and said, "You have to come to the campus Christmas. We're having a Parent-Child Week." I was early in the composition of a novel, *The Seventh Game,* and said I'd be glad to come up for a day but not a week.

"This is, like, important," she said. "If you don't come up for the week, we won't be responsible if like Roger commits, like, suicide."

A few nights before Christmas thirty people gathered in a large oval within the great room of the DeSisto mansion. DeSisto and two therapists sat in armchairs. The rest of us, parents and children, sat on bridge chairs. DeSisto spouted rules. Everyone, parents and children, would be equal. The children were not to drink, nor were the parents, except for one glass of wine at dinner. Everyone should get in touch with his or her feelings and feel free to talk about anything at all, no matter how intimate. We shouldn't worry about privacy because this was a therapeutic session. We would be meeting eight hours a day for seven days. He then asked people to introduce themselves. A man with a camera said he was Michael O'Brien, a photographer from *Life* magazine. A woman with a notepad said she was Jan Mason, a reporter from *Life*.

"Whoa," I said. "What about privacy?"

DeSisto plunged on. "We meet again at nine tomorrow morning. Have a good night's sleep, everybody."

Awake at three A.M. I walked down to a small sunroom where I saw a slim, handsome man puffing a cigarette and wearing pajamas and a plaid bathrobe. He was Gower Champion, the dancer and choreographer, who had taken time away from whipping the musical *42nd Street* into shape for a Broadway revival. We knew one another by reputation.

"I'd rather be off skiing somewhere with my son, Blake," Champion said. "Smoke?" Blake, a tall, blond boy of about eighteen, had been seated next to me during orientation. Like his dad, Blake was remarkably handsome. "What do you think about press being here?" Champion said.

"Dreadful idea."

"You and I are the only parents here with much experience with the press. You've been reviewed, interviewed, quoted, and misquoted, and so have I." Gower puffed hard. "I'm not trying to influence anybody else, but if press stays, I'll leave."

"If everybody comes from the guts, as DeSisto demands," I said, "we'll be talking about what? Adultery, money battles, drugs, booze, and worse."

"Exactly," Champion said. His former wife and dance partner, Marge Belcher Champion, was not attending Parent-Child Week, and he told me after a while that he had become quite taken with a beautiful ingenue named Wanda Rickert, who would play opposite Jerry Orbach in *42nd Street*. "That attachment may become an issue here, and my personal romantic life is exactly what I don't want to see bandied about in *Life*."

I said first thing next morning I'd move to expel the outside journalists. Champion said that he would second the motion. After bickering that consumed three hours, Gower and I forced a vote. A healthy majority directed O'Brien and Mason to leave. But after lunch the two journalists from *Life* returned to the great room.

"We voted," I told DeSisto. "They have to go. Right now. We have a clear majority."

"You have a majority," DeSisto said, "but no consensus."

"You're playing games," I said. "We're wasting time talking about *Life* when we ought to be talking about the children. I know you want publicity, but you told nobody in advance that press would be here. You're being duplicitous."

"Duplicitous," DeSisto repeated, smiling unpleasantly. "An excellent word. I'll have to remember to use it sometime myself." There was a DeSisto School term for DeSisto's own behavior. At DeSisto, ducking an issue was called "sliming."

Gower Champion rose and said, "I'm leaving." He snapped his fingers, and blond, handsome Blake Champion stood up beside me. Gower embraced Blake. I looked away. Suddenly my chair began to shake. The bodies of Gower and Blake were touching the chair and Gower was weeping so hard that his entire body trembled. At length, with a hand at his face, he returned to his own chair. Press or no, he could not leave his son.

Some, but not all of the families, came forward with problems: drug use, drug dealing, alcoholism, promiscuity, physical battering. One woman pointed to her husband and said, "I caught that son of a bitch fucking the maid."

"Is the maid still working for you?" I said. People giggled, but I was serious. The woman said yes, because she needed the maid to run her household.

"Then don't complain," a sharp-featured woman said.

Another woman described how her mother had saved her from suicide when at the age of thirteen she climbed out on a ledge high above Park Avenue. "My mother saw me and said, if I jumped everybody would be sorry, but only I would be dead. Then she walked away. If my mother had tried to grab me, I really would have jumped to defy her. It was her calm tone that saved my life."

Moving with surprising agility, DeSisto put a bridge chair in the center of the oval and placed a pillow on it. "Place your own chair out in the center," DeSisto said. "The pillow is your mother. Tell Mother how you feel." The woman, blond and attractive, paled. "Oh," she said, "that would be as hard for me as it would be to stand in the center of this room in front of everybody completely naked." The group thought about that for a bit and moved on. Gradually the group was developing a collective personality. It made suggestions, passed judgments, and found faults.

In my divorce Alice had agreed to put the proceeds from the sale of the Ridgefield house into a trust fund "for the health, education, and welfare of the children." As part of the settlement, she insisted on administering the trust herself. Later she took the cash and bought a summer home on Martha's Vineyard. "We really need that money now for the kids, Alice" I said in the big DeSisto oval. "Why don't you sell the Vineyard place and put the proceeds back in the trust?"

Alice avoided my eyes. She had no answer. A few minutes later she stood up and screamed, "I'm dizzy. Somebody hold me."

"Nobody touch her," a therapist said sharply.

Alice began to wail. I was shocked. She had always put great stock in appearing controlled. Roger bent in his chair and looked down, hands pressed against his temples. Alice continued to wail and swayed from side to side. At length one parent, a white-haired dentist from New Jersey, came forward and embraced her.

"We'll take a fifteen-minute break," DeSisto said.

"She was sliming away from the question," I said to a female gestalt therapist named Diane. "You realize that those hysterics were fake."

"Of course. But do *you* realize that fake hysterics are just as tough to do through as real hysterics."

I had not realized that.

Roger came up to me and said, "That proves it."

"Proves what?

"Mom belongs in here, not me."

The story in *Life* ran under a headline "School That Mends Wrecked Lives." The writer, Harriet Heyman, called the place "a human safety net" and repeated DeSisto's claim that 90 percent of his students attended college. The article neglected to mention that the school had not been licensed by the State of Massachusetts. There was no explicit discussion of failures, no mention of dismayed parents who had withdrawn their children, and no reporting, none at all, on the question of suicide. In its June 1980 issue, *Life* published a piece of puff.

"I think it's great," Alice said. "Now people in Oregon will find out about this wonderful place." Rather than wonderful, I thought a suitable description would have been "experimental." To his credit, DeSisto was always trying to break new ground, and certainly his student body was a difficult bunch. He helped some, harmed others. Sometimes his innovations were brilliant. Some were ludicrous.

"I want you and Alice to start acknowledging each other physically again," DeSisto said early one evening. "You are going to tickle one another. Kindly lie down on your stomach." This man is forever playing power games, I thought, but I complied. "Now, Alice, lie on top of him." She did. "Start tickling," DeSisto commanded. Alice had strong potter's fingers, and she dug them into my ribs, gently at first, but then with as much pressure as she could apply. The effort made her grunt. When the pain intensified, I rolled away.

"Now lie on top of Alice," DeSisto said, "and start tickling her." Having known Alice through an ardent romance, I recalled which areas of her body, aside from the obvious ones, were particularly responsive. I also was aware that Roger was staring at us. Getting Alice aroused would be a power trip of my own within DeSisto's power trip, and wholly inappropriate. I tickled her only in neutral zones. She didn't stir.

"Enough," DeSisto said. "Great going, you guys! I call that Tickle Therapy. It's going to be the next big thing."

I have asked myself, and more than once, why I didn't pull Roger out of the strange and troubling DeSisto School. What may appear to be a simple question does not yield a simple answer. First, as I've mentioned, I was not the custodial parent. Under prevailing law I was empowered only to pay Roger's bills. The American Puritan heritage made divorced fathers second-class citizens, as other heritages have discriminated against American blacks and retarded children.

Suppose I had said, "Enough of tickle therapy and butterflies. I'm not going to support this nonsense one day longer." I felt certain that Alice figuratively would have dragged me into court, borrowing money from the Biddle side of her family to harness the necessary lawyers, and slam me with a heinous charge: failure to support my child.

That in no way makes her a villainess. By this time Alice had become, in the current phrase, a battered person. Not physically, but emotionally. Her first marriage failed and her second marriage was not satisfactory. Her efforts to become a part of the New York artistic scene had come to nothing. Her beloved son was spinning out of control. She was forty years old and had gained weight. Where once Alice relished haute couture, she now knocked about in shapeless slacks and sneakers. Her solution, or as much of a solution as she seemed able to find in difficult circumstances, was to demonize her first husband, Roger's father, me.

"I liked your hair the way you had it tinted at Henri Bendel," I told her at DeSisto. "Why have you let your hair go mouse brown?" I meant this as encouragement. I meant, *Alice, come on, kid. Spruce up. You can look great again.* But that is not the way Alice took it.

"I'd rather have mouse-brown hair like mine," she snapped, "than hair like yours, rat gray."

Ideally her hectoring would have stopped and we jointly would have found Roger a safer place than the DeSisto School. But we could do nothing jointly, and that was a family dynamic in which the head-master flourished. In advertising jargon his manner constantly suggested, "You got problems? I got solutions." For a time Alice was totally taken by him, and since she *was* the custodial parent that locked Roger into the school until his eighteenth birthday.

After Alice's second marriage failed, she moved to Martha's Vineyard year-round, but continued to dispute me on issues of money and Roger's education. This led us to a court in White Plains where my attorney, Stephen Feldman, put her on the stand and drew her admission under oath that she had used the children's trust money to buy her Vineyard house. The presiding justice, John C. Marbach, looked dismayed and said, "Madam, did it occur to you that you might have been committing grand larceny?"

Alice went pale and made moaning sounds, "Oh, no, no, no."

Surprisingly I felt a rush of sympathy. Some old love still lingered for my onetime Quaker bride. Alice a felon? Alice in jail? The idea made me shudder. I appreciated Judge Marbach's outrage on the children's behalf, but I suspect he realized as I did that the trust fund was gone for good. I suspect also that his stern words to Alice were mostly an admonition aimed at having her behave more responsibly in the future.

I published my baseball novel, *The Seventh Game,* in 1982, and that kept everyone clothed, housed, and fed. To my delight Budd Schulberg wrote the publisher a letter that ended, "Move over, Ring Lardner. We've got Roger Kahn." The other Roger, Roger Laurence Kahn, left DeSisto after his eighteenth birthday, as was his right, and moved into an apartment in Westchester County with his brother, Gordon.

"I'm never going back to that damn school," Roger said. "They won't give me a diploma unless I go through more consensus shit, which I refuse. I got great marks. I was the star on the baseball team. I was high scorer on the hockey team. Now DeSisto won't even give me back my clothing. All I have is what I'm wearing. DeSisto is jealous of me. I'm through putting up with his fucking humiliations."

When I telephoned, DeSisto said, "Roger is a simple truant. Until he comes back and faces the consequences of his truancy, I'll continue holding his clothing and his sneakers, his [$200] hockey skates, his baseball glove, and his shoes."

"You almost literally are stealing the shirt off my son's back."

"If you don't like what I'm doing," DeSisto said, playing power games again, "take me to court. We have a staff of lawyers on retainer." In my memory, these trying events out of the early 1980s remain as vivid as the high noon that graces this summer day on which I write. It startles me to consider that now, in the twenty-first century, Roger, De-Sisto, Gower Champion, and Gower's tall son, Blake, are dead.

After the clothes-napping incident, neither Roger nor I spoke to De-Sisto again. Gordon, who was working toward his license as an architect, described his roommate, the post-DeSisto Roger, as a changed person. The younger Roger, he said, was pretty much a model Republican. Conservative. Comfortable with jackets and neckties. Clean-spoken. The new Roger walked about with baseball cap on backward and sneaker laces united. Gordon wondered if all the outrageous behavior Roger had seen at the DeSisto School made him feel that such behavior somehow was acceptable.

Worse, Roger erupted into outbursts of uncontrollable rage, without apparent cause. In time I learned that this was one symptom of what therapists formerly described as a manic-depressive personality. Now they call the condition bipolar disorder. Roger sometimes telephoned and began the conversation, "You better listen to me, Dad, or you are one dead man." Then, half an hour later, "Dad, can we go to the Yankee game tonight?" Bipolar disorder is terrifying, perhaps most of all for the person suffering from it.

Roger found work selling towels at Bloomingdale's, but one night, for no discernable reason, he threatened Gordon with a kitchen knife. He held the knife at Gordon's throat for twenty minutes. Accompanied by police, I took Roger to a hospital. A young admitting psychiatrist said that a single incident was not sufficient reason for institutionalizing any-one. I said a that few days of observation surely were in order. The doc-tor walked away.

Roger moved into my home in Croton-on-Hudson, and when he made several threats to kill me, I took to sleeping with a baseball bat beside my bed. Roger possessed great physical strength. At length, quite cheerfully, he said he had decided to make a new start in California. One of his friends from the DeSisto School had a place for him in Topanga Canyon, where the boy lived with his parents in a large, hillside house.

"But I need a car," Roger said.

I bought him a sturdy used Volvo for $2,000, and together we packed his new clothing. "Promise me one thing," I said. "It's a long road out to the Coast. Drive carefully."

"I will," Roger said. He hugged me. "I love you, Dad," he said.

And then he bloomed. He found a series of jobs, bought a lunch cart, connected with a partner, and went into the business of selling soft drinks and hot snacks near the beach at Marina del Rey. He found an apartment of his own in southwestern Los Angeles. Somehow, without a high school diploma, he talked his way into Santa Monica City College and began posting straight A's. He liked history, he said, and seventeenth-century poetry, particularly *Absalom and Achitophel,* a complex satire by John Dryden, published in 1681, that proceeds from the biblical story of David and Absalom. "I enjoy studying stuff that's hermeneutic," Roger said.

"Beg pardon."

He laughed. "At last. I've used a word you don't know. Hermeneutic."

"Sounds like a name."

"It describes poetry based on the Scriptures."

I said I preferred nineteenth-century lyrics.

"The hermeneutic stuff has more in the way of ideas," Roger said, "but there is one of those lyrics that I do like a lot. By Shelley. You know the one. It begins:

> *When the lamp is shattered,*
> *The light in the dust lies dead."*

I noticed on a transcript that in addition to academic courses Roger was taking something called modern dance. "What's that?"

"Good place to meet girls," Roger said. On trips to California I met two of them. One, whom I'll call "Juanita," was a pert, affectionate, dark-haired college girl from Mexico. "Sylvia," an extraordinary beauty with silvery blond hair, came from Mexican and German stock. Unfortunately, she was suffering from chlamydia, an annoying but treatable venereal disease. She infected Roger, and for a time they kept reinfecting one another. "I don't know what to do," Roger told me.

"Stay away from her for a while. Get cured. Then start making it with somebody else. Leave her alone until she gets cured herself."

"That way I'll lose her," Roger said. He lost her anyway. Among other things, the stress of chlamydia broke them up.

Roger wasn't ready to marry. He wanted first to get straightened out on a career. He thought he might become a historian, or possibly go into psychology, with an eye toward helping troubled youngsters. The lunch wagon business was only fair, but he was picking up extra money playing center field in a fast-pitch softball league. "Some NBA guys, basketball players with the Lakers, are on my team. They do it for fun. I need the money." I sent him checks as often as I could.

After one softball game, as Roger would tell me later, one of the basketball players invited him to "a really sleek condo" on Wilshire Boulevard. The place had indirect lighting, stainless-steel furniture, and a huge television set that appeared from nowhere at the push of a button. Amid the opulence, the two were not meeting for a postgame beer. The basketball player produced a mortar and pestle. He opened a glassine packet containing heroin crystals. Then he showed Roger how to grind the stuff into powder, hold it close to his nostrils, and sniff. Roger told me the basketball player's name. The man had achieved some renown as an athlete, but in my view he was and is a dangerous criminal.

Research on an article pretty much forced upon me by some friends at *The New York Times*—how did the winning 1980s Los Angeles Dodgers match up against Brooklyn's *Boys of Summer?*—brought me to Los Angeles for a few days. I visited Roger's apartment, modest but neat, in a mixed Anglo-Mexican neighborhood. I met his cat. Roger smacked the rug beside her. "What's that?"

"No fleas."

He had swapped his Volvo for a motorcycle. "And there's big news," he said. "I've been accepted at UCLA."

"Steak dinner," I said. "Name your place."

"I'd rather go to the ball game. Orel Hershiser is pitching against the Cubs."

The Dodgers won, 3 to 1. Afterward, I took Roger into the club-house, where Hershiser was icing his arm. Before becoming an all-star major-leaguer, Hershiser had been a prep-school hockey player, and he and Roger fell into easy hockey talk. Say, wasn't that team from Cherry Hill, New Jersey, a rugged bunch? A reporter for the *Los Angeles Times* approached and said, "In the fifth inning, when that guy knocked in the run, what kind of pitch did he hit?"

Hershiser looked at Roger and said, "Excuse me. I have to go to work. The pitch was a breaking ball, a bit higher than it was supposed to be." Then Orel and Roger went back to talking hockey. This was perhaps a small incident, but I have never forgotten a great pitcher's courtesy and kindness to my son.

When we went upstairs, Al Campanis, the Dodger general manager, a man I had known for thirty-five years, invited us into his office. "I understand you play ball," he said to Roger. "I can tell by the way you move that you're an athlete." He stared. "And I like your face. I've signed thousands of kids and whatever the books may say, first I study the face. You have a fine face. What are you up to?."

"I'm starting UCLA, sir, as a junior in the fall."

"I could offer you a contract to play in a rookie league," Campanis said. "I know what's going on around this town. I hear you can hit. But, son, only three percent of the boys in the rookie leagues ever get even to sit on a bench in the majors. Only three out of a hundred. Your Dad's a friend, and we could sign you, but the minor-league life isn't much. I'm sure you're an intelligent person. Stay in school. Keep playing ball, but do that for fun." I mouthed, without actually saying the words, *Thank you, Al.*

I felt hopeful for Roger, but this was, in Hemingway's term, a false spring.

A few months later on a long-distance line, I heard desperation hone an edge on Roger's voice. Heroin had gotten him into trouble, he said. Some drug dealers were after him because he hadn't paid them, and "Dad, these guys pack guns." His only hope was to enter a private hospital that was offering a twenty-eight-day program to cure addiction. The up-front fee was $15,000.

I burst out, "Why in the name of hell are you using heroin?"

Roger's tone became patronizing and angry. "Dad. You drink."

"Drinking is legal. I don't have to go to crooks to buy scotch. And scotch doesn't cost me a hundred dollars a day."

"If you don't do what I ask," Roger said, abruptly sounding calm, "you are going to have one dead son. I know you paid for my student health insurance, but the insurance company won't help. They say the drug stuff isn't covered because it was a pre-existing condition. Can you fly out here with fifteen thousand dollars? Please?"

Roger's story did not wholly make sense. Would a private hospital be a safe haven from murderous drug dealers who might appear with drawn pistols at three A.M.? Where were the police? As I was learning, heroin addicts tend to be fabricators, exaggerating and making things up in their grinding need, one way or another, to support their habit. I stopped researching a book I was trying to prepare with the ballplayer and gambler Pete Rose, flew to Los Angeles, and gave the private hospital its $15,000.

(The Mickey Rooney experience had not encouraged further collaborative efforts, but I accepted Rose's request to work with him in order to cover the expenses I faced in raising my flawed and gifted child. Once Rose collared his half of the publisher's advance, Pete, like Rooney before him, became evasive. Rose lied a great deal, sounding sincere as he did, and after our relationship collapsed he had the temerity to accuse me of making a play for his wife, Carol. Truth here triumphs over fantasy. Carol Rose simply was not my type of woman.)

The California hospital was situated in a quiet neighborhood in Westwood. A pleasant and concerned young psychiatrist—"Call me Doug, Mr. Kahn"—explained that the institution treated only three conditions: alcoholism, compulsive gambling, and drug addiction. As at DeSisto, group therapy was part of the program, and I sat in on several sessions, hearing sad stories from men and women who ranged in age from eighteen to sixty. The psychiatrist concluded after a bit that Roger was bipolar and prescribed lithium, which he said was a successful treatment 80 percent of the time. "So if your son kicks heroin, and that's what he's here for, the prognosis is good."

I mentioned that the aberrant behavior all around Roger at the DeSisto School seemed to have been damaging.

"That's a risk here as well," Doug said. "I've told Roger once and

I'll tell him again, he is here to recover from addiction, not to make friends."

On his release Roger continued seeing the psychiatrist and met regularly with a drug therapist, a kind, forlorn man, who himself had been an addict. Roger told me something about those sessions and then mentioned "this terrific guy I met at the hospital." That turned out to be a dashing character, six years Roger's senior, a compulsive gambler. One weekend, I never found out which, the gambler drove Roger to Las Vegas. By Monday morning the money Roger had earned from his lunch wagon and playing softball was gone. The gambler found out about an emergency account I had set up in Roger's name at a Los Angeles bank. He pilfered the checkbook and forged Roger's name. The emergency money disappeared as well. "I'd kill him," Roger said, "but I can't find him." The gambler simply vanished into the undergrowth of sidewinders and grifters that was his native land.

I told Roger to dress decently so that he would look like a substantial citizen and go to a district attorney's office. He said he did. I'm not sure. Disheartened as he now was with his money gone, he quit taking lithium and stopped seeing the psychiatrist. I called the doctor and the drug therapist and said I was flying west, so we could meet with Roger and devise a recovery plan.

"A very bad idea," the psychiatrist said. "There is an element of infantilism in Roger's behavior. He feels that he was not mothered properly, so in a way you represent not only yourself but also, uh, what is the mother's name again?"

"Alice."

"Of course. Roger acts out, with anger, with drugs, and now irresponsible gambling. You arrive to help him, as though he were still a little child. Then he acts out again, but more severely. The more often you come out here, the more extreme his conduct may become. I don't want him holding up filling stations. He's almost twenty-three and he has to assume responsibility for his own actions, his own life. He's bright and he's strong. As long as he takes his lithium, the prognosis is far from hopeless."

"He doesn't want to take lithium. He wants to sniff heroin."

"All I can do is prescribe," the psychiatrist said. "Excuse me. I have a patient waiting."

In the early hours of April 7, 1987, Roger and I had our last rational conversation. The night before, I traveled to a studio in New York to appear on the ABC program *Nightline,* moderated by Ted Koppel. The occasion was the fortieth anniversary of Jackie Robinson's first major-league season. Koppel asked if I thought Robinson would be pleased with the state of blacks in major-league baseball at the time. A waffled answer was available. In Robinson's era marginal blacks did not last in the big leagues. A black ballplayer was either a star or he was released. By 1987, most teams were using black utility men and that certainly would have pleased Robinson. But Robinson believed in capitalism. Staying as true to his memory as I knew how, I started to say that he would be unhappy that there were then no black major-league field managers, general managers, or club owners. I paused for breath at field managers. Koppel, who was in Washington, quickly turned to the other guest, my old friend, Al Campanis, who was sitting in the Houston Astrodome, where the Dodgers had just been defeated. "Is Mr. Kahn's statement true," Koppel asked, "and if it is, to what do you attribute it?"

"Blacks lack the necessities to manage," Campanis said. His voice was thick. He may have been drinking.

"We'll take a break," Koppel said.

Campanis had misused the word "necessities." He appeared to mean "qualifications" or perhaps even "intelligence." He shocked me, and he would shock much of the nation. Born on the island of Kos, which he often cited as the birthplace of Hippocrates, Alexander Sebastian Campanis grew up New York and became a multisports star at NYU. His major-league playing career consisted of only seven games, but he was a competent and intelligent infielder with the Dodgers' Montreal farm club during the season of 1946. There, he told me more than once, always with great pride, he had shown Jackie Robinson how to make the various pivots a second baseman must master to complete double plays.

After some commercials, Koppel repeated his question to Campanis, a fair chance for Al to maneuver out of trouble. But Campanis repeated his statement about "necessities." Presently he likened the managing situation to blacks' limited success in swimming. Blacks lack "buoyance," Campanis said.

"How about lack of access to pools?" Koppel said.

I had never before heard a hint of racial profiling from Campanis, but now as he blundered on, I could not remain silent. The memory of Jackie Robinson commanded me to speak. "I get it, Al," I said. "Do blacks have the intelligence to work in the fields, the cotton fields and the ball fields? Yes. But do they have the intelligence to manage? No."

On the television monitor in front of me, Campanis looked confused. When the show ended, Koppel said he hoped my telephone number was unlisted, like his, because the ABC switchboard was lighting up "like a hundred Christmas trees." A long white ABC limousine drove me home through a downpour. Roads were flooded, and I didn't arrive until 1:45 A.M. I was aware something unfortunate had happened, and sleep eluded me.

Roger telephoned a few minutes after three AM, just after *Nightline* ran in Los Angeles. "Dad, I was never prouder of you in my whole life than I was tonight."

"Thanks. I don't know what got into Campanis."

"That doesn't matter. I remember when Jackie Robinson let me play with his football. I remember he was nice to a little kid. And I know about prejudice. A lot. Juanita is Mexican. You can't imagine some of the stuff she's had to go through."

"Maybe Campanis was only saying what he'd heard said for years behind closed doors in the Dodger offices."

"That doesn't matter, either," Roger said. "Tonight, Dad, you have one very proud son."

All his ensuing calls were requests for money. Roger stopped seeing the psychiatrist but continued seeing the drug therapist. "Don't you think," I said, "that if I flew out I could give you a hand."

"Look, heroin is tough, but I'm working hard with Roger. With all due respect, Mr. Kahn, the last thing I need and absolutely the last thing Roger needs in a hovering parent."

On his twenty-third birthday, July 1, 1987, Roger asked me to wire "a few hundred dollars" to him care of Western Union in National City, a largely Hispanic town about eight miles from San Diego. "You can use a credit card," he said. "They'll want a password. Tell them

'Dodger.'" He next asked his mother to send him what she could. "The password you have to give," he told Alice, "is 'death.'"

He used some of the money to buy a garden hose at a hardware store, then leased a sedan from the Ugly Duckling Rent-a-Car Company. On the night of July 3 he drove to Malibu, parked, and connected the hose to the exhaust pipe. He closed the windows tight, leaving one open just wide enough to admit the hose. He turned on the ignition. The cabin filled with carbon monoxide.

Roger's sister Alissa, a pretty twenty-year-old redhead, walked up to his bed in the intensive care unit at La Robles Hospital and said, "Stop this nonsense, Roger. Sit up." The only sound that followed was the respirator that was keeping Roger breathing. Roger's Uncle Jim Brackbill, the Massachusetts surgeon, chattered compulsively in grief. Like Alice, Alissa wanted Rogers vital organs donated to help others. The nearest transplant team, at UCLA, would not be available for two days.

The vigil overwhelmed me. I reserved a room at a nearby motel and called for a taxi. "You can use some rest yourself," I said to Gordon. He shook his head. He would not leave his brother's side. "You'll have to buy a coffin," someone told me.

"Alice," I said, "come with me." When the taxi arrived, I couldn't find her. She reappeared carrying little toy animals, teddy bears, bunny rabbits, puppies she had found at the hospital gift shop. She said, "I want these in the coffin with my baby."

The end, on July 7, 1987, was not dramatic. I signed forms authorizing organ transplants. The transplant team, which arrived by helicopter, brusquely assumed command. Someone disconnected machines. The digital readouts, recording what remained of Roger's life, went blank. Or faded, as the saying is, to black.

"Those doctors from UCLA should have been more compassionate," a small, white-haired nurse said.

"Yes," I said. "I suppose they should have been."

But I didn't care.

The lamp was shattered.

The light in the dust lay dead.

# CHAPTER 7

# *Coda*

I HAVE not gotten over Roger's death, nor will I, nor do I want to. As the poker players say, you play the hand you are dealt.

Out of respect for Alice and her family, I chose the Friends Meeting House in Manhattan as the site for a memorial service in mid-July 1987. Outside the immediate family, Rachel Robinson was the first person to arrive. "I had to come," she said, "after all the help you were when we lost young Jack. Now don't fuss about me. I have a newspaper to read until the service starts." Then she saw Gordon. They fell into each other's arms in tears.

I asked my friend, the late violinist Erick Friedman to play, but he had known Roger, played tennis with him, and said he was afraid he might break down. Erick sent instead Joseph Seiger, a wonderful pianist who had been Mischa Elman's accompanist. Joe Seiger played consoling music, mostly Bach. He refused to accept a fee.

Frances Chaney, an actress who was married to Ring Lardner Jr., spoke a powerful eulogy. "Alice," she cried, "Roger. This is a terrible tragedy, but it is not your tragedy alone. These have been terrible times for young people to grow up. Wicked war. Terrible bigotry. Poisonous drugs. Drugs that kill!

"Let's make a *real* memorial to Roger. Let's all of us pledge right now to make the world a warmer, safer, and more loving place for children. Let's work for that, no matter how hard it is to do or how many years or decades that it takes us. We owe that to all the children. We owe that to ourselves. We owe that to the memory of Roger."

Since Katy and I began our marriage seventeen years ago, in the wake of Roger's death, I have published more books than I did in the preceding sixty years. Katharine Colt Johnson, LCSW, is a psychotherapist specializing in troubled children. I know she has uncertain moments, but I can only imagine how many youngsters she has helped, the number of lives that she has resurrected.

Put briefly, we have come to believe that the art of living begins with a wholehearted appreciation of life itself and the understanding that going on with life, especially in the clutch of tragedy, cannot be accomplished through denial, anger, or passivity. It demands courage. It requires loving and love. *It takes life to love life.*

As I consider the memories which are my life, I marvel at the characters who have walked besides me: Stanley Woodward, Pee Wee Reese, Robert Frost, Jackie Robinson, Eugene McCarthy, and Roger Laurence Kahn. I learned from each, sometimes joyously, sometimes in pain; they all broadened my understanding of the human experience and the gift of living. I have tried to set down what they taught me and what I have learned. With this book I hope we reach many others, most of whom I have not met, my readers.

Each night Katy and I try to look forward to morning. Like Robert Frost, we remember our old loves and our old poems, but most of the time we look ahead. Now, in my eighth decade, I continue to follow the great creed of intellectuality with Brahms and Shakespeare and Milton's mighty line.

But still, too, I relish thieves, gypsies, and, lest I forget, ballplayers.

# INDEX

12-5-61

To Roger with respect
and admiration. It has
been good working with you
and knowing you over the
years

Jackie Robinson